The Sixties in America
Primary Sources

The Sixties in America
Primary Sources

Tom Pendergast
and Sara Pendergast

Allison McNeill,
Project Editor

U·X·L
An imprint of Thomson Gale,
a part of The Thomson Corporation

REFERENCE

THOMSON

GALE

Detroit • New York • San Francisco • San Diego • New Haven, Conn. • Waterville, Maine • London • Munich

THOMSON
™
GALE

The Sixties in America: Primary Sources
Tom Pendergast and Sara Pendergast

Project Editor
Allison McNeill

Rights Acquisition and Management
Mari Masalin-Cooper

Imaging and Multimedia
Denay Wilding, Lezlie Light, Mike Logusz

Product Design
Kate Scheible and Pamela Galbreath

Composition
Evi Seoud

Manufacturing
Rita Wimberley

For permission to use material from this product, submit your request via Web at http://www.gale-edit.com/permissions, or you may download our Permissions Request form and submit your request by fax or mail to:

Permissions Department
Thomson Gale
27500 Drake Rd.
Farmington Hills, MI 48331-3535
Permissions Hotline:
248-699-8006 or 800-877-4253, ext. 8006
Fax: 248-699-8074 or 800-762-4058

Cover photographs reproduced by permission of © Jack Moebes/Corbis (first Woolworth's department store lunch counter sit-in) and AP/Wide World Photos (Miss America pageant protest; Vietnam veterans protest).

While every effort has been made to ensure the reliability of the information presented in this publication, Thomson Gale does not guarantee the accuracy of the data contained herein. Thomson Gale accepts no payment for listing; and inclusion in the publication of any organization, agency, institution, publication, service, or individual does not imply endorsement by the editors or publisher. Errors brought to the attention of the publisher and verified to the satisfaction of the publisher will be corrected in future editions.

LIBRARY OF CONGRESS CATALOGING-IN-PUBLICATION DATA

Pendergast, Tom.
Sixties in America. Primary sources / Tom Pendergast and Sara Pendergast.
    p. cm.
Includes bibliographical references and index.
    ISBN 0-7876-9248-4 (hardcover : alk. paper)
1. United States—History—1961-1969—Sources—Juvenile literature. I. Pendergast, Sara. II. Title.

E841.P383 2004
973.923—dc22

2004016602

Contents

Reader's Guide

Many Americans realized by the middle of the 1960s that their nation was going through a period of intense change and disruption. The decade had begun in relative peace, with the election of a vibrant, young president, John F. Kennedy, a Democrat. Yet Kennedy faced several key issues that would come to define the decade. First, he clashed with the Soviet Union over the spread of communist influence in Europe and in Cuba. Then, he faced domestic tensions as the civil rights movement in the South grew increasingly intense and even violent. When Kennedy was assassinated in November of 1963, the nation was shocked and saddened, for many Americans had invested great hopes in Kennedy.

Kennedy's successor, Lyndon B. Johnson, struggled with the existing tensions and new pressures as well. He had an ambitious agenda for domestic policies that he called the Great Society, which included passing civil rights legislation, using federal funds to wage a "war on poverty," and creating programs to support public education, housing, and jobs. He succeeded in passing many of his programs. But Johnson's political career was undone by American involvement in the expanding war in Vietnam, which American combat troops entered in 1965. A powerful grassroots movement rose up against the war, and its dramatic demonstrations helped turn public sentiment against the war. Johnson did not seek reelection in 1968. Republican Richard M. Nixon won a hard-fought election by promising to return law and order to what he depicted as an unruly nation.

Domestic and international politics were not the only source of high drama in the 1960s. The colorful hippie subculture emerged as a growing youth movement, bringing changes in music, education, fashion, art, and other areas of culture. Thanks to television, American sports became more commercial and more dramatic, and American sports figures like Muhammad Ali, Vince Lombardi, and Joe Namath became important cultural figures. Riots in major cities and the assassinations of the Rev. Dr. Martin Luther King Jr., Malcolm X, and Robert Kennedy caused many Americans to worry about rising violence in their society. An increase in sexual content in books and movies, as well as a new openness about homosexuality at the end of the decade, raised worries about declining morality. There was, of course, much, much more, as changes in one area of American society encouraged or clashed with other movements and trends.

The dramatic, stirring, and sometimes violent events of the 1960s make it an important decade for students to study in their quest to understand American society as it exists today. Many aspects of American culture in the 2000s can be traced back to that era. In some ways, the 1960s are still close at hand. Classic rock radio stations continue to play music from the decade. In fact, the Beatles remain one of the top-selling bands, just as they were in the 1960s. Fashion trends introduced in the 1960s—bell-bottoms and paisley fabric, for example—make periodic comebacks. Politicians continue to refer to the legacy of President John F. Kennedy and civil rights leader Martin Luther King Jr. to inspire audiences. Political leaders and activists also point to the lessons of the Vietnam War to help Americans understand foreign policy. Many Americans who experienced the 1960s firsthand are in positions of power in American society in the 2000s, and their experiences of that decade inform their actions.

In some ways, however, the 1960s can seem quite distant. For example, during that era, television was still a relatively new phenomenon. Nightly coverage of war on television was something new to Americans. In addition, the Cold War (1945–91) between the United States and the Soviet Union—and the threat of nuclear war—informed every decision about foreign policy. And, sexuality, especially homosexuality, was never discussed in polite company, much less on television. One of the features that make this decade so fascinating is the fact that the 1960s are so close, yet so far away.

The Sixties in America: Primary Sources tells the story of the 1960s in the words of the people who lived and shaped the decade. Approximately twenty-five excerpted and full-text documents provide a wide range of perspectives on this period of history. Included are excerpts from political speeches and proclamations; manifestos from civil rights groups and antiwar protesters; influential books of the era; magazine articles; and reflections by individuals who lived through the tumultuous times.

Format

The excerpts in *The Sixties in America: Primary Sources* are divided into six chapters. Each of the chapters focuses on a specific theme: The Struggle for Civil Rights, Feminist Perspectives, The War in Vietnam, The Antiwar Movement, "The Times They Are a Changin'": Radicals on the Left and Right, and Debating the Power of Television. Every chapter opens with a historical overview, followed by reprinted documents.

Each excerpt (or section of excerpts) includes the following additional features:

- **Introductory material** places the document and its author in a historical context.

- **Things to remember while reading** offers important background information about the featured text.

- **Excerpt** presents the document in its original spelling and format.

- **What happened next...** discusses the impact of the document and/or relevant historical events following the date of the document.

- **Did you know...** provides interesting facts about the document and its author.

- **Consider the following...** poses questions about the material for the reader to consider.

- **For More Information** offers resources for further study of the document and its author as well as sources used by the authors in writing the material.

Other features of *The Sixties in America: Primary Sources* include sidebar boxes highlighting interesting, related information. More than sixty black-and-white photos illustrate the text. In addition, each excerpt is accompanied by a glossary running in the margin alongside the reprinted document that defines terms, people, and ideas. The volume begins with a timeline of events and a "Words to Know" section, and concludes with a general bibliography and subject index of people, places, and events discussed throughout *The Sixties in America: Primary Sources*.

The Sixties in America Reference Library

The Sixties in America: Primary Sources is only one component of the three-part U•X•L Sixties in America Reference Library. The other two titles in this set are:

- ***The Sixties in America: Almanac*** (one volume) presents, in fifteen chapters, a comprehensive overview of events that occurred within the United States during the 1960s. The introduction asks readers to consider the themes that make the decade worthy of study. This includes: the unfolding dramas of the civil rights movement; the Vietnam War, and antiwar movement; the expansion of the federal government under Democratic presidents; the birth of a counterculture and its impact on American entertainment; and a variety of other cultural developments. These issues and others are considered closely in the thematic chapters that follow. Finally, the conclusion asks readers to consider the extent to which the experiences and events of the 1960s shaped American society in the years that followed.

- ***The Sixties in America: Biographies*** (one volume) presents the life stories of twenty-six men and women who played crucial roles in the social, cultural, and political developments of the 1960s. Readers will find coverage of the most notable figures of the decade, including John F. Kennedy, Lyndon B. Johnson, Martin Luther King Jr., and

Malcolm X. Essays are also provided on a number of lesser-known though no less interesting figures, including labor activist Dolores Huerta, atheist activist Madalyn Murray O'Hair, scientist Frances Oldham Kelsey, feminist author and activist Betty Friedan, and Native American activist Richard Oakes.

- A cumulative index of all three titles in the U•X•L Sixties in America Reference Library is also available.

Special Thanks

The authors wish to thank U•X•L's Allison McNeill for being the ideal editor for this set, pointing out pitfalls to avoid while ably steering us toward creating books that would best serve an audience of young readers.

The authors note that work on this book was both enriched and complicated by the growing and diverse body of historical knowledge that exists on the 1960s. The 1960s may be considered a part of the distant past to many of the readers of this book, but many of those who have written about the period lived through it or, in the case of the authors of this book, had parents who lived through it. It was such a dramatic, eventful decade that those with direct experience have not always seen it clearly. As such, the authors have tried to develop an approach to the decade that is without undue bias, though it may take another generation before the decade is seen clearly.

Comments and Suggestions

We welcome your comments on *The Sixties in America: Primary Sources* and suggestions for other topics to consider. Please write: Editors, *The Sixties in America: Primary Sources,* U•X•L, 27500 Drake Rd., Farmington Hills, Michigan 48331-3535; call toll-free: 1-800-877-4253; fax to (248) 699-8097; or send e-mail via http://www.gale.com.

Timeline of Events

1960   Dolores Huerta and César Chávez form the United Farm Workers of America (UFW), an agricultural workers labor union.

January 4, 1960 The United Steel Workers agree on a settlement to end the longest steel strike in U.S. history. The strike had started in July 1959.

February 1, 1960 Four black students request service at a whites-only lunch counter at a Woolworth's store in Greensboro, North Carolina. They politely begin a "sit-in" to protest not being served. Their nonviolent protest sparks a new form of civil rights protest that quickly spreads throughout the American South.

May 1960 The oral contraceptive pill, known as "the pill," is approved for distribution throughout the United States.

May 6, 1960 The Civil Rights Act of 1960 is approved to protect black voting rights. However, the law's loopholes make it very difficult for blacks to register or to vote.

May 10, 1960 Nashville, Tennessee, becomes the first large city to desegregate public places.

May 13, 1960 College students protesting the House Un-American Activities Committee hearing outside the San Francisco, California, city hall are dispersed by police who blast the protestors with fire hoses.

July 25, 1960 The first African American eats a meal at the Woolworth's lunch counter in Greensboro, North Carolina.

September 1960 The Young Americans for Freedom, a group of conservative activists, release a set of principles known as the "Sharon Statement." This is considered the founding document on the modern conservative movement.

Fall 1960 Democrat John F. Kennedy and Republican Richard M. Nixon engage in a series of televised presidential debates, the first such debates to air on national television.

January 3, 1961 The United States severs diplomatic ties with Cuba.

January 20, 1961 In his inaugural speech as president, John F. Kennedy urges Americans to "Ask not what your country can do for you—ask what you can do for your country." Kennedy takes office with Lyndon B. Johnson as vice president.

January 31, 1961 The United States launches a chimpanzee into space in a test flight of Project Mercury, a space mission of the National Aeronautics and Space Administration (NASA).

February 17-23, 1961 A six-day airline strike grounds flights by American, Eastern, Flying Tiger, National, and TWA airlines.

March 20, 1961 Louisiana's legislation enforcing segregation is deemed unconstitutional.

April 12-May 5, 1961 Two Soviet cosmonauts become the first men in space.

April 17, 1961 U.S.-supported Cuban exiles invade Cuba in the Bay of Pigs invasion. To the embarrassment of President Kennedy, they are defeated within three days.

May 4, 1961 Black and white civil rights activists begin their "freedom rides" to various southern cities in an attempt to end segregation in interstate transportation.

May 9, 1961 In a speech to the National Association of Broadcasters, Federal Communications Commission chairperson Newton Minow makes the famous statement that television is a "vast wasteland."

May 14, 1961 Ku Klux Klan members attack freedom riders and burn the riders' bus in Anniston, Alabama.

May 25, 1961 President Kennedy announces that the United States intends to land a man on the moon and return him safely, beginning the "space race" between the Soviets and Americans.

July 21, 1961 Astronaut Gus Grissom blasts off in the second American manned rocket flight, though he does not enter orbit.

August 13, 1961 East Germany begins construction of the Berlin Wall.

October 26-28, 1961 U.S. and Soviet tanks confront each other along the border of East and West Berlin.

November 3, 1961 U.S. government officials return from South Vietnam and suggest that decisive military action will lead to a quick victory.

December 1961 President Kennedy forms the Commission on the Status of Women to investigate barriers to women's full enjoyment of basic rights.

1962 Nationally distributed *Harper's Bazaar* magazine includes a full-page color advertisement featuring a nude model, making nudity in advertising a subject of national discussion.

1962 Scientist Rachel Carson publishes *Silent Spring,* which is credited with giving birth to the modern environmental movement.

January 12, 1962 The U.S. State Department denies Americans who are members of the Communist Party the ability to travel abroad.

February 20, 1962 U.S. astronaut John Glenn is the first American to orbit Earth; all three television networks cover the event.

February 26, 1962 The Supreme Court rules that segregation in interstate and intrastate transportation is unconstitutional.

June 1962 The Students for a Democratic Society (SDS) issues the "Port Huron Statement," a manifesto for the emerging New Left student movement.

June 25, 1962 The Supreme Court ruling in *Engel v. Vitale* holds that prayer in schools is unconstitutional.

July 8, 1962 The U.S. government initiates a study on the impact of television on young children.

July 9-August 1, 1962 Artist Andy Warhol exhibits a series of paintings of Campbell's soup cans at the Ferus Gallery in Los Angeles, California.

July 26, 1962 The public schools in Prince Edward County, Virginia, are opened by federal order after being closed for three years in an attempt to avoid desegregation. The schools remain closed on appeal, however, and the case is sent to the U.S. Supreme Court.

October 1962 President Kennedy faces off with Soviet Premier Nikita Khrushchev over the Soviets' placement of long-range missiles on the island nation of Cuba, eventually forcing the removal of the missiles.

October 1, 1962 James Meredith becomes the first black student to enroll at the University of Mississippi. The event sparks fifteen hours of rioting, leaving two dead. He had been blocked from enrollment by Mississippi governor Ross Barnett on September 24, by Lt. Governor Paul Johnson on September 26, and by riots on campus on September 30.

1963 Betty Friedan publishes *The Feminine Mystique*, a major book on the role of women in U.S. society.

January 14, 1963 In his inaugural speech as governor of Alabama, George Wallace declares his support for "segregation now, segregation tomorrow, segregation forever!"

January 26, 1963 A New York City newspaper strike ends after 114 days with lost revenues of $100 million. It becomes the costliest newspaper strike in history.

January 28, 1963 The first black student enrolls at Clemson College in South Carolina—without incident.

April 2, 1963 The Rev. Dr. Martin Luther King Jr. and the Southern Christian Leadership Conference begin efforts to desegregate the city of Birmingham, Alabama.

June 11, 1963 Alabama Governor George Wallace blocks the steps of the University of Alabama to prevent the enrollment of two black students. However, a court order secures the enrollment of the students.

June 17, 1963 In the case of *Murray v. Curlett,* the U.S. Supreme Court issues a definitive ruling against prayer in public schools. The case launched the career of Madalyn Murray O'Hair, who became America's most vocal atheist activist.

June 26, 1963 President John F. Kennedy pledges that the United States will help West Germany resist communism, proclaiming "Ich bin ein Berliner" (I am a Berliner).

July 16, 1963 Barry Goldwater accepts the Republican presidential nomination, announcing that "extremism in the defense of liberty is no vice."

August 18, 1963 James Meredith becomes the first black to graduate from the University of Mississippi with a bachelor's degree.

August 28, 1963 At the March on Washington for Jobs and Freedom, attended by more than 100,000 supporters of the civil rights movement, the Rev. Dr. Martin Luther King Jr. delivers his "I Have a Dream" speech.

September 15, 1963 Four young black girls are murdered when a bomb explodes under the steps of the Sixteenth Street Baptist Church in Birmingham, Alabama.

November 1, 1963 South Vietnamese president Ngo Dinh Diem is killed in a U.S.-backed coup.

November 22, 1963 President John F. Kennedy is assassinated in Dallas, Texas. Lyndon B. Johnson is sworn in as president.

December 16, 1963 President Lyndon B. Johnson signs an aid-to-higher-education bill into law as a "monument to President Kennedy."

January 8, 1964 President Johnson declares a "War on Poverty."

February 1964 The Beatles begin their first U.S. concert tour.

February 1964 Boxer Cassius Clay defeats Sonny Liston to become world heavyweight champion. The next day he publicly changes his name, first to Muhammad X and then to Muhammad Ali. He also embraces the Nation of Islam as his religion.

March 1964 Black activist Malcolm X breaks with the Nation of Islam, a black separatist group, and begins his own group, the Organization of Afro-American Unity. The new association promotes peaceful coexistence between whites and blacks as well as equal rights for blacks.

May 25, 1964 The U.S. Supreme Court holds that the Prince Edward County, Virginia, schools must open.

June 1964 Three civil rights workers are killed during the voter-registration drive called "freedom summer" in Mississippi.

July 2, 1964 President Johnson signs the Civil Rights Act of 1964 into law.

July 18, 1964 Riots break out in the black neighborhoods of New York City.

August 3, 1964 North Vietnamese patrol boats attack U.S. ships in the Gulf of Tonkin.

August 7, 1964 The U.S. Congress passes the Tonkin Gulf Resolution, granting President Lyndon B. Johnson congressional approval to wage war in Vietnam.

August 30, 1964 President Johnson signs the Equal Opportunity Act, which provides $950 million for antipoverty programs, small-business loans, and youth programs, and also forms the Job Corps.

September 1964 The Warren Commission issues a report declaring that Lee Harvey Oswald acted alone in the assassination of John F. Kennedy.

October 12, 1964 The first space flight with more than one man is launched by the Soviet Union.

December 3, 1964 Nearly eight hundred students sitting in at the administration building of the University of California, Berkeley, are arrested.

December 10, 1964 The Rev. Dr. Martin Luther King Jr. is awarded the Nobel Peace Prize for his work promoting equal rights for all Americans.

January 25, 1965 The federal budget contains the largest increase in welfare and education spending since President Franklin Delano Roosevelt's New Deal of the 1930s.

February 8, 1965 The Soviet Union commits military support to the North Vietnamese.

February 21, 1965 Black leader Malcolm X is shot and killed after delivering a speech in Harlem, New York.

March 2, 1965 U.S. bombing campaigns begin over North Vietnam.

March 7, 1965 Civil rights activists, marching from Selma to Montgomery, Alabama, to protest the lack of voting rights for blacks, are attacked by Alabama state police.

March 8, 1965 The first U.S. combat troops leave for Vietnam; earlier on-ground personnel were advisers or other support personnel.

March 18, 1965 Soviet cosmonaut Aleksei Leonev walks in space for ten minutes.

March 25, 1965 Twenty-five thousand civil rights activists gather in Montgomery, Alabama.

April 17, 1965 The first mass protest against the Vietnam War is organized by Students for a Democratic Society and attracts more than 15,000 protestors to Washington, D.C.

April 25, 1965 The United States confirms that North Vietnamese troops are fighting within South Vietnam.

June 5, 1965 U.S. officials announce the active engagement of U.S. troops in combat in Vietnam.

June 18, 1965 Nguyen Cao Cy becomes South Vietnamese premier.

June 28, 1965 President Johnson increases the military draft from 17,000 to 35,000 men per month.

July 17, 1965 The first close-up photos of Mars taken in space are sent to Earth by U.S. spacecraft *Mariner 4.*

July 28, 1965 125,000 U.S. troops are committed to the fight in Vietnam.

August 6, 1965 President Johnson signs the Voting Rights Act of 1965 into law.

August 11-16, 1965 The Watts section of Los Angeles, California, erupts in riots that kill thirty-five people and damage $200 million in property.

September 16, 1965 Labor leader Dolores Huerta helps organize a strike of 5,000 United Farm Workers of America (UFW) farmworkers in Delano, California. The strike ends in 1970—following a two-year national boycott of grapes—with the recognition of the labor union.

October 15, 1965 Protests against the war in Vietnam spread to forty U.S. cities.

November 27, 1965 Twenty-five thousand antiwar demonstrators converge on Washington, D.C.

December 20, 1965 U.S. field commanders pursue enemy troops into Cambodia, which borders on South Vietnam.

December 21, 1965 The Soviet Union announces increased support for North Vietnam.

1966 The National Organization for Women (NOW), a political action group formed to win equal rights for women, is founded with author Betty Friedan as its first president.

1966 The Student Nonviolent Coordinating Committee (SNCC) changes its official policy from integration to separatism, changes its name to the Student National

Coordinating Committee, and expels all whites from its organization.

January 1966 In the Haight-Ashbury neighborhood of San Francisco, California, a group of young people organize the Trips Festival, which is widely seen as the start of the hippie movement. Within months, Haight-Ashbury becomes the center of this loosely based youth movement.

February 3, 1966 The unmanned Soviet spacecraft, *Luna 9,* makes the first landing on the moon.

February 4, 1966 Televised congressional hearings on U.S. policy regarding the Vietnam War begin.

March 16, 1966 With *Gemini 8,* U.S. astronauts Neil Armstrong and David Scott perform the first space docking of an orbiting spacecraft.

April 3, 1966 The unmanned Soviet spacecraft, *Luna 10,* becomes the first man-made object to orbit the moon.

April 6, 1966 The National Farm Workers Union, headed by César Chávez, is recognized as the bargaining agent for farmworkers at Schenley Industries after nearly a year-long strike.

May 12, 1966 To protest the University of Chicago's cooperation with the military draft, students stage a sit-in at the administration building.

May 15, 1966 Ten thousand antiwar demonstrators picket the White House.

July 1, 1966 The first U.S. health-insurance plan for the elderly, Medicare, starts.

July 11, 1966 The Soviet Union refuses to send athletes to participate in the annual U.S.–Soviet track meet because of U.S. policy in Vietnam.

July 12, 1966 Riots erupt in Chicago, Illinois, and occur in twenty other cities during the summer.

August 30, 1966 Communist China agrees to send aid to North Vietnam.

September 1966 In a famous *Playboy* magazine interview, LSD advocate Timothy Leary urges Americans to "turn on, tune in [and] drop out."

September 1, 1966 French President Charles de Gaulle asks the United States to withdraw from Vietnam.

September 9, 1966 The Traffic Safety Act is signed by President Johnson. It enforces safety standards for automobiles.

October 1966 Huey P. Newton and Bobby Seale establish the Black Panthers, a militant black nationalist group.

1967 College student protests of the Vietnam War and the draft increase throughout the country.

1967 The "summer of love" begins when more than 75,000 young people migrate to San Francisco's Haight-Ashbury district with the hope of building a new society based on peace, "free love," and drugs. During the summer, bad drug experiences, crime, rape, and violence escalate in the district. The summer ends with a march proclaiming the death of the hippie movement.

1967 The use of LSD is made illegal nationwide.

January 15, 1967 Led by fiery coach Vince Lombardi, the Green Bay Packers win the National Football League's inaugural (first) Super Bowl.

January 27, 1967 Gus Grissom, Edward White, and Roger Chaffee are killed aboard the rocket *Apollo 1* after a fire on the launch pad.

April 1967 Large antiwar protests occur in San Francisco and New York City.

May 13, 1967 New York City hosts a pro-Vietnam War parade that attracts 70,000 people.

June 23-25, 1967 In Glassboro, New Jersey, Soviet Premier Aleksei Kosygin and U.S. President Johnson discuss nuclear arms control, Vietnam, and the Middle East.

July 12, 1967 Riots break out in Newark, New Jersey.

July 23, 1967 Riots in Detroit, Michigan, kill forty-three people and damage $200 million in property; the National Guard is called in to restore order.

August 3, 1967 President Johnson announces plans to send 45,000 to 50,000 additional troops to Vietnam in order to raise troop strength to 525,000 by the end of 1968.

October 21-22, 1967 More than 250,000 people organized by the National Mobilization to End the War in Vietnam (MOBE) gather to protest the Vietnam War in Washington, D.C. The protest ends in a lighthearted attempt, led by activist Abbie Hoffmann, to levitate the Pentagon.

January 25, 1968 Secretary of Health, Education, and Welfare John Gardner's doubts about the "Great Society" lead him to resign.

January 31, 1968 The North Vietnamese army launches the Tet Offensive, a major military campaign against South Vietnamese and American forces in South Vietnam.

February 6, 1968 Sweden grants asylum (political protection) to six American soldiers opposed to the war in Vietnam.

February 27, 1968 News anchor Walter Cronkite announces on national television that he believes the war in Vietnam has become a stalemate (a situation in which progress is at a standstill).

March 8, 1968 The first statewide teacher's strike in U.S. history ends after almost half of Florida's public-school teachers spend more than two weeks on picket lines.

March 16, 1968 The My Lai massacre leaves hundreds of South Vietnamese men, women, and children dead at the hands of U.S. soldiers. (Reports of the deaths are suppressed for more than a year.)

March 31, 1968 President Johnson announces that he will not seek reelection as president of the United States.

April 4, 1968 Civil rights leader Rev. Dr. Martin Luther King Jr. is assassinated in Memphis, Tennessee.

May 6-30, 1968 Student demonstrations in Paris, France, spark a general strike throughout the country that eventually involves 10 million workers.

May 12, 1968 Peace talks to end the Vietnam War begin in Paris.

June 5, 1968 Democratic presidential candidate Robert Kennedy is assassinated in Los Angeles shortly after winning the California primary.

August 26-29, 1968 At the Democratic presidential nominating convention in Chicago, Illinois, Vice President Hubert Humphrey secures the party's nomination. Protests rage, both inside and outside the convention center, and police and National Guard forces attack and beat demonstrators on national television. A radical group known as the Yippies nominates a pig for president.

September 7, 1968 More than one hundred women's liberation protestors gather outside the Miss America Pageant proceedings to throw out bras, girdles, and high-heeled shoes to protest women's subordination to men in American society.

October 14-28, 1968 American 200-meter-dash gold medalist Tommie Smith and bronze medalist John Carlos bow their heads and raise their fists in a Black Power salute during the playing of the "Star-Spangled Banner" at the Olympic Games in Mexico. As a result, they are stripped of their medals and suspended from their team.

November 5, 1968 Republican Richard M. Nixon is elected president, defeating Democrat Hubert Humphrey and independent candidate George Wallace.

December 4, 1968 The U.S. government enforces the 1964 Civil Rights Act in the North by ordering the public schools in Union, New Jersey, to comply with desegregation.

December 21, 1968 With *Apollo 8,* the United States becomes the first to orbit a manned spacecraft around the Moon.

1969 The "Great Society" programs give educational aid to 9 million children from low-income families, offer Head Start primary care to 716,000, and support the vocational education of 4 million high school and 845,000 technical students.

1969 President Nixon continues negotiations to end the Vietnam War.

1969 The Supreme Court orders the immediate desegregation of all public schools.

June 8, 1969 President Nixon orders the removal of 25,000 American troops from Vietnam, thus beginning the American withdrawal from the war.

June 18-22, 1969 The Students for a Democratic Society holds its national convention, which concludes with the organization breaking up into the Progressive Labor Party and the Revolutionary Youth Movement (RYM).

June 27, 1969 Homosexuals and police clash at the Stonewall Inn in New York following a police raid on the bar; the Stonewall riot is the symbolic start of the gay liberation movement.

July 20, 1969 The United States lands the first manned spacecraft, *Apollo 11,* on the Moon. Neil Armstrong and Edwin "Buzz" Aldrin walk on the Moon's surface.

August 1969 Members of the Manson Family, a cult led by Charles Manson, murder seven people outside Los Angeles, California.

August 15-17, 1969 The Woodstock Music Festival is held in upstate New York, drawing more than 500,000 music lovers.

September 3, 1969 North Vietnamese president Ho Chi Minh dies at age seventy-nine.

October 15, 1969 Various antiwar groups label this day "Moratorium Day" and organize hundreds of thousands of marchers in protests across the United States.

November 15, 1969 250,000 antiwar demonstrators march on Washington, D.C.

November 21, 1969 A group of Native American activists, led by Richard Oakes, takes possession of Alcatraz Island in the bay near San Francisco, California. The event marks one of the most dramatic moments in the growing Native American rights movement.

1973 Following the landmark decision by the U.S. Supreme Court in *Roe v. Wade,* abortion is legalized in the United States. For many involved in the struggle for women's rights, particularly women's reproductive rights, this is a major victory for their cause.

April 23, 1975 President Gerald Ford, who succeeded Richard Nixon, announces that the war in Vietnam is "finished."

April 30, 1975 The South Vietnamese surrender to officially end the war in Vietnam.

January 21, 1977 President Jimmy Carter fulfills his campaign promise to pardon those who had peacefully avoided the draft during the Vietnam War. This allowed draft dodgers, who had fled the country to avoid mandatory military service, to return home to the United States without fear of being prosecuted for their actions.

1980 The conservative movement, begun under Senator Barry Goldwater, shows its strength as Republican Ronald Reagan soundly defeats incumbent president Jimmy Carter in the presidential election.

1982 The Equal Rights Amendment, which states that equal legal rights cannot be denied based on gender, fails to be ratified. Although the amendment passed in both the House and Senate in 1972, it needed to be ratified by three-fourths (thirty-eight) of the states before it could become part of the U.S. Constitution. The ERA fell three states short of ratification by its deadline in 1982. President Ronald Reagan was among those opposed to the amendment; earlier, he became the first major presidential candidate to voice his opposition to the ERA.

November 13, 1982 The Vietnam Veterans Memorial, also known as "The Wall," is dedicated in Washington,

D.C. Designed by twenty-one-year-old artist/architect Maya Lin, the memorial records the names of the more than 58,000 American men and women who did not return from the war.

1991 The communist government of the Soviet Union collapses, thus ending the Cold War between the United States and the Soviet Union.

November 2000 The first crew takes up residence on the International Space Station, a joint effort by the Canadian, European, Japanese, Brazilian, Russian, and U.S. space agencies. The crew consists of two Russians and one American.

August 2003 On August 20, Alabama Chief Justice Roy Moore refuses to abide by a U.S. District Court order to remove a Ten Commandments monument from the state's judicial building. The U.S. District Court had ruled that the monument violated the separation of church and state. On August 27, workers remove the monument from public view. Later, Moore loses his job for refusing to comply with the court order. The monument itself begins a tour of U.S. cities in mid-2004.

2004 Twin robots, part of NASA's Mars Exploration Rover program, transmit photos to scientists back on Earth as the agency studies the geology of the red planet.

2004 Senator John Kerry, a Vietnam veteran who later spoke against the war, runs for president against incumbent George W. Bush.

Words to Know

A

activist: A person who campaigns vigorously for or against a political, social, or economic issue.

authentic: True to one's spirit or character. In the 1960s, the idea of being authentic was important to many young people because they considered the behavior of their parents to be inauthentic or something that compromised their own values.

B

black nationalism: An ideology held among militant groups of American blacks that called for the formation of self-governing black communities that were separate from those of whites.

Black Power: A movement among American blacks to gain economic and political rights and improve their social condition.

C

civil rights: The legal, political, and human rights guaranteed by the U.S. constitution and various legislative acts, including the right to vote, the right to equal protection under the law, to right to equal use of public facilities, and the right to freedom of speech.

Cold War: A prolonged conflict for world dominance from 1945 to 1991 between the two superpowers, the democratic, capitalist United States and the communist Soviet Union. The weapons of conflict were commonly words of propaganda and threats, not military conflicts.

communal living: A shared living space formed by a group of like-minded individuals. Those living in communes work together for the common good of the group and share material possessions.

communism: A political system in which most aspects of social and economic life are dictated by the government. Under communism, all property is owned by the government and, theoretically, wealth is distributed evenly throughout society.

conservatism: A political ideology based on the concept of a limited federal government, one that protects individual's freedoms by maintaining domestic order, providing for national defense, and administering justice. This ideology is generally opposed to the use of federal powers for the protection or preservation of civil rights.

counterculture: Literally, a cultural group whose values run counter to the majority. In the late 1950s and through the 1960s, several distinct groups criticized developments in American society and worked for social change. Some historians use the term to refer only to hippies, but the counterculture also included groups such as the New Left and racial and ethnic political action groups.

D

democracy: A political system that places the power of the government in the hands of citizens. During the Cold War, democracy was generally considered to include a capitalist economic system, in which individual property owners made the decisions that determined economic activities.

desegregation: To end the practice of separating races, as in schools, buses, restaurants, or other public facilities.

discrimination: The singling out of minority groups for unfavorable treatment.

draft (selective service): A system by which persons are chosen for mandatory service in a nation's military.

draft dodgers: Persons who hide in or flee from a country in order to avoid mandatory military service.

drop out: To reject the social and economic norms of society by living an alternative lifestyle.

E

establishment: A term used by members of the counterculture to refer to the established power structures and authority figures of the time, including parents, employers, and the government.

F

feminism: A theory and organized social movement based on the idea that male and female genders are socially, politically, and economically equal.

G

grassroots: An effort formed by ordinary people at a local community level.

Great Society: The social vision of President Lyndon B. Johnson that would use the federal government to improve the American quality of life. This would be achieved by enacting legislation to regulate air and water quality, to offer medical care, to provide civil rights, to enforce safety issues with regard to citizens and industry, and to support the arts and humanities, among other things.

H

hallucinogenic: A drug that disrupts the nervous system to produce perceptions of objects or sounds without regard to reality.

hippies: People, usually young, who rejected the established customs of society by engaging in such activities as taking drugs, living in communal societies, dressing in unconventional ways, and wearing their hair in long, flowing styles. Some historians refer to hippies as "the counterculture."

I

integration: A social plan in the United States to involve African Americans as equals in white society, especially in areas where the races were formerly separated or segregated.

L

liberalism: A political ideology based on the concept of a federal government that protects individual's freedoms by maintaining domestic order, providing for national defense, and administering justice, but also protects and preserves civil rights of citizens by maintaining programs to aid certain social groups.

LSD (lysergic acid diethylamide): A hallucinogenic drug that disrupts the normal functioning of the nervous system to cause a loss of connection to reality.

P

prejudice: A negative opinion or attitude about a person, race, or group of people that is not based on fact or one's experiences with such people or groups. Instead, such opinions are based on unfounded ideas about how that person, race, or group might be or act.

protest: An organized public demonstration of discontent with the governance of or social circumstances within a society.

psychedelic: Often used as a descriptor relating to a drug that causes hallucinogenic effects, such as the perception of distorted sounds or images. As an adjective, psychedelic is used to describe music and art associated with the hippie movement.

R

radical: Someone who supports an extreme political cause.

riot: A violent, public disturbance by a disorderly group of people.

S

segregation: The separation of social groups based on racial differences. Segregation was legally mandated in some southern states and culturally practiced in some northern states. Segregation was practiced on buses and trains as well as in schools, concert halls, restaurants, and other areas. In some places, bathrooms and water fountains were designated "whites only" or "coloreds only."

sexual revolution: A period in which sexual practices, sexual orientation, and sexual issues—such as public displays of nudity, unmarried couples living together, homosexuality, and abortion—became more openly discussed and accepted.

Space Race: A competition between the United States and the Soviet Union to build space programs that launched rockets and men outside the Earth's orbit. One of the chief objectives of the Space Race was to land a man on the moon.

U

Uncle Tom: A derogatory term used to refer to a black person who acts in submissive ways toward whites.

V

Vietcong: Guerilla forces in South Vietnam who allied themselves with the North Vietnamese Army in an effort to unify the country under communist rule. The Vietcong fought the U.S. forces that came to aid South Vietnam in its quest to remain independent. Guerilla forces are those involved in unconventional warfare practices, including sabotage and terrorist activities.

W

War on Poverty: The central program of President Lyndon B. Johnson's "Great Society," this effort tried to end poverty by providing poor Americans with education, job training, food, housing, and money.

welfare: Government aid to the needy in the form of money or other necessities, such as foodstuffs or housing.

Text Credits

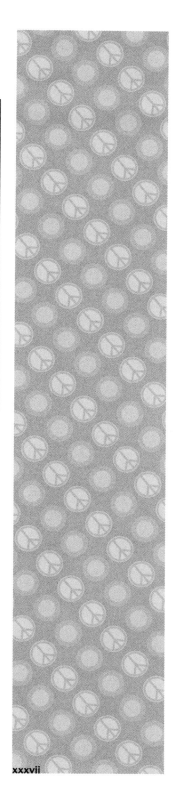

The following is a list of the copyright holders who have granted us permission to reproduce excerpts from primary source documents in *The Sixties in America: Primary Sources.* Every effort has been made to trace copyright; if omissions have been made, please contact us.

Copyrighted excerpts were reproduced from the following sources:

Friedan, Betty. From *The Feminine Mystique.* W.W. Norton & Company, 1997. Copyright © 1997, 1983, 1974, 1973, 1963, by Betty Friedan. All rights reserved. Reproduced by permission of W. W. Norton & Company, Inc.

From "Invitation to Action," in *American Women: The Report of the President's Commission on the Status of Women and Other Publications of the Commission.* Edited by Margaret Mead and Frances B. Kaplan. Charles Scribner's Sons, 1965. Copyright © 1965 Charles Scribner's Sons. All rights reserved. Reproduced by permission of the Gale Group.

King, Jr., Martin Luther. From "Where Do We Go From Here?," in *A Call to Conscience: The Landmark Speeches of Dr. Martin Luther King, Jr.* Edited By Clayborne Carson and Kris Shepard. Copyright © 1967 Martin Luther King Jr., copyright renewed 1991 Coretta Scott King. All rights reserved. Reproduced by arrangement with the Estate of Martin Luther King, Jr., c/o Writers House Inc. as agent for the proprietor New York, NY.

Malcolm X. From "The Ballot or the Bullet," in *Malcolm X Speaks: Selected Speeches and Statements.* Edited with Prefatory Notes by George Breitman. Grove Weidenfeld, 1990. Copyright © 1965 by Merit Publishers and Betty Shabazz. All rights reserved. Reproduced by permission of the Estate of Malcolm X.

McDonald, Joe. From "I-Feel-Like-I'm-Fixin'-to-Die Rag." Words and music by Joe McDonald © 1965 by Alkatraz Corner Music Co, BMI. Reproduced by permission.

McLuhan, Marshall. From an introduction and "The Medium Is the Message," in *Understanding the Media: The Extensions of Man.* Introduction by Lewis H. Lapham. The MIT Press, 1997. © 1964, 1994 Corinne McLuhan. Introduction © 1994 Massachusetts Institute of Technology. All rights reserved. Reproduced by permission of The MIT Press, Cambridge, MA.

The Sixties
in America
Primary Sources

The Struggle for Civil Rights

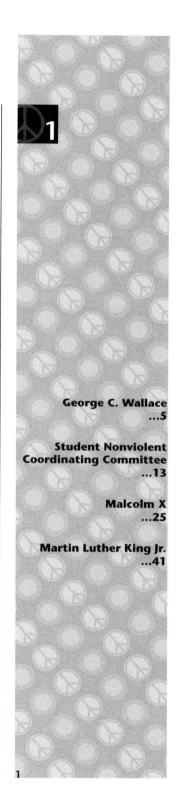

Civil rights for blacks was not a new idea in the 1960s. African Americans had been struggling for racial justice since slavery was ended following the American Civil War (1861–65). While they had gained their independence and a few social privileges by World War II (1939–45), the war against racist fascists (people who believe in a political philosophy that prefers a dictatorial government with severe economic and social distinctions between citizens, often based on racial differences) in Europe brought the reality of American racism to light. America sent troops to secure freedom in other parts of the world but maintained a segregated (separated by race; in the South, many public buildings and services, such as schools, buses, and lunch counters, had separate facilities for whites and blacks) society that denied basic rights, such as voting, to people based on race.

World War II served as the catalyst for the dramatic changes in the 1960s. President Harry S. Truman (1884–1972; served 1945–53)) ended segregation in the armed forces and the federal civil service in 1948. The National Association for the Advancement of Colored People (NAACP) Legal Defense

Fund then mounted a series of legal actions that led to the 1954 *Brown* v. *Board of Education* Supreme Court ruling, which declared racial segregation in American schools unconstitutional. More protests followed. In 1955, Rosa Parks (1913–) triggered the Montgomery, Alabama, bus boycott, a protest against racial discrimination on the local bus service that lasted more than a year and helped to make Martin Luther King Jr. (1929–1968) a civil rights leader. King and other ministers, thrilled with the results of their efforts, formed the Southern Christian Leadership Conference (SCLC) in 1957 to spread their message of nonviolent protest against segregation.

As blacks won these and other smaller civil rights victories, some Americans, especially white southerners, threatened to resist the integration of blacks into white society. Southern politicians spoke out against the end of segregation and tried to resist federal court rulings that required mixing races in schools, on public transportation, and elsewhere. Membership in violent organizations such as the Ku Klux Klan, a white supremacist group, boomed. News of these organizations' frightening raids intended to intimidate and harm blacks permeated American society. Tensions grew between supporters and opponents of civil rights for African Americans.

The 1960s opened with four black college students sitting down at a whites-only lunch counter in North Carolina and refusing to budge until they could buy a cup of coffee. Within months, tens of thousands of student protestors organized "sit-in" demonstrations throughout the South to protest racial segregation. Their actions led to the founding of the Student Non-Violent Coordinating Committee (SNCC) in 1960. These nonviolent, mass protests were often met with violent reaction. Protestors were sometimes brutally beaten and terrorized. One of the most violent clashes occurred in Birmingham, Alabama, in 1961. There members of the Ku Klux Klan attacked a bus filled with a racially mixed group of men and women calling themselves "freedom riders" who were attempting to travel from Washington, D.C., to Alabama in protest of white southerners' refusal to end segregation of interstate bus and train travel. In the coming years, more and more protestors were harmed as they worked to win civil rights legislation. In 1963 television news programs and newspapers publicized the police attack of nonviolent protestors, including many schoolchildren, in Birmingham, Alabama. The protestors were beaten with clubs, sprayed with fire hoses, and attacked by police dogs.

As it became clear that enduring civil rights victories required both federally mandated legal protections and government enforcement—not just isolated protests of segregated schools, buses, and lunch counters—civil rights supporters debated how to best meet their goals. Could they affect a dramatic change in the government with peaceful methods or would they need to carry out acts of violence? Several different strategies for victory emerged, splitting civil rights activists into groups of peaceful and militant protestors.

The documents selected for this chapter offer a peek into the tensions over civil rights during the 1960s. In his inaugural speech on January 13, 1964, Alabama governor **George C. Wallace** promised segregation "forever." His speech affected whites living in the state much differently than it affected Alabama blacks without the right to vote. The various strategies for winning civil rights are represented here with speeches from **Martin Luther King Jr.** and Malcolm X (1925–1965). Martin Luther King Jr. maintained throughout his life that nonviolent protest was the only political strategy worth pursuing. In his last speech to the SCLC on August 16, 1967, published as "Where Do We Go From Here?," King assessed a decade of various types of protest and reconfirmed his commitment to nonviolence. Nonviolent strategies frustrated some activists, including **Malcolm X**, and in the early 1960s Malcolm X outlined a different philosophy for success. In his April 3, 1964 speech, "The Ballot or the Bullet," given in Cleveland, Ohio, Malcolm X described when civil rights activism should shift from nonviolence to determined violent protest.

The struggle between advocates for and against violence within the civil rights movement is highlighted with the organizing documents of the **Student Nonviolent Coordinating Committee** (SNCC). In its position paper of 1966, the SNCC offered a description of the roots of the civil rights problem and hopes for the future. This organization, which had opened the decade with a firm commitment to nonviolence, had shifted its view dramatically by 1966. Each in its own way, the diverse civil rights philosophies presented here helped to shape the decade and to change the lives of Americans forever.

George C. Wallace

Excerpt from his inaugural speech, delivered January 14, 1963
Reprinted from *Our Nation's Archive*.

Published in 1999.

G eorge Corley Wallace (1919–1998) made himself a national symbol of racism in the 1960s. During his five-year
tenure as an Alabama judge starting in 1953, he established a
reputation as an opponent of all civil rights legislation.

Born on August 25, 1919, the son of a cotton farmer
in rural Clio, Alabama, **George Corley Wallace** spent most of
his life as an "underdog," someone who was unlikely to succeed. However, he worked hard from an early age to help
earn money for his family and to eventually pay his way
through college. His first taste of politics came when he was
fifteen; he took a part-time position as a page in the Alabama
Senate. In college, he launched a campaign to appeal to independent and out-of-state students to beat the favored, frater-
nity-backed candidates in the race for presidency of his fresh-
man class. After college he joined the Air Force in 1942 and
flew several missions during World War II (1939–45).

After his military discharge, Wallace became assistant
to the attorney general of Alabama in 1946. The next year he
launched his political career, winning a seat in the state legislature. Throughout the 1950s Wallace had a reputation as a

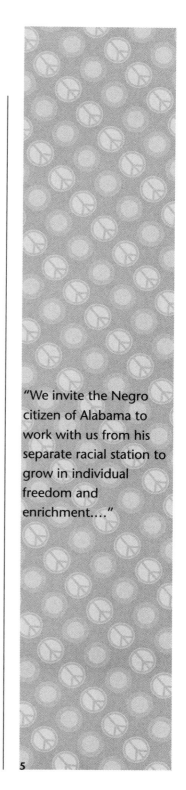

"We invite the Negro
citizen of Alabama to
work with us from his
separate racial station to
grow in individual
freedom and
enrichment...."

Governor George C. Wallace at a 1964 rally to support Republican presidential candidate Barry Goldwater. *AP/Wide World Photos. Reproduced by permission.*

racially tolerant liberal. When he first ran for governor in 1958, the National Association for the Advancement of Colored People endorsed his candidacy. After losing the Alabama governorship to a strident racist, though, Wallace revised his moderate political agenda to a platform that promised to defy federal pressure for racial integration. With his new strong position, Wallace won the governor's race in 1962, backed by the Ku Klux Klan, a militant white supremacist group.

His inaugural speech captured the anger of those in southern states who felt that the federal government had overstepped its authority by passing federal desegregation laws. While Wallace's stance on segregation brought him into the national limelight, he committed himself as governor to fight for states' right to determine their own laws. Wallace believed that the federal government should be very limited in its authority to regulate laws in individual states. He worked hard to curb the federal government's attempts to pass laws that he believed should be decided by the residents of each state.

Things to remember while reading the excerpt from George Wallace's 1963 inaugural speech:

- While serving as an Alabama judge, George Wallace drew public attention and the nickname "The Fighting Judge" when he publicly refused to turn over voter registration records to the United States Civil Rights Commission. Later, he quietly ordered the records to be given to the commission, but his new nickname stuck.

- Wallace contended that his stance on racial segregation had more to do with states' rights than race.

- Wallace established a large political following in Alabama because of his opposition to racial segregation.

Excerpt from George Wallace's inaugural speech, January 14, 1963

Today I have stood where once **Jefferson Davis** stood and took an oath to my people. It is very appropriate then that from this Cradle of the Confederacy, this very heart of the great Anglo-Saxon Southland, that today we sound the drum for freedom [....]

Let us rise to the call of freedom-loving blood that is in us and send our answer to the **tyranny** that clanks its chains upon the South. In the name of the greatest people that ever trod this earth, I **draw the line in the dust** and **toss the gauntlet** before the feet of tyranny, and I say: segregation now, segregation tomorrow, segregation forever [....]

Government has become our God. It is a system that is the very opposite of Christ. The **international racism** of the liberals seeks to persecute the **international white** minority to the whim of the **international colored** so that we are **footballed** about according to the favor of the Afro-Asian bloc.... [If the races] **amalgamate** into the one unit...then we become a **mongrel unit of one** under a single, all-powerful government....

We invite the Negro citizen of Alabama to work with us from his separate racial station to grow in individual freedom and enrichment....

But we warn those of any group who would follow the false doctrines of **communistic amalgamation** that we will not surrender our system of government, our freedom of race and religion [that] was won at a hard price; and if it requires a hard price to retain it, we are able—and quite willing—to pay it.

Jefferson Davis (1808–1889): The president of the Confederate States of America during the Civil War.

Tyranny: In this case, tyranny refers to the U.S. federal government, which passed laws that overruled some laws of Southern states.

Draw the line in the dust: Similar to "Draw a line in the sand," meaning to mark the point at which an opponent should not pass.

Toss the gauntlet: Similar to "Throw down the gauntlet," meaning to open a challenge.

International racism, international white, and international colored: Wallace is referring to the theory that white southerners are being persecuted by those who want to eliminate racial differences.

Footballed: Tossed.

Amalgamate: Combined.

Mongrel unit of one: A racially mixed citizenry.

Communistic amalgamation: Social mixing that results in the unification of people into a single, mixed race.

What happened next...

George Wallace spent the duration of the 1960s working to prevent desegregation. While he served as governor of Alabama, civil rights activists suffered violence at the hands

George C. Wallace pledges "segregation now, segregation tomorrow, segregation forever" during his inaugural address as governor of Alabama, January 14, 1963. © *Bettmann/Corbis. Reproduced by permission.*

of state troopers. Several blacks were killed in racially motivated acts in Alabama, including four small black girls who were killed after a bomb placed under the steps of the Sixteenth Street Baptist Church by a Ku Klux Klan member exploded on September 13, 1963.

Nationally recognized as a desegregationist, Wallace ran for the U.S. presidency in 1968 on a racist platform but lost to Richard Nixon. Four years later, Wallace ran another presidential campaign and received a great deal of southern support. While campaigning, Wallace was shot five times by Arthur H. Bremer in a failed assassination attempt that left him paralyzed from the waist down. He withdrew from the race. (Bremer, whose motives for the shooting remain unclear, was sentenced to fifty-three years in prison.)

Wallace did not retire permanently from politics despite using a wheelchair. In 1982 he regained the governorship of Alabama and served out a fifth term in the office with the support of many blacks. In the 1980s, Wallace reinvented himself as a more moderate politician and reversed his position about many racial issues. During his last term in office, Wallace worked to increase the numbers of black voters in Alabama and appointed approximately 150 blacks to legislative committees and other advisory groups.

Wallace tried to explain the dramatic shift in his political opinions to Carl T. Rowan of the *Washington Post* in 1991. About saying the words "segregation now, tomorrow and forever," Wallace said, "I have regretted it all my life." He went on to explain that "When I first ran for governor...I had to stand up for segregation or be defeated, but I never insulted black people by calling them inferior, that statement in 1963 about 'segregation forever' and my stand in the classroom door reflected my vehemence, my belligerence, against the federal court system that seemed to be taking over everything in the South." Wallace's shift in stances may have had less to do with his true feelings about the issues and more to do with his desire to hold political office. According to Hank Sanders, a black member of the Alabama Senate quoted in the *New York Times,* Wallace was "a man who just had a keen sense of which way the political winds were blowing, and the nose to follow them."

Did you know...

- George Wallace tried to physically prevent two black students from entering the University of Alabama in 1963. His refusal to admit them to the campus prompted President John F. Kennedy to send National Guard troops to ensure the students' enrollment.

- During his first term as governor, Wallace authorized state troopers to prevent the desegregation of Alabama's public schools. Alabama was the last southern state to desegregate schools in 1963.

- On March 7, 1965, civil rights activists began a march from Selma to Montgomery, Alabama, to bring attention to the voting rights cause. Wallace sent mounted state troopers to prevent them. Using tear gas and clubs, the troopers stopped the march at the Pettus Bridge just out-

George Wallace, facing a National Guardsman, blocks a doorway at the University of Alabama to try to prevent two black students from entering, 1963.
AP/Wide World Photos. Reproduced by permission.

side Selma. On March 9, police blocked yet another march, which leader Martin Luther King Jr. turned back. When the activists eventually won court permission to proceed, thousands of supporters marched to Montgomery, winning national publicity for their cause. Soon after, the Voting Rights Act of 1965 passed through Congress.

- The percentage of black students attending integrated schools in the seventeen southern states rose from 6.4 percent in 1960 to 84.3 percent in 1970.

Consider the following...

- Near the end of his life, George C. Wallace tried to reverse his reputation as a racist, saying that his efforts were not anti-black but anti-federal government. His actions reflected his anger at the federal court system, which he believed was stripping the states of their authority. Can you make a case for this distinction?

- Do you think Wallace could have won the governorship of Alabama without taking a stand on segregation? Explain your reasoning.

- When Wallace ran for presidency in 1968, he campaigned mostly as an opponent of desegregation. Do you think his choice to run as an opponent of desegregation was more effective than a choice to run as a proponent of states' rights? Why?

For More Information

Books

Bruun, Erik, and Jay Crosby, eds. *Our Nation's Archive: The History of the United States in Documents.* New York: Black Dog & Leventhal, 1999.

Crass, Philip, *The Wallace Factor.* New York: Mason/Charter, 1976.

Dorman, Michael, *The George Wallace Myth.* New York: Bantam, 1976.

Lesher, Stephan, *George Wallace: American Populist.* Addison-Reading, MA: Wesley, 1994.

Schneider, Gregory L., ed. *Conservatism in America since 1930.* New York: New York University Press, 2003.

Periodicals

Hirsley, Michael. "Ex-Alabama Gov. George Wallace; Opposed Integration in the 1960s." *Chicago Tribune* (September 14, 1998): p. 7.

Pearson, Richard. "Former Ala. Gov. George C. Wallace Dies." *Washington Post* (September 14, 1998): p. A1.

Raines, Howell. "George Wallace, Symbol of the Fight to Maintain Segregation, Dies at 79." *New York Times* (September 15, 1998): p. B10.

Rowan, Carl T. "The Rehabilitation of George Wallace." *Washington Post* (September 5, 1991): p. A21.

Web sites

Alabama Department of Archives and History. http://www.archives.state.al.us/govs_list/inauguralspeech.html (accessed on August 4, 2004).

Student Nonviolent Coordinating Committee

Excerpt from "The Basis of Black Power," 1966

Reprinted from *"Takin' It to the Streets:"A Sixties Reader,* **2003; also available online at www.hartford-hwp.com/archives/45a/387.html**

On February 1, 1960, four black students from North Carolina Agricultural and Technical College sat down at an all-white Woolworth's lunch counter in Greensboro, North Carolina, to order some coffee. When the waitress refused to serve them, the students stayed, stating that they would not leave until they could place an order. The four remained sitting at the counter quietly without service for about an hour until the store closed. The next day, nearly thirty students occupied the lunch counter for about two hours, attracting the attention of local news reporters. The day after that, sixty-six black students filled nearly every seat at the lunch counter. After a week of steady protests, no black student had been served at the lunch counter, and the Woolworth's manager decided to close the store temporarily. Students at other colleges became inspired to organize their own sit-ins. By the end of April, more than 50,000 protestors, mostly students, had staged nonviolent sit-ins in every southern state.

To organize their efforts, several of the student sit-in protestors gathered at a conference at Shaw University in Raleigh, North Carolina, on April 16, 1960. The result of the

"Negroes in this country have never been allowed to organize themselves because of white interference. As a result of this, the stereotype has been reinforced that blacks cannot organize themselves."

conference was the formation of the Student Nonviolent Co-ordinating Committee (SNCC, pronounced "snick"). One of the founding principles of the organization was nonviolence. Members agreed that in order to win the support of non-blacks, they must never respond with acts of violence, even if attacked. During the first half of the 1960s, SNCC members strictly followed their doctrine of nonviolence. Some members were beaten; others shot. And when these attacks hit newsstands and aired on television, SNCC won supporters.

Cooperative black and white civil rights activism culminated on August 28, 1963, when 250,000 people rallied at the Lincoln Memorial in Washington, D.C., in support of the proposal of civil rights legislation introduced by President John F. Kennedy. During the rally, Martin Luther King Jr. gave his "I have a dream" speech that envisioned a color-blind society. All three television networks broadcast the speech to millions of viewers. But for SNCC, this rally marked not a victory, but a real disappointment with the struggle for civil rights. SNCC chairman John Lewis (1940–) had planned to publicly criticize the Kennedy administration for proposing civil rights legislation that did too little to really help blacks. Although other civil rights leaders at the rally persuaded Lewis to temper his speech that day, Lewis and other SNCC members did not let go of their angry disappointment at the slowness of progress within the civil rights movement.

By the mid-1960s, the strategy of SNCC officially changed when Stokely Carmichael (1941–1998) gained control of the organization. Speaking in Greenwood, Mississippi, in 1966, Carmichael announced: "The only way we gonna stop them white men from whuppin' us is to take over. We've been saying *freedom* for six years—and we ain't got nothin'. What we gonna start saying now is 'Black Power,'" according to *The Columbia Guide to America in the 1960s*. Under Carmichael's leadership, SNCC produced a position paper, titled "The Basis of Black Power," in 1966 that outlined a new strategy for success: one that would exclude whites from the organization and made a case for excluding interaction between blacks and whites in all facets of society.

Things to remember while reading the excerpt from "The Basis of Black Power":

- While SNCC members had hoped that white support would help their efforts to win civil rights, by the late 1960s SNCC members found support from whites complicated. White protestors often did not receive the same harsh treatment as black SNCC protestors. And if they were killed, white protestors were mourned by the nation but the deaths of black protestors were often ignored by national news organizations.

- In 1964 SNCC members and other civil rights activists organized the Mississippi Freedom Democratic Party (MFDP) as an alternative to the established all-white Democratic Party. When the MFDP candidates failed to gain entrance to the 1964 Democratic National Convention, SNCC and other activists felt betrayed and angry, and they believed that the established white community would never live up to the promise of a fully integrated, equal society.

Aaron Henry, leader of the Mississippi Freedom Democratic Party, argues for seats at the Democratic National Convention at a meeting of the credentials committee, Atlantic City, New Jersey, August 22, 1964. *AP/Wide World Photos. Reproduced by permission.*

Dialect: A variation of a language that is distinguished by unique vocabulary, grammar, and pronunciation, and is used by a distinct group or in a particular region.

- By 1964 SNCC had abandoned its regular seminars to promote nonviolence and completely abandoned the idea by the end of the 1960s.

- SNCC membership voted to expel all whites from the organization in 1967.

Excerpt from "The Basis of Black Power"

The myth that the Negro is somehow incapable of liberating himself, is lazy, etc., came out of the American experience. In the books that children read, whites are always good (good symbols are white), blacks are evil or seen as savages in movies, their language is referred to as a **dialect,** *and black people in this country are supposedly descended from savages.*

The Sixties in America: Primary Sources

Any white person who comes into the movement has the concepts in his mind about black people, if only subconsciously. He cannot escape them because the whole society has geared his subconscious in that direction.

*Miss America coming from Mississippi has a chance to represent all of America, but a black person from either Mississippi or New York will never represent America. Thus the white people coming into the movement cannot relate to the black experience, cannot relate to the word black, cannot relate to the **nitty gritty**, cannot relate to the experience that brought such a word into existence, cannot relate to **chitterlings**, **hog's head cheese**, **pig feet**, **ham hocks**, and cannot relate to slavery, because these things are not a part of their experience. They also cannot relate to the black religious experience, nor to the black church, unless, of course, this church has taken on white manifestations.*

White Power

Negroes in this country have never been allowed to organize themselves because of white interference. As a result of this, the stereotype has been reinforced that blacks cannot organize themselves. The white psychology that blacks have to be watched, also reinforces this stereotype. Blacks, in fact, feel intimidated by the presence of whites, because of their knowledge of the power that whites have over their lives. One white person can come into a meeting of black people and change the complexion of that meeting.... People would immediately start talking about brotherhood, love, etc.; race would not be discussed.

If people must express themselves freely, there has to be a climate in which they can do this. If blacks feel intimidated by whites, then they are not liable to vent the rage that they feel about whites in the presence of whites—especially not the black people whom we are trying to organize, i.e., the broad masses of black people. A climate has to be created whereby blacks can express themselves. The reasons that whites must be excluded is not that one is anti-white, but because the effects that one is trying to achieve cannot succeed because whites have an intimidating effect. Ofttimes, the intimidating effect is in direct proportion to the amount of degradation that black people have suffered at the hands of white people.

Roles of Whites and Blacks

It must be offered that white people who desire change in this country should go where that problem (racism) is most manifest.

Nitty gritty: The everyday experiences.

Chitterlings, hog's head cheese, pig feet, ham hocks: Various pork dishes traditional to Southern black culture.

*The problem is not in the black community. The white people should go into white communities where the whites have created power for the express purpose of denying blacks human dignity and self-determination. Whites who come into the black community with ideas of change seem to want to absolve the power structure of its responsibility for what it is doing, and saying that change can only come through black unity, which is the worst kind of **paternalism**. This is not to say that whites have not had an important role in the movement. In the case of Mississippi, their role was very key in that they helped give blacks the right to organize, but that role is now over, and it should be.*

People now have the right to picket, the right to give out leaflets, the right to vote, the right to demonstrate, the right to print.

These things which revolve around the right to organize have been accomplished mainly because of the entrance of white people into Mississippi, in the summer of 1964. Since these goals have now been accomplished, whites' role in the movement has now ended. What does it mean if black people, once having the right to organize, are not allowed to organize themselves? It means that blacks' ideas about inferiority are being reinforced. Shouldn't people be able to organize themselves? Blacks should be given this right. Further, white participation means in the eyes of the black community that whites are the brains behind the movement, and that blacks cannot function without whites. This only serves to perpetuate existing attitudes within the existing society, i.e., blacks are dumb, unable to take care of business, etc. Whites are smart, the brains behind the whole thing.

[…]

*In the beginning of the movement, we had fallen into a trap whereby we thought that our problems revolved around the right to eat at certain lunch counters or the right to vote, or to organize our communities. We have seen, however, that the problem is much deeper. The problem of this country, as we had seen it, concerned all blacks and all whites and therefore if decisions were left to the young people, then solutions would be arrived at. But this negates the history of black people and whites. We have dealt **stringently** with the problem of **Uncle Tom**, but we have not yet gotten around to **Simon Legree**. We must ask ourselves, who is the real villain— Uncle Tom or Simon Legree? Everybody knows Uncle Tom, but who knows Simon Legree? So what we have now in SNCC is a closed society, a clique. Black people cannot relate to SNCC because of its un-*

Paternalism: The practice of governing or managing individuals in a manner similar to that of a father dealing with his children.

Stringently: Severely.

Uncle Tom: The character in the book *Uncle Tom's Cabin,* whose name became slang for any black acting in a submissive or deferential way toward whites.

Simon Legree: The character of the brutal slave trader in the book *Uncle Tom's Cabin* whose name became slang for any harsh authority figure.

realistic, nonracial atmosphere; denying their experience of America as a racist society. In contrast, the Southern Christian Leadership Conference of Martin Luther King, Jr., has a staff that at least maintains a black facade. The front office is virtually all black, but nobody accuses SCLC of being racist.

If we are to proceed toward true liberation, we must cut ourselves off from white people. We must form our own institutions, credit unions, co-ops, political parties, write our own histories.

To proceed further, let us make some comparisons between the Black Movement of the early 1900s and the movement of the 1960s—i.e., compare the National Association for the Advancement of Colored People with SNCC. Whites subverted the Niagara movement (the forerunner of the NAACP) which, at the outset, was an all-black movement. The name of the new organization was also very revealing, in that it presupposed blacks have to advanced to the level of whites. We are now aware that the NAACP has grown reactionary, is controlled by the black power structure itself, and stands as one of the main roadblocks to black freedom. SNCC, by allowing the whites to remain in the organization, can have its efforts subverted in much the same manner, i.e., through having them play important roles such as community organizers, etc. Indigenous leadership cannot be built with whites in the positions they now hold.

These facts do not mean that whites cannot help. They can participate on a voluntary basis. We can contract work out to them, but in no way can they participate on a policy-making level.

Black Self-Determination

The charge may be made that we are racists, but whites who are sensitive to our problems will realize that we must determine our own destiny.

In an attempt to find a solution to our dilemma, we propose that our organization (SNCC) should be black-staffed, black-controlled, and black-financed. We do not want to fall into a similar dilemma that other civil rights organizations have fallen into. If we continue to rely upon white financial support we will find ourselves entwined in the **tentacles** of the white power complex that controls this country. It is also important that a black organization (devoid of **cultism**) be projected to our people so that it can be demonstrated that such organizations are **viable**.

Tentacles: Extensions of a larger body with the ability to grasp.

Cultism: Like a cult, a group obsessively committed to an idea.

Viable: Capable of working.

Fire consumes a building during the Detroit race riots, Detroit, Michigan, July 28, 1967. The eruption of riots helped cement SNCC members' belief that nonviolent protest was no longer effective. © *Bettmann/Corbis. Reproduced by permission.*

More and more we see black people in this country being used as a tool of the white liberal establishment. Liberal whites have not begun to address themselves to the real problem of black people in this country—witness their bewilderment, fear, and anxiety when **nationalism** is mentioned concerning black people. An analysis of the white liberal's reaction to the word nationalism alone reveals a very meaningful attitude of whites of an **ideological persuasion** toward blacks in this country. It means previous solutions to black problems in this country have been made in the interests of those whites dealing with these problems and not in the best interests of black people in the country. Whites can only subvert our true search and struggles for **self-determination**, self-identification, and liberation in this country. Reevaluation of the white and black roles must now take place so that white no longer designate roles that black people play but rather black people define white people's roles.

Too long have we allowed white people to interpret the importance and meaning of the cultural aspects of our society. We have allowed them to tell us what was good about our Afro-American *music, art, and literature. How many black critics do we have on the jazz scene? How can a white person who is not part of the black psyche (except in the oppressor's role) interpret the meaning of the blues to us who are manifestations of the song themselves?*

*It must be pointed out that on whatever level of contact blacks and whites come together, that meeting or confrontation is not on the level of the blacks but always on the level of the whites. This only means that our everyday contact with whites is a reinforcement of the **myth of white supremacy**. Whites are the ones who must try to raise themselves to our humanistic level. We are not, after all, the ones who are responsible for a genocidal war in Vietnam; we are not the ones who are responsible for **neocolonialism** in Africa and Latin America; we are not the ones who held a people in animalistic bondage over 400 years. We reject the American dream as defined by white people and must work to construct an American reality defined by Afro-Americans....*

What happened next...

In 1967 more than 150 American cities reported riots or, as black activists called them, "rebellions." Huge numbers of rioters burned city blocks and fought with police and National Guardsmen. The eruption of riots helped cement SNCC members' belief that nonviolent protest was no longer effective. Activists banded together with a sense of resistance to white society and common brother and sisterhood that came to be called "Black Power."

SNCC became an increasingly radical group throughout the later years of the 1960s. SNCC cooperated with the Black Panther Party starting in 1968, sharing offices and organizing rallies and violence. The Black Panther Party came to be known as one of the most violent groups supporting "Black Power." Many of the group's members were killed or imprisoned after conflicts with police in Chicago, Illinois, and Oakland, California.

SNCC leaders Stokely Carmichael (1941–1998) and H. Rap Brown (1943–) gained national reputations as black radicals. Although Carmichael was kicked out of SNCC in 1968 for

Nationalism: Devotion to and promotion of the interests and culture of a particular nation.

Ideological persuasion: A certain mind-set or attitude.

Self-determination: The free choice of a people about their own political status.

Myth of white supremacy: The idea of white superiority.

Neocolonialism: A governmental policy of influencing a less powerful nation by economic and political means.

advocating violence in cities, when Brown succeeded him as chairman he took the word "Nonviolent" out of the name and renamed SNCC the Student National Coordinating Committee, to reflect the organization's willingness to react violently if necessary.

The surge of violent protests united blacks, but also gave rise to conservative, white politicians who began focusing attention on liberal government policies that they linked to riots and other civil rights violence. Some of the most prominent conservative politicians during the era were Ronald Reagan (1911–2004), who won the California governorship in 1966, and George Wallace (1919–1998), who began campaigning for the presidency in 1967.

Ultimately, as protestors grew more violent and others grew more conservative, both blacks and whites, no matter their opinion of the civil rights movement, had a hard time figuring out the truth about the causes of riots and the solutions for the civil strife. By the early 1970s, SNCC lost its momentum as its leaders spent increasing amounts of time dodging legal troubles. Brown was imprisoned in 1971 for robbing a tavern, and without his leadership SNCC dissolved as a forceful political group.

Black Power advocates Stokely Carmichael (left) and H. Rap Brown (right) talk to the news media outside of Hamilton Hall, one of five Columbia University buildings taken over by demonstrators, New York City, April 26, 1968.
© Bettmann/Corbis. Reproduced by permission.

Did you know...

- In 1960 blacks made up approximately 10 percent of the American population.

- In 1967 the prominent African American newspaper, the *Amsterdam News* of New York, announced that it would no longer use the term "Negro."

- Martin Luther King Jr. and the leaders of the NAACP vocally opposed the embrace of violence promoted by SNCC and other groups in the late 1960s.

- Many members of SNCC became powerful politicians: Marion Barry became mayor of Washington, D.C., Julian Bond served as a Georgia senator, and John Lewis served as a Georgia congressman.

Consider the following...

- Explain why SNCC members may have changed their view from nonviolent protest.

- Do you think nonviolent protests would be effective if violent attacks from opponents to these protests were not reported by television cameras or newspapers? Explain your opinion.

- What do you think SNCC gained from expelling white supporters from membership?

For More Information

Books

Bloom, Alexander, and Wini Breines, eds. *"Takin' It to the Streets": A Sixties Reader*. New York: Oxford University Press, 2003.

Farber, David. *The Age of Great Dreams: America in the 1960s*. New York: Hill and Wang, 1994.

Farber, David, and Beth Bailey, with others. *The Columbia Guide to America in the 1960s*. New York: Columbia University Press, 2001.

Gitlin, Todd. *The Sixties: Years of Hope, Days of Rage*. New York: Bantam, 1987; revised, 1993.

Malcolm X

Excerpt from "The Ballot or the Bullet," a speech delivered in Cleveland, Ohio, April 3, 1964

Reprinted from *Malcolm X Speaks: Selected Statements and Speeches*, 1965; also available online at: www.indiana.edu/ ~rterrill/Text-BorB.html

Although the civil rights movement of the 1960s started with a commitment to nonviolent protest, activists' opinions about how best to gain civil rights diverged by mid-decade. Malcolm X became a prominent leader of activists who doubted that nonviolent protest would ever produce the desired changes in the lives of blacks.

Malcolm X was born Malcolm Little on May 19, 1925, in Omaha, Nebraska. His father, Earl Little, was a minister and activist who supported a "back-to-Africa" movement encouraging blacks to unite and separate from America's oppressive, white society. Because of his father's activism, Malcolm and his family were often harassed by white supremacist groups such as the Ku Klux Klan, and the family moved often. In Lansing, Michigan, white supremacists burned the family's home and killed Malcolm's father. Malcolm's mother, Louise Little, then raised her eight children on welfare until the stress of her life caused her to enter a mental hospital, and her children were dispersed to foster homes.

Despite the turmoil in his family life, Malcolm X did well in school and hoped to become a lawyer. Upon hearing

"Now in speaking like this, it doesn't mean that we're anti-white, but it does mean we're anti-exploitation, we're anti-degradation, we're anti-oppression. And if the white man doesn't want us to be anti-him, let him stop oppressing and exploiting and degrading us."

Elijah Muhammad, leader of the Black Muslim Nation of Islam, pictured in 1972.
AP/Wide World Photos. Reproduced by permission.

his dream of becoming a professional, a teacher counseled him to set his sights lower because of his race. Discouraged, Malcolm X quit school at age fifteen and soon became a drug addict and street-hustling criminal. Just weeks before his twenty-first birthday in 1946, he was sentenced to ten years in prison for burglary.

While in prison Malcolm X discovered the Muslim religion from books in the library. He began corresponding with Elijah Muhammad, a man who proclaimed himself to be the direct messenger of the Muslim deity, Allah, and the leader of the Black Muslims religious group. His discovery of the Muslim faith prompted Malcolm X to drop his surname Little. Little was the surname of his family's white owners; in its place he took the name X to signify that he had cast off the oppression of his former life. Released from prison in 1952, Malcolm X moved to Chicago to become a student of Muhammad. Before long, Malcolm X became a minister in Detroit, Philadelphia, and Harlem mosques.

By the mid-1950s, Malcolm X emerged as a leader of the Black Muslims. Speaking from Muslim mosques, street corners, and university campuses, Malcolm X praised the virtues of embracing black pride and separatism. A charismatic speaker, Malcolm X encouraged his mainly black audiences to embrace their race. He preached that whites were "devils" and that blacks were a superior race. Over time Malcolm X grew increasingly frustrated with the doctrine of Elijah Muhammad, and a rivalry for power within the Black Muslims developed between the two men in the early 1960s.

In 1964 Malcolm X traveled to Mecca in Saudi Arabia, the most sacred city of the Muslim faith, and returned with a vision of uniting blacks, regardless of religious faith or nationality, and with a more moderate opinion of whites. He broke away from the Black Muslims to start his own groups,

which eventually came to be known as the Organization of Afro-American Unity and the Muslim Mosque, Inc. The following excerpt from his speech "The Ballot or the Bullet," given on April 3, 1964, in Cleveland, Ohio, outlined his plan for action.

Malcolm X speaks to a crowd in New York City's Harlem section. *AP/Wide World Photos. Reproduced by permission.*

Things to remember while reading the excerpt from "The Ballot or the Bullet":

- The ideas presented in this speech were developed in speeches Malcolm X gave in Harlem, New York City, earlier in 1964.

- Throughout his career as spokesman for the Black Muslims and after, Malcolm X expressly rejected the philosophy of Martin Luther King Jr.

- Malcolm X's opinions, like those of many other activists, changed throughout the 1960s. Malcolm X never avoided changing his mind or considering new ideas.

- "The Ballot or the Bullet" was presented at the Cory Methodist Church in Cleveland, Ohio, at a Congress of Racial Equality (CORE) symposium called "The Negro Revolt—What Comes Next?"

- In his speech Malcolm X described a growing sentiment for black nationalism, a belief that blacks should create a separate society, within activist groups, such as the NAACP and CORE.

Excerpt from "The Ballot or the Bullet"

Mr. Moderator, Brother Lomax, brothers and sisters, friends and enemies: I just can't believe everyone in here is a friend and I don't want to leave anybody out. The question tonight, as I understand it, is "The Negro Revolt, and Where Do We Go From Here? or What Next?" In my little humble way of understanding it, it points toward either the ballot or the bullet.

Before we try and explain what is meant by the ballot or the bullet, I would like to clarify something concerning myself. I'm still a Muslim, my religion is still Islam. That's my personal belief. Just as Adam Clayton Powell is a Christian minister who heads the Abyssinian Baptist Church in New York, but at the same time takes part in the political struggles to try and bring about rights to the black people in this country; and Dr. Martin Luther King is a Christian minister down in Atlanta, Georgia, who heads another organization fighting for the civil rights of black people in this country; and Rev. Galamison, I guess you've heard of him, is another Christian minister in New York who has been deeply involved in the school boycotts to eliminate segregated education; well, I myself am a minister, not a Christian minister, but a Muslim minister; and I believe in action on all fronts by whatever means necessary.

Although I'm still a Muslim, I'm not here tonight to discuss my religion. I'm not here to try and change your religion. I'm not here to argue or discuss anything that we differ about, because it's time for us to submerge our differences and realize that it is best for us to first see that we have the same problem, a common problem, a problem that will make you catch hell whether you're a Baptist, or a

Methodist, or a Muslim, or a nationalist. Whether you're educated or illiterate, whether you live on the boulevard or in the alley, you're going to catch hell just like I am. We're all in the same boat and we all are going to catch the same hell from the same man. He just happens to be a white man. All of us have suffered here, in this country, political oppression at the hands of the white man, **economic exploitation** at the hands of the white man, and **social degradation** at the hands of the white man.

Now in speaking like this, it doesn't mean that we're anti-white, but it does mean we're anti-exploitation, we're anti-degradation, we're anti-oppression. And if the white man doesn't want us to be anti-him, let him stop oppressing and exploiting and degrading us. Whether we are Christians or Muslims or nationalists or **agnostics** or **atheists**, we must first learn to forget our differences. If we have differences, let us differ in the closet; when we come out in front, let us not have anything to argue about until we get finished arguing with the man. If the late President Kennedy could get together with **Khrushchev** and exchange some wheat, we certainly have more in common with each other than Kennedy and Khrushchev had with each other.

If we don't do something real soon, I think you'll have to agree that we're going to be forced either to use the ballot or the bullet. It's one or the other in 1964. It isn't that time is running out—time has run out! 1964 threatens to be the most explosive year America has ever witnessed. The most explosive year. Why? It's also a political year. It's the year when all of the white politicians will be back in the so-called Negro community jiving you and me for some votes. The year when all of the white political crooks will be right back in your and my community with their false promises, building up our hopes for a let-down, with their trickery and their **treachery**, with their false promises which they don't intend to keep. As they nourish these dissatisfactions, it can only lead to one thing, an explosion; and now we have the type of black man on the scene in America today—I'm sorry, Brother Lomax—who just doesn't intend to turn the other cheek any longer.

Don't let anybody tell you anything about the odds are against you. If they draft you, they send you to Korea and make you face 800 million Chinese. If you can be brave over there, you can be brave right here. These odds aren't as great as those odds. And if you fight here, you will at least know what you're fighting for.

I'm not a politician, not even a student of politics; in fact, I'm not a student of much of anything. I'm not a Democrat, I'm not a Repub-

Economic exploitation: The utilization of a group for selfish, unjust profit.

Social degradation: The act of lowering the social standing of a group or person.

Agnostics: Persons who hold the view that the existence or nonexistence of God is unknowable.

Atheists: Persons who do not believe in a god.

Nikita Sergeyevich Khrushchev: 1894–1971; The Soviet premier who was the main architect of the Soviet Union's Cold War policies.

Treachery: Violation of faith or allegiance.

lican, and I don't even consider myself an American. If you and I were Americans, there'd be no problem. Those **Hunkies** that just got off the boat, they're already Americans; **Polacks** are already Americans; the Italian refugees are already Americans. Everything that came out of Europe, every blue-eyed thing, is already an American. And as long as you and I have been over here, we aren't Americans yet.

Well, I am one who doesn't believe in deluding myself. I'm not going to sit at your table and watch you eat, with nothing on my plate, and call myself a diner. Sitting at the table doesn't make you a diner, unless you eat some of what's on that plate. Being here in America doesn't make you an American. Being born here in America doesn't make you an American. Why, if birth made you American, you wouldn't need any legislation, you wouldn't need any amendments to the Constitution, you wouldn't be faced with civil-rights **filibustering** in Washington, D.C., right now. They don't have to pass civil-rights legislation to make a Polack an American.

No, I'm not an American. I'm one of the twenty-two million black people who are the victims of **Americanism**. One of the twenty-two million black people who are the victims of **democracy**, nothing but **disguised hypocrisy**. So, I'm not standing here speaking to you as an American, or a patriot, or a flag-saluter, or a flag-waver—no, not I. I'm speaking as a victim of this American system. And I see America through the eyes of the victim. I don't see any American dream; I see an American nightmare.

These twenty-two million victims are waking up. Their eyes are coming open. They're beginning to see what they used to only look at. They're becoming politically mature. They are realizing that there are new political trends from coast to coast. As they see these new political trends, it's possible for them to see that every time there's an election the races are so close that they have to have a recount. They had to recount in Massachusetts to see who was going to be governor, it was so close. It was the same way in Rhode Island, in Minnesota, and in many other parts of the country. And the same with Kennedy and Nixon when they ran for president. It was so close they had to count all over again. Well, what does this mean? It means that when white people are evenly divided, and black people have a bloc of votes of their own, it is left up to them to determine who's going to sit in the White House and who's going to be in the dog house.

It was the black man's vote that put the present administration in Washington, D.C. Your vote, your dumb vote, your ignorant vote,

Hunkies: A negative term for Hungarians.

Polacks: A negative term for those of Polish descent.

Filibustering: Tactics used to delay legislative action.

Americanism: The customs and political principles and practices of America.

Democracy: A political system that places the power of the government in the hands of citizens.

Disguised hypocrisy: The false appearance of virtue.

your wasted vote put in an administration in Washington, D.C., that has seen fit to pass every kind of legislation imaginable, saving you until last, then filibustering on top of that. And your and my leaders have the **audacity** to run around clapping their hands and talk about how much progress we're making. And what a good president we have. If he wasn't good in Texas, he sure can't be good in Washington, D.C. Because Texas is a lynch state. It is in the same breath as Mississippi, no different; only they lynch you in Texas with a Texas accent and lynch you in Mississippi with a Mississippi accent. And these Negro leaders have the audacity to go and have some coffee in the White House with a Texan, a **Southern cracker**—that's all he is—and then come out and tell you and me that he's going to be better for us because, since he's from the South, he knows how to deal with the Southerners. What kind of logic is that?

[…]

So it's time in 1964 to wake up. And when you see them coming up with that kind of conspiracy, let them know your eyes are open. And let them know you got something else that's wide open too. It's got to be the ballot or the bullet. The ballot or the bullet. If you're afraid to use an expression like that, you should get on out of the country, you should get back in the cotton patch, you should get back in the alley. They get all the Negro vote, and after they get it, the Negro gets nothing in return. All they did when they got to Washington was give a few big Negroes big jobs. Those big Negroes didn't need big jobs, they already had jobs. That's camouflage, that's trickery, that's treachery, **window-dressing**. I'm not trying to knock out the Democrats for the Republicans, we'll get to them in a minute. But it is true—you put the Democrats first and the Democrats put you last.

[…]

I say again, I'm not anti-Democrat, I'm not anti Republican, I'm not anti-anything. I'm just questioning their sincerity, and some of the strategy that they've been using on our people by promising them promises that they don't intend to keep. When you keep the Democrats in power, you're keeping the **Dixiecrats** in power. I doubt that my good Brother Lomax will deny that. A vote for a Democrat is a vote for a Dixiecrat. That's why, in 1964, it's time now for you and me to become more politically mature and realize what the ballot is for; what we're supposed to get when we cast a ballot; and that if we don't cast a ballot, it's going to end up in a situation where we're going to have to cast a bullet. It's either a ballot or a bullet.

[…]

Audacity: Arrogance.

Southern cracker: A derogatory term for a poor white southerner.

Window-dressing: The act of making something appear attractive or favorable.

Dixiecrats: Southern Democrats whose support for the party relies on the promise that progress on civil rights will be very gradual.

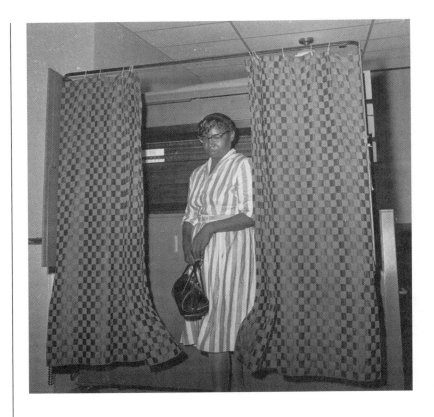

Mary E. Johnson casts a vote at the polls in Lake Providence, Louisiana, on July 28, 1962, the first black person to cast a vote in this area since 1922. *AP/Wide World Photos. Reproduced by permission.*

So, what I'm trying to impress upon you, in essence, is this: You and I in America are faced not with a segregationist conspiracy, we're faced with a government conspiracy. Everyone who's filibustering is a senator—that's the government. Everyone who's finagling in Washington, D.C., is a congressman—that's the government. You don't have anybody putting blocks in your path but people who are a part of the government. The same government that you go abroad to fight for and die for is the government that is in a conspiracy to deprive you of your voting rights, deprive you of your economic opportunities, deprive you of decent housing, deprive you of decent education. You don't need to go to the employer alone, it is the government itself, the government of America, that is responsible for the oppression and exploitation and degradation of black people in this country. And you should drop it in their lap. This government has failed the Negro. This so-called democracy has failed the Negro. And all these white liberals have definitely failed the Negro.

So, where do we go from here? First, we need some friends. We need some new allies. The entire civil-rights struggle needs a new interpretation, a broader interpretation. We need to look at this civil-rights thing from another angle—from the inside as well as from the outside. To those of us whose philosophy is **black nationalism**, the only way you can get involved in the civil-rights struggle is give it a new interpretation. That old interpretation excluded us. It kept us out. So, we're giving a new interpretation to the civil-rights struggle, an interpretation that will enable us to come into it, take part in it. And these **handkerchief-heads** who have been **dillydallying** and **pussy footing** and compromising—we don't intend to let them pussyfoot and dillydally and compromise any longer.

How can you thank a man for giving you what's already yours? How then can you thank him for giving you only part of what's already yours? You haven't even made progress, if what's being given to you, you should have had already. That's not progress. And I love my Brother Lomax, the way he pointed out we're right back where we were in 1954. We're not even as far up as we were in 1954. We're behind where we were in 1954. There's more segregation now than there was in 1954. There's more racial **animosity**, more racial hatred, more racial violence today in 1964, than there was in 1954. Where is the progress?

And now you're facing a situation where the young Negro's coming up. They don't want to hear that "turn the-other-cheek" stuff, no. In Jacksonville, those were teenagers, they were throwing **Molotov cocktails**. Negroes have never done that before. But it shows you there's a new deal coming in. There's new thinking coming in. There's new strategy coming in. It'll be Molotov cocktails this month, hand grenades next month, and something else next month. It'll be ballots, or it'll be bullets. It'll be liberty, or it will be death. The only difference about this kind of death—it'll be **reciprocal**. You know what is meant by "reciprocal"? That's one of Brother Lomax's words, I stole it from him. I don't usually deal with those big words because I don't usually deal with big people. I deal with small people. I find you can get a whole lot of small people and whip hell out of a whole lot of big people. They haven't got anything to lose, and they've got every thing to gain. And they'll let you know in a minute: "**It takes two to tango**; when I go, you go."

[...]

I might stop right here to point out one thing. When ever you're going after something that belongs to you, anyone who's depriving you of the right to have it is a criminal. Understand that. Whenever you are going after something that is yours, you are within your

Black nationalism: Devotion to the creation of a separate, self-governing black nation.

Handkerchief-heads: A disparaging term used to refer to blacks who act submissively toward whites.

Dillydallying: Delaying.

Pussy footing: Proceeding timidly without committing oneself to a certain direction.

Animosity: Ill will.

Molotov cocktail: A homemade bomb made of a bottle filled with flammable liquid.

Reciprocal: Felt by both sides.

It takes two to tango: In this case, an expression used to mean that blacks must join together in their fight against whites.

A policeman holds back a police dog who tries to attack a black demonstrator during an anti-segregation protest in Birmingham, Alabama, May 3, 1963.

AP/Wide World Photos. Reproduced by permission.

legal rights to lay claim to it. And anyone who puts forth any effort to deprive you of that which is yours, is breaking the law, is a criminal. And this was pointed out by the Supreme Court decision. It outlawed segregation. Which means segregation is against the law. Which means a segregationist is breaking the law. A segregationist is a criminal. You can't label him as anything other than that. And when you demonstrate against segregation, the law is on your side. The Supreme Court is on your side.

Now, who is it that opposes you in carrying out the law? The police department itself. With police dogs and clubs. Whenever you demonstrate against segregation, whether it is segregated education, segregated housing, or anything else, the law is on your side, and anyone who stands in the way is not the law any longer. They are breaking the law, they are not representatives of the law. Any time you demonstrate against segregation and a man has the audacity to put a police dog on you, kill that dog, kill him, I'm telling you, kill that dog. I say it, if they put me in jail tomorrow, kill that dog. Then you'll put a stop to it. Now, if these white people in here don't want to see that kind of action, get down and tell the mayor to tell the police department to pull the dogs in. That's all you have to do. If you don't do it, someone else will.

If you don't take this kind of stand, your little children will grow up and look at you and think "shame." If you don't take an **uncompromising** stand—I don't mean go out and get violent; but at the same time you should never be nonviolent unless you run into some nonviolence. I'm nonviolent with those who are nonviolent with me. But when you drop that violence on me, then you've made me go insane, and I'm not responsible for what I do. And that's the way every Negro should get. Any time you know you're within the law, within your legal rights, within your moral rights, in accord with justice, then die for what you believe in. But don't die alone. Let your dying be **reciprocal**. This is what is meant by equality. **What's good for the goose is good for the gander**.

[...]

Black people are fed up with the dillydallying, pussyfooting, compromising approach that we've been using toward getting our freedom. We want freedom now, but we're not going to get it saying **"We Shall Overcome."** We've got to fight until we overcome.

[...]

Our gospel is black nationalism. We're not trying to threaten the existence of any organization, but we're spreading the gospel of black nationalism. Anywhere there's a church that is also preaching and practicing the gospel of black nationalism, join that church. If the NAACP is preaching and practicing the gospel of black nationalism, join the NAACP. If CORE is spreading and practicing the gospel of black nationalism, join CORE. Join any organization that has a gospel that's for the **uplift** of the black man. And when you get into it and see them pussyfooting or compromising, pull out of it because that's not black nationalism. We'll find another one.

And in this manner, the organizations will increase in number and in quantity and in quality, and by August, it is then our intention to have a black nationalist convention which will consist of delegates from all over the country who are interested in the political, economic and social philosophy of black nationalism. After these delegates convene, we will hold a seminar, we will hold discussions, we will listen to everyone. We want to hear new ideas and new solutions and new answers. And at that time, if we see fit then to form a black

Uncompromising: Non-negotiable, unyielding.

Reciprocal: Done by both sides; mutual.

What's good for the goose is good for the gander: Malcolm X is using this expression to say that if blacks must die in their fight for equality, whites must die during the fight as well.

"We Shall Overcome": Malcolm X is referring to the words of Martin Luther King, who insisted on nonviolent measures to gain civil rights.

Uplift: Improvement of the social, spiritual, or intellectual well being of an individual.

nationalist party, we'll form a black nationalist party. If it's necessary to form a black nationalist army, we'll form a black nationalist army. It'll be the ballot or the bullet. It'll be liberty or it'll be death.

It's time for you and me to stop sitting in this country, letting some **cracker** senators, Northern crackers and Southern crackers, sit there in Washington, D.C., and come to a conclusion in their mind that you and I are supposed to have civil rights. There's no white man going to tell me anything about my rights. Brothers and sisters, always remember, if it doesn't take senators and congressmen and presidential proclamations to give freedom to the white man, it is not necessary for legislation or proclamation or Supreme Court decisions to give freedom to the black man. You let that white man know, if this is a country of freedom, let it be a country of freedom; and if it's not a country of freedom, change it.

[...]

If a Negro in 1964 has to sit around and wait for some cracker senator to **filibuster** when it comes to the rights of black people, why, you and I should hang our heads in shame. You talk about a march on Washington in 1963, you haven't seen anything. There's some more going down in '64. And this time they're not going like they went last year. They're not going singing ''We Shall Overcome.'' They're not going with white friends. They're not going with **placards** already painted for them. **They're not going with round-trip tickets.** They're going with one way tickets.

And if they don't want that non-nonviolent army going down there, tell them to bring the filibuster to a halt. The black nationalists aren't going to wait. Lyndon B. Johnson is the head of the Democratic Party. If he's for civil rights, let him go into the Senate next week and declare himself. Let him go in there right now and declare himself. Let him go in there and denounce the Southern branch of his party. Let him go in there right now and take a moral stand— right now, not later. Tell him, don't wait until election time. If he waits too long, brothers and sisters, he will be responsible for letting a condition develop in this country which will create a climate that will bring seeds up out of the ground with vegetation on the end of them looking like something these people never dreamed of. In 1964, it's the ballot or the bullet. Thank you.

Cracker: A derogatory term for whites.

Filibuster: Delay the action of a legislative body.

Placards: Public notices.

They're not going with round-trip tickets: The statement means that the protestors are going to protest with all their conviction, that they will die if necessary for their cause.

What happened next...

Between 1952 and 1964, Malcolm X rallied blacks around the idea that whites oppressed them and should be brought to justice for their "evils." But more than just preaching hatred of whites, Malcolm X nurtured black pride in African and African American culture and history. His spellbinding speeches taught African Americans about their past. Nurturing the notion of creating a separate black nation, he championed Black Power, an idea that blacks should take control of their culture, their work life, and their politics. This rough opposition to white society that Malcolm X had so vehemently upheld for more than a decade fostered the rise of militant black activist groups that vowed to fight for civil rights "by any means necessary," as Malcolm X had preached.

To many of Malcolm X's followers, his official split with the Black Muslims in 1964 promised new hope that he would help create a separate black nation. But when he returned from his trip to Mecca preaching a more tolerant view of whites, some were angry with him. For these activists, "The Ballot or the Bullet" speech was a signal that Malcolm X would now consider the integration of blacks and whites, an idea he had vehemently protested for more than a decade. To others, who had grown frustrated with the slow progress gained by followers of the nonviolent teachings of Martin Luther King Jr., Malcolm X's speech suggested that there were times when it was necessary to fight violently for their rights.

Shortly after his split from the Black Muslims, Malcolm X learned that the Black Muslims wanted him dead. Nevertheless, he worked constantly to get his new message to blacks, giving speeches in cities across America and traveling to Africa, the Middle East, and Europe to appeal to African nations and the United Nations for help. On February 13, 1965, his home was firebombed; he, his wife, and four daughters escaped unharmed. While he was giving a speech on February 21, 1965, assassins linked to the Black Muslims gunned him down, in front of his daughters and pregnant wife.

Within a year, the Student Nonviolent Coordinating Committee (SNCC), which had started the decade steadfast in its commitment to nonviolence, shifted from the preaching of Martin Luther King Jr. to a militant platform. SNCC

Malcolm X in front of his damaged Queens, New York City, home one day after it was firebombed in February 1965. He, his wife, and four daughters escaped unharmed. © Bettmann/Corbis. Reproduced by permission.

leader Stokely Carmichael proclaimed in 1966, "The only way we gonna stop them white men from whuppin' us is to take over," according to David Farber in *The Great Age of Dreams*. Despite the urging of King, SNCC made a decisive shift toward violence. Other groups such as the Black Panther Party formed that year under the banner of Black Power. Black Panther members considered themselves revolutionaries and often wore black military uniforms. By the end of the decade, Black Power revolutionaries squared off in deadly battles with police in American cities.

Did you know...

- Malcolm X embodied the black dignity that he encouraged other blacks to embrace. Despite growing up in difficult social circumstances, with an abbreviated education, Malcolm X grew to see himself as a worthy individual and to live his life with pride.

- After his return from Mecca in 1964, Malcolm X adopted the name El Hajj Malik El-Shabazz.

- Malcolm X returned from the Middle East a changed man. He claimed to understand that not all white people were the "devil," as he had said countless times before. Many of his followers were angered, while others admired his ability to rethink old positions when faced with new facts.

- The Black Power movement the Malcolm X advocated peaked with the formation of the militant Black Panther Party in 1966. Violence escalated until the early 1970s when many Black Power groups broke up because of the deaths or arrests of their members.

Consider the following...

- Do you think Malcolm X's modification of his opinions helped or hurt his position as a civil rights leader? Explain your reasoning.

- Malcolm X often called for the formation of a separate black nation. How do you think such a nation could form within the United States?

- Do you think Malcolm X gave adequate advice for distinguishing between times it would be best to vote and times when violence would be necessary for change? Explain your reasoning.

- What themes of Malcolm X's speech seem to speak directly to nonviolent protestors?

For More Information

Books

Benson, Michael. *Malcolm X*. Minneapolis, MN: Lerner Publications, 2002.

Breitman, George, ed. *Malcolm X Speaks: Selected Speeches and Statements*. New York: Grove Weidenfeld, 1965.

Farber, David. *The Age of Great Dreams: America in the 1960s*. New York: Hill and Wang, 1994.

Farber, David, and Beth Bailey, with others. *The Columbia Guide to America in the 1960s.* New York: Columbia University Press, 2001.

Malcolm X. *Malcolm X Talks to Young People: Speeches in the U.S., Britain, and Africa.* New York: Pathfinder, 1991.

Malcolm X, with the assistance of Alex Haley. *The Autobiography of Malcolm X.* New York: Grove Press, 1965.

Myers, Walter Dean. *Malcolm X: By Any Means Necessary: A Biography.* New York: Scholastic, 1993.

Stine, Megan. *The Story of Malcolm X, Civil Rights Leader.* New York: Dell, 1994.

Web sites

Malcolm X Museum. www.themalcolmxmuseum.org (accessed on August 4, 2004).

Martin Luther King Jr.

Excerpt from "Where Do We Go from Here?," a speech delivered at the annual convention of the Southern Christian Leadership Conference, Atlanta, Georgia, August 16, 1967.

Reprinted from *A Call to Conscience: The Landmark Speeches of Dr. Martin Luther King, Jr.,* **2001.**

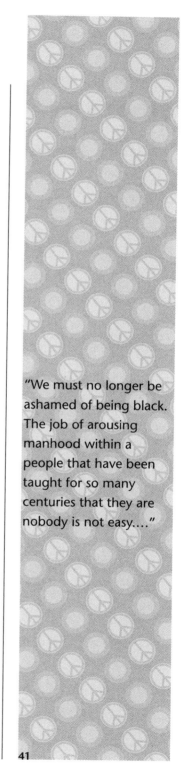

"We must no longer be ashamed of being black. The job of arousing manhood within a people that have been taught for so many centuries that they are nobody is not easy...."

Martin Luther King Jr. (1929–1968) was by far the best known of all the 1960s civil rights leaders. Hundreds of thousands of civil rights activists at rallies across the country and millions watching his speeches on the three television networks found inspiration in his words. King's opinions either gave people encouragement to forge ahead or stirred them up to fight against the coming change.

Martin Luther King Jr. was born Michael Luther King, on January 15, 1929, in Atlanta, Georgia. Early in his childhood his name was changed to Martin, Jr., after his father, a Baptist minister. King had a keen intellect. He graduated from Morehouse College in 1948 and went on to earn doctoral degrees in theology and philosophy by the end of the 1950s. Ordained a minister in 1948, King accepted his first position at the Dexter Avenue Baptist Church in Montgomery, Alabama, that same year.

King rose to national prominence during the Montgomery bus boycott in 1955. King and others formed the Montgomery Improvement Association (MIA) to organize the boycott in support of Rosa Parks (1913–), the black woman who had re-

Two black men ride in the first seat behind the driver of a city bus in Montgomery, Alabama, December 21, 1956, soon after racial segregation on buses was ended by federal court order. *AP/Wide World Photos. Reproduced by permission.*

fused to give up her seat to a white man and move to the back of the bus, as required by Alabama law, when the driver directed her to. As president of the MIA, King advocated nonviolent protest as the most effective method to achieve racial justice. Blacks, who made up the largest percentage of bus riders in Montgomery, refused to ride city buses until the bus system was desegregated. Despite harassment and arrests, the peaceful protests continued for more than a year. When the U.S. Supreme Court declared bus segregation laws illegal in 1956, King and his followers were energized to do more. They formed the Southern Christian Leadership Conference (SCLC) with the goal of increasing black voter registration and eliminating segregation.

King's masterful gift for speechmaking propelled the civil rights movement forward, inspiring protestors at rallies and marches throughout the South. *Time* magazine recognized King in 1957, saying that he had "risen from nowhere to become one of the nation's remarkable leaders of men." By 1964 King had become an international symbol of peace.

That year *Time* honored him as "Man of the Year," and he received the Nobel Peace Prize.

The nonviolent protests King led, such as marches, served the civil rights movement well at first. Reports of attacks by police and others on peaceful protestors repulsed many. Nonviolent protestors gave their cause a dignified air. As the decade wore on, however, violent reaction against protestors became less visible, occurring behind closed doors or in the dead of night. Without the horrible pictures of violent opponents attacking calm protestors, the shock value of nonviolent protestors wore off, and public support became less enthusiastic.

By the mid-1960s civil rights activists were divided in their opinions about violence. Radical groups formed and some, such as SNCC, shifted their policies toward more violent methods of activism. King, however, remained steadfast in his belief in nonviolent protest. His example was Mohandas Gandhi (1869–1948), who led massive nonviolent protests in India to end British colonial rule there. In the following speech, given in 1967, King assessed the victories of nonviolent versus violent protest. In King's mind, nonviolent protest remained the only answer to the plight of the black man.

Martin Luther King Jr. displays his 1964 Nobel Peace Prize medal. *AP/Wide World Photos. Reproduced by permission.*

Things to remember while reading the excerpt of "Where Do We Go from Here?":

- Martin Luther King Jr. became a pastor in 1954 at Dexter Avenue Baptist Church in Montgomery, Alabama, and emerged as a political leader during the Montgomery bus boycott in 1955.

- King was a highly educated man; he earned a Ph. D. in 1955 from Boston University.

- Though King suffered threats, intimidation, arrests, a bombing of his house, and even a stab in the chest in 1958, he never wavered in his commitment to nonviolence.

- King was known to a vast majority of Americans by the 1960s. All three television networks broadcast King's "I Have a Dream" speech that he delivered at the Lincoln Memorial in Washington, D.C., in 1963; he appeared on numerous popular magazine covers; and he was honored with a Nobel Peace Prize in 1964.

- When King gave the following speech, violent civil rights protestors were advocating for uprisings against white society and even the formation of a black "nation."

- In his speech King evaluated the decade of nonviolent protest to persuade his followers that their nonviolent efforts had been more successful in winning civil rights.

Excerpt of "Where Do We Go from Here?"

Ten years ago during the piercing chill of a January day and on the heels of the year-long Montgomery bus boycott, a group of approximately one hundred Negro leaders from across the South assembled in this church and agreed on the need for an organization to be formed that could serve as a channel through which local protest organizations in the South could coordinate their protest activities. It was this meeting that gave birth to the Southern Christian Leadership Conference.

And when our organization was formed ten years ago, racial segregation was still a structured part of the architecture of southern society. Negroes with the pangs of hunger and the anguish of thirst were denied access to the average lunch counter. The downtown restaurants were still off-limits for the black man. Negroes, burdened with the fatigue of travel, were still barred from the motels of the highways and the hotels of the cities. Negro boys and girls in dire need of recreational activities were not allowed to inhale the fresh air of the big city parks. Negroes in desperate need of allowing their mental buckets to sink deep into the wells of knowledge were confronted with a firm no when they sought to use the city libraries. *Ten years ago, legislative halls of the South were still ringing loud with such words as **interposition** and **nullification**. All types of **conniving** methods were still being used to keep the Negro from becoming a registered voter. A decade ago, not a single Negro entered the legislative chambers of the South except as a porter or a chauffeur. Ten years ago, all too many Negroes were still harried by day and haunted by night by a corroding sense of fear and a nagging sense of nobody-ness.*

*But things are different now. In assault after assault, we caused the sagging walls of segregation to come tumbling down. And during this era the entire **edifice** of segregation was profoundly shaken. This is an accomplishment whose consequences are deeply felt by every southern Negro in his daily life. It is no longer possible to count the number of public establishments that are open to Negroes. Ten years ago, Negroes seemed almost invisible to the larger society, and the facts of their harsh lives were unknown to the majority of the nation. But today, civil rights is a dominating issue in every state, crowding the pages of the press and the daily conversation of white Americans. In this decade of change, the Negro stood up and confronted his oppressor. He faced bullies and the guns, the dogs and the tear gas. He put himself squarely before the vicious mobs and moved with strength and dignity toward them and decisively defeated them. And the courage with which he confronted enraged mobs dissolved the stereotype of the grinning, submissive **Uncle Tom**. He came out of his struggle integrated only slightly in the external society, but powerfully integrated within. This was a victory that had to precede all other gains.*

*In short, over the last ten years the Negro decided to straighten his back up, realizing that a man cannot ride your back unless it is bent. We made our government write new laws to alter some of the cruelest injustices that affected us. We made an indifferent and unconcerned nation rise from **lethargy** and **subpoenaed** its conscience to appear before the judgment seat of morality on the whole question of civil rights. We gained manhood in the nation that had always called us "boy."...But in spite of a decade of significant progress, the problem is far from solved. The deep rumbling of discontent in our cities is indicative of the fact that the plant of freedom has grown only a bud and not yet a flower....*

Now in order to answer the question, "Where do we go from here?," which is our theme, we must first honestly recognize where we are now. When the Constitution was written, a strange formula to de-

Interposition: The placing of a state's sovereignty (independence) between its citizens and the federal government.

Nullification: A state impeding or attempting to prevent the enforcement within its territory of a U.S. federal law.

Conniving: Scheming; wrongful.

Edifice: A structure.

Uncle Tom: The character in the book *Uncle Tom's Cabin,* whose name became slang for any black acting in a submissive or deferential way toward whites.

Lethargy: Laziness.

Subpoenaed: Summoned.

President Lyndon Johnson shakes hands with Martin Luther King Jr. after signing the Civil Rights Act of 1964 on July 2, 1964.
© Bettmann/Corbis. Reproduced by permission.

termine taxes and representation declared that the Negro was sixty percent of a person. Today another curious formula seems to declare he is fifty percent of a person. Of the good things in life, the Negro has approximately one-half those of whites. Of the bad things of life, he has twice those of whites. Thus, half of all Negroes live in substandard housing. And Negroes have half the income of whites. When we turn to the negative experiences of life, the Negro has a double share: There are twice as many unemployed; the rate of infant mortality among Negroes is double that of whites; and there are twice as many Negroes dying in Vietnam as whites in proportion to their size in the population.

In other spheres, the figures are equally alarming. In elementary schools, Negroes lag behind whites, and their segregated schools receive substantially less money per student than the white schools. One-twentieth as many Negroes as whites attend college. Of employed Negroes, seventy-five percent hold menial jobs. This is where we are.

Where do we go from here? First we massively assert our dignity and worth. We must stand up amid a system that still oppresses us and develop an **unassailable** and majestic sense of values. We must no longer be ashamed of being black. The job of arousing manhood within a people that have been taught for so many centuries that they are nobody is not easy....

Psychological freedom, a firm sense of self-esteem, is the most powerful weapon against the long night of physical slavery. No **Lincolnian Emancipation Proclamation**, no **Johnsonian civil rights bill** can totally bring this kind of freedom. The Negro will only be free when he reaches down to the inner depths of his own being and signs with the pen and ink of assertive manhood his own emancipation proclamation....[T]he Negro must...say to himself and to the world, "I am somebody. I am a person. I am a man with dignity and honor. I have a rich and noble history, however painful and exploited that history has been. Yes, I was a slave through my foreparents, and now I'm not ashamed of that. I'm ashamed of the people who were so sinful to make me a slave." Yes, yes, we must stand up and say, "I'm black, but I'm black and beautiful." This, this self-affirmation is the black man's need, made compelling by the white man's crimes against him.

Now another basic challenge is to discover how to organize our strength into economic and political power. No one can deny that the Negro is in dire need of this kind of legitimate power. Indeed, one of the great problems that the Negro confronts is his lack of power. From the old plantations of the South to the newer **ghettos** of the North, the Negro has been confined to a life of voicelessness and powerlessness. Stripped of the right to make decisions concerning his life and destiny, he has been subject to the authoritarian and sometimes whimsical decision of the white power structure. The plantation and the ghetto were created by those who had power, both to confine those who had no power and to perpetuate their powerlessness. Now the problem of transforming the ghetto, therefore is a problem of power, a confrontation between the forces of power demanding change and the forces of power dedicated to the preserving of the **status quo**. Now, power properly understood is nothing but the ability to achieve purpose. It is the strength required to bring about social, political, and economic change.

[...]

Now we got to get this thing right. What is needed is a realization that power without love is reckless and abusive, and that love without power is sentimental and **anemic**. Power at its best, power at its best is love implementing the demands of justice, and justice

Unassailable: Not open to attack or question.

Lincolnian Emancipation Proclamation: President Abraham Lincoln's Emancipation Proclamation of 1862, which ended legal slavery.

Johnsonian civil rights bill: The Civil Rights Act of 1964 signed by President Lyndon B. Johnson.

Ghettos: Sections of cities where minority groups live because of social, legal, or economic pressures.

Status quo: The existing legal, social, or cultural state.

Anemic: Used here to mean lacking force.

A scene from the Watts riot in Los Angeles, California, June 1965. Martin Luther King Jr. felt riots did nothing positive to improve the rights of black Americans. © Bettmann/Corbis. Reproduced by permission.

at its best is love correcting everything that stands against love. And this is what we must see as we move on.

Now what has happened is that we've had it wrong and mixed up in our country, and this has led Negro Americans in the past to seek their goals through love and **moral suasion** devoid of power, and white Americans to seek their goals through power devoid of love and conscience. It is leading a few extremists today to advocate for Negroes the same destructive and conscienceless power that they have justly **abhorred** in whites. It is precisely this collision of immoral power with powerless morality which constitutes the major crisis of our times.

[...]

Now let me rush on to say we must reaffirm our commitment to nonviolence. And I want to stress this. The futility of violence in the struggle for racial justice has been tragically etched in all the recent Negro riots. Now yesterday, I tried to analyze the riots and deal with the causes for them. Today I want to give the other side. There is something painfully sad about a riot. One sees screaming youngsters and angry adults fighting hopelessly and aimlessly against impossible odds. Deep down within them, you perceive a desire for self-destruction, a kind of suicidal longing.

Occasionally, Negroes contend that the **1965 Watts riot** and the other riots in various cities represented effective civil rights action. But those who express this view always end up with stumbling words when asked what concrete gains have been won as a result. At best the riots have produced a little additional anti-poverty money allotted by frightened government officials, and a few water sprinklers to cool the children of the ghettos. It is something like improving the food in the prison while the people remain securely **incarcerated** behind bars. Nowhere have the riots won any concrete improvement such as have the organized protest demonstrations.

And when one tries to pin down advocates of violence as to what acts would be effective, the answers are **blatantly** illogical. Sometimes they talk of overthrowing racist state and local governments and they talk about **guerrilla warfare**. They fail to see that no internal revolution has ever succeeded in overthrowing a government by violence unless the government had already lost the allegiance and effective control of its armed forces. Anyone in his right mind know that this will not happen in the United States. In a violent racial situation, the power structure has the local police, the state troopers, the National Guard, and finally, the Army to call on, all of which are predominantly white. Furthermore, few, if any, violent revolutions have been successful unless the violent minority had the sympathy and support of the non-resisting majority....It is perfectly clear that a violent revolution on the part of American blacks would find no sympathy and support from the white population and very little from the majority of the Negroes themselves.

Moral suasion: Persuasion or influence based on a conception of righteous behavior.

Abhorred: Hated.

1965 Watts riot: A violent riot in the Watts section of Los Angeles, California.

Incarcerated: Imprisoned.

Blatantly: Obviously; clearly.

Guerrilla warfare: Informal fighting by independent groups within a nation.

Romantic illusions: Unrealistic, optimistic images or visions.

Tactical: Carefully planned.

*This is no time for **romantic illusions** and empty philosophical debates about freedom. This is a time for action. What is needed is a strategy for change, a **tactical** program that will bring the Negro into the mainstream of American life as quickly as possible. So far, this has only been offered by the nonviolent movement. Without recognizing this we will end up with solutions that don't solve, answers that don't answer, and explanations that don't explain.*

And so I say to you today that I still stand by nonviolence. And I am still convinced, and I'm still convinced that it is the most potent weapon available to the Negro in his struggle for justice in this country.

[....]

What happened next...

At the time of King's speech, the militant civil rights groups, such as the Black Panthers, the Congress of Racial Equality (CORE), the Nation of Islam, and SNCC (renamed the Student National Coordinating Committee), advocated for urgent militant efforts to gain rights for blacks. These groups rejected, and many directly threatened, white society. American cities, including Los Angeles and Detroit, exploded in rioting in which businesses and homes were burned and looted.

Knowing that the right to vote and participate in white society was not enough, King had outlined a plan for economic equality that would help blacks compete on an equal footing with whites. But King would not live to reach these goals. When he was killed by a gunshot on April 4, 1968, his followers scrambled to keep his dream alive.

Reverend Ralph Abernathy tried to lead King's proposed Poor People's Campaign in May of 1968, erecting a tent city in Washington, D.C., with several hundred demonstrators in protest of economic inequalities. Abernathy did not exert King's moral hold on the demonstrators, however, and the tent city deteriorated into violence among the protestors. The failure of the Poor People's Campaign signaled how strong King's leadership had been. Washington police evicted the protestors in June, marking an end to the demonstration.

No leader could match King's leadership, and by the end of the decade civil rights groups had splintered into several small, less effective organizations. But King's legacy lived on. The legal changes made during the 1960s laid the foundation for dramatic improvement in lives of blacks and other minorities in America. The oppressive regime that King had been born into was gone.

Did you know...

- Although the civil rights movement lost momentum with King's death, it had already transformed American society. America was a much fairer society by the end of the 1960s, but not the "colorblind" society King envisioned.

- During the 1970s, affirmative action policies, which gave racial minorities an advantage in job and university applications, helped many minorities and some women get education and jobs with better salaries.

Rev. Ralph Abernathy tried to carry on Martin Luther King Jr.'s work after King's 1968 assassination in 1968. *© Bettmann/Corbis. Reproduced by permission.*

- The affirmative action programs that gave racial minorities an advantage in university enrollment and employment hiring procedures fostered racial resentment in white society. Instead of seeing affirmative action programs as remedies for eliminating the past practices that banned blacks from universities and jobs, some whites came to see these programs as "reverse" racism.

Consider the following...

- Martin Luther King Jr. is credited with possessing a moral leadership that inspired civil rights activists to subject themselves to dangerous, life-threatening situations.

What qualities would a leader have to display for you become such an activist?

- In his speech, King described the improvements nonviolent protest had made in society by 1967. Do you think these improvements prove that nonviolent protest really worked? Explain your reasoning.

- Without King, the civil rights protestors had a difficult time assembling peacefully in large numbers. Why do you think this happened?

For More Information

Books

Bennett, Lerone, Jr. *What Manner of Man: A Biography of Martin Luther King, Jr.* Chicago, IL: Johnson, 1964.

Bruun, Erik, and Jay Crosby, eds. *Our Nation's Archive: The History of the United States in Documents.* New York: Black Dog & Leventhal, 1999.

Carson, Clayborne, and Kris Shepard, eds. *A Call to Conscience.* New York: Warner Books, 2001.

Farber, David. *The Age of Great Dreams: America in the 1960s.* New York: Hill and Wang, 1994.

Farber, David, and Beth Bailey, with others. *The Columbia Guide to America in the 1960s.* New York: Columbia University Press, 2001.

Haskins, James. *The Life and Death of Martin Luther King, Jr.* New York: Beech Tree Books, 1992.

January, Brendan. *Martin Luther King, Jr.: Minister and Civil Rights Activist.* Chicago, IL: Ferguson Publishing, 2000.

King, Coretta Scott. *My Life with Martin Luther King, Jr.* New York: Holt, Rinehart & Winston, 1969, revised, 1993.

King, Rev. Martin Luther, Jr. *The Words of Martin Luther King, Jr.,* edited by Coretta Scott King. New York: Newmarket Press, 1983.

Pettit, Jayne. *Martin Luther King, Jr.: A Man with a Dream.* New York: Franklin Watts, 2001.

Unger, Irwin, and Debi Unger, eds. *The Times Were a Changin'.* New York: Random House, 1998.

Wukovits, John F. *Martin Luther King, Jr.* San Diego, CA: Lucent Books, 1999.

Web sites

National Civil Rights Museum. www.civilrightsmuseum.org (accessed on August 4, 2004).

The King Center. www.thekingcenter.org (accessed on August 4, 2004).

"Martin Luther King, Jr.: Biography." *Nobel eLibrary.* www.nobel.se/peace/laureates/1964/king-bio.html (accessed on August 4, 2004).

Feminist Perspectives

2

The women's liberation movement of the 1960s and 1970s was not a political and social reaction limited to conditions of that time, but rather a reaction against many years of social and legal constraints on women in America. Life for women, as for all people, in any country at any time is shaped by custom, law, and circumstance. In the colonial times and the early years of the United States, women could not own property, earn wages, or vote. The lives of women in rural areas focused on the domestic work that accompanied farming, on cooking, and on storing the annual harvest. Traditionally, women also tended to take charge of poultry and would take the eggs into the market to sell or exchange for goods they could not produce at home, like salt and coffee. In both rural and urban areas, women were responsible for quilting and rug making, and for making their family's clothes, nursing the sick, and teaching children. To further add to the family's economic well-being, some women took in other people's laundry or sewing work and were often paid with goods or supplies rather than money. Few worked outside the home.

Through the nineteenth century with mechanization of production, both men and women living in urban areas could find work for wages in factories. Lower-class women worked in domestic service or textile mills. Women's wages were lower than men's wages, in part because men were paid a "family wage" that was expected to provide enough for the entire family. Working women earned about one-half the wages of men. Working women, if they had a family, were also responsible for all the household duties.

As more people moved onto the western frontier in the mid-1800s, opportunities and rights for many women increased. Many frontier women owned their own property and worked their own farms. Some women even worked as doctors, a profession that did not require a university degree until the late 1800s. These frontier women worked hard and were allowed to participate in society in meaningful ways earlier than women living in more established towns in the East. Wyoming, Utah, Colorado, and Idaho all granted women the right to vote before 1870, for example. It would take until the passage of the Nineteenth Amendment in 1920 for all U.S. women to be able to vote.

In towns in both the East and West, educational opportunities for women also increased in the nineteenth century. Before this time, the extent of many women's education was learning to read the Bible. The first public high school for girls opened in Worcester, Massachusetts, in 1824. In 1837, Oberlin College in Ohio became the first university to admit women; however, female students were required to do the laundry and cook for the male students in addition to attending to their own studies. Women had the chance to focus completely on their own studies at women's universities. The first, Mount Holyoke Female Seminary, opened in Massachusetts in 1837. Between the 1860s and 1890s six more women's universities opened. Together these women's universities came to be known as "The Seven Sisters." Although opportunities for education had increased, only a small percentage of women earned advanced degrees at universities. Those who did most often became nurses or teachers.

As the United States became increasingly industrialized throughout the nineteenth century and growing numbers of people moved to urban centers, new job opportunities emerged for all. Women held clerical jobs in businesses and sales positions in new retail stores. By the late nineteenth century, women were becoming telephone operators and held switchboard positions in telephone companies. By 1918 all states had passed compulsory education for children laws, so more women found jobs as teachers. Others with some level of formal education could work as nurses and librarians. But women were restricted from certain kinds of work, were excluded from some areas of study, and in some cases restricted from certain work because of their marital status. Nonetheless, by 1930, one out of every six married women worked outside the home, at least part-time.

When American men left to serve in World War II (1939–45), women were encouraged to replace them in the traditionally male positions in industry, particularly in factory work that supported the war effort. These wartime positions in U.S. industry paid well, and women eagerly tackled the new work. But at war's end, women were expected to vacate these positions to make way for returning veterans. Women who wanted to continue working after the war often had to accept lower wages. In the post–World War II period, women were urged to embrace their domestic roles as wives and mothers and to focus on the private sphere of the home.

Throughout the 1950s, American culture revered the home and family. Wives and mothers were glorified as homemakers. Women began marrying at earlier ages, having more children, and ending their schooling in order to support their husbands' careers. The popular belief was that a woman's place was in the home, providing stability and a haven for both her husband and their children. In the 1950s the national economy grew well, and middle-class women were increasingly the consumers in the marketplace. They had money to spend and took charge of the shopping, buying the family's clothes and decorating the house.

But by the 1960s, women found themselves increasingly aware of conflicting messages in a culture that at once glorified the homemaker and promoted increasing consumption of new products. More and more couples believed that both spouses had to work in order to afford larger suburban homes, cars, appliances, and fashionable clothing. Then too, since women typically lived longer than men, older women started to think about careers after their roles as wife and mother had ended. The 1960s civil rights movement asserted equal rights, and women began to question cultural beliefs that limited them or denied them the options men enjoyed. Women grew increasingly frustrated with gender-based limitations in career opportunities and in earning power.

In 1961 President John F. Kennedy (1917–1963; served 1961–63) created the **Commission on the Status of Women** to analyze the lives of American women and make recommendations for improving various aspects of their lives, including education, health care, and job opportunities. This chapter includes an excerpt from "American Women: The Report of the President's Commission on the Status of Women," which was presented to the president in 1963.

Helen Gurley Brown in her 1962 book *Sex and the Single Girl* and **Betty Friedan** in her 1963 book *Feminine Mystique* articulated the frustrations of a generation of women. Brown made it clear that adult females were sexual beings, and she offered single women guidance for living happy, guilt-free lives in a society that revered marriage. The excerpt from Brown's book included in this chapter indicates how her opinions differed from mainstream America on the subject of single women's sexuality. Betty Friedan reported on the emptiness felt by many suburban homemakers who wanted to be more than wives or mothers, and her book offered advice to married women seeking fuller lives. The first chapter of Betty Friedan's *The Feminine Mystique* describes married women's suffering.

These publications helped trigger the women's liberation movement of the 1960s and 1970s and sparked the idea to create the political action group called the National Organization for Women (NOW) in 1966. The movement promoted change in women's lives. It raised people's awareness of the need for increased career opportunities, helped women gain access to medical and law schools, and shaped corporate and political decisions regarding women's roles in business and government. The movement also helped establish government programs committed to improving education opportunities and extending health care and childcare. This chapter includes the "Bill of Rights for Women in 1968" written by the **National Organization for Women**. These excerpts provide a picture of American women's lives during the 1960s and how their lives had begun to change by the 1970s.

Commission on the Status of Women

Excerpt from "American Women: The Report of the President's Commission on the Status of Women," which was presented to President John F. Kennedy on October 11, 1963

Reprinted from *American Women: The Report of the President's Commission on the Status of Women and Other Publications of the Commission*.

Published in 1965.

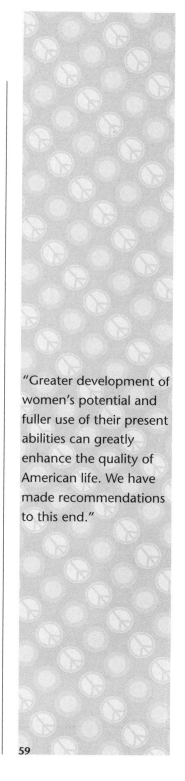

"Greater development of women's potential and fuller use of their present abilities can greatly enhance the quality of American life. We have made recommendations to this end."

President John F. Kennedy established the President's Commission on the Status of Women on December 14, 1961. Eleanor Roosevelt (1884–1962), one of the most influential woman in America at the time, chaired the twenty-member commission until her death in 1962. The president requested the commission to analyze employment policies affecting women, such as labor laws pertaining to hours and wages, the availability and quality of legal representation for women, and the availability and quality of education and counseling for working women.

The commission's findings were published in the "American Women" report, presented to President John F. Kennedy on October 11, 1963. "American Women" came to be commonly known as the Peterson Report after the commission's executive vice chairman Esther Peterson (1906–1997). The commission reported extensive discrimination against women. The commission recommended several changes in bureaucratic organization and laws to remedy the discrimination they documented. Some of the broadest recommendations were for paid maternity leave, affordable

President John Kennedy meets with the commission he appointed to examine the status of women in the United States. Eleanor Roosevelt, to the left of Kennedy, was chairperson of the committee.
© Bettmann/Corbis. Reproduced by permission.

childcare, and hiring practices that did not distinguish between men and women.

The President's Commission on the Status of Women, which was dissolved in October 1963 after it submitted its report, triggered significant legal and social support for women. Even before the commission's final report was presented to President Kennedy, he issued an executive order to establish an Interdepartmental Committee on the Status of Women and a Citizens' Advisory Council to continue the work outlined by the commission. President Lyndon B. Johnson (1908–1973; served 1963–69) following Kennedy's lead, had by 1964 appointed fifty-six women to federal positions. States also established commissions to advise on the status of women on local, regional, and state levels. Perhaps most tellingly the Equal Pay Act passed through the legislature in 1963, prohibiting wage discrimination between men and women performing under similar working conditions at the same establishment.

Things to remember while reading the excerpt from "American Women: The Report of the President's Commission on the Status of Women":

- Women had been marrying at younger and younger ages since the first two world wars. In 1890 the median age of marriage was 22 years for women, but by 1962 the median had dropped to 20.3 years. In the 1960s, 750,000 women between the ages of 14 and 19 had married and begun families.

- In 1900 two out of every five families lived on a farm or in small, rural towns without electricity or plumbing. By1962 fewer than one in ten families lived in similar places, and the vast majority of homes had electricity and plumbing.

- In 1900 women were expected to know how to cook, to regulate the temperature in a wood or coal cooking stove, to preserve the farm harvest in order to feed their families throughout the year, to sew clothing, nurse common ailments, and teach their children, if no school was nearby.

- By the 1960s, women managed households very differently. They could purchase canned or frozen food and such modern conveniences as instant coffee and minute rice from grocery stores and prepare food on gas or electric stoves. They visited doctors and dentists to care for their health and bought ready-to-wear clothing at department stores. More children attended schools than were taught at home.

- In 1962, the Department of Health, Education, and Welfare reported that 58 percent of male high school graduates and 42 percent of female graduates continued their education at colleges and universities.

- Eleanor Roosevelt served mainly as a figurehead of the commission. Her failing health limited her contributions to advising committees, signing letters, and publicizing the commission. She died on November 7, 1962.

- Esther Peterson, assistant secretary of labor and director of the Women's Bureau, the highest-ranking woman in the Kennedy administration, emerged as a leader in the commission, serving as its executive vice chairman.

- The commission established seven committees to study education and counseling available to women; home and community services; employed women; labor standards; levels of women's income; laws affecting women; and women's position as U.S. citizens. Two special examinations of African American women and the portrayal of women in the media were also conducted.

Excerpt from American Women: The Report of the President's Commission on the Status of Women

Invitation to Action

This report is an invitation to action. When President John F. Kennedy appointed our Commission, he said: "we have by no means done enough to strengthen family life and at the same time encourage women to make their full contribution as citizens....It is appropriate at this time...to review recent accomplishments, and to acknowledge frankly the further steps that must be taken. This is a task for the entire nation."

*The 96 million American women and girls include a range from infant to **octogenarian**, from **migrant** farm mother to suburban homemaker, from file clerk to research scientist, from Olympic athlete to college president. Greater development of women's potential and fuller use of their present abilities can greatly enhance the quality of American life. We have made recommendations to this end.*

*We invite response to our recommendations by **citizen initiative** exercised in many ways—through individual **inventiveness**, voluntary agencies, community cooperation, commercial enterprise, corporate policy, foundation support, governmental action at various levels. In making our proposals, we have had in mind the well-being of the entire society; their adoption would in many cases be of direct benefit to men as well as women.*

Octogenarian: An 80-year-old person.

Migrant: A person who moves to different places in order to find work harvesting seasonal crops.

Citizen initiative: Action taken by citizens in order to improve their lives.

Inventiveness: Creativeness or ingenuity.

Tenets: Beliefs or principles.

Democracy: A political system that places the power of the government in the hands of citizens.

Levers: Compelling forces.

Discrepancies: Differences or variances.

Social lag: The slow implementation of social equalities to all citizens.

Illumined: Enlightened or informed.

Certain **tenets** have guided our thinking. Respect for the worth and dignity of every individual and conviction that every American should have a chance to achieve the best of which he—or she—is capable are basic to the meaning of both freedom and equality in this **democracy**. They have been, and now are great **levers** for constructive social change, here and around the world. We have not hesitated to measure the present shape of things against our convictions regarding a good society and to note **discrepancies** between American life as it is in 1963 and as it might become through informed and intelligent action.

The human and national costs of **social lag** are heavy; for the most part, they are also avoidable. That is why we urge changes, many of them long overdue, in the conditions of women's opportunity in the United States.

Responsible Choice

We believe that one of the greatest freedoms of the individual in a democratic society is the freedom to choose among different life patterns. Innumerable private solutions found by different individuals in search of the good life provide society with basic strength far beyond the possibilities of a dictated plan.

Illumined by values transmitted through home and school and church, society and heritage, and informed by present and past experience, each woman must arrive at her contemporary expression of purpose, whether as a center of home and family, a participant in the community, a contributor to the economy, a creative artist or thinker or scientist, a citizen engaged in politics and public service. **Part and parcel** of this freedom is the obligation to assume corresponding responsibility.

Yet there are social as well as individual determinants of freedom of choice; for example, the city slum and the poor **rural crossroad** frustrate natural gifts and innate human powers. It is a bitter fact that for millions of men and women **economic stringency** all but eliminates choice among alternatives.

Esther Peterson assumed leadership of the President's Commission on the Status of Women after Eleanor Roosevelt's death in late 1962. *AP/Wide World Photos. Reproduced by permission.*

Part and parcel: A basic or fundamental element.

Rural crossroad: Small community.

Economic stringency: Scarcity of money.

A common sight in the United States prior to the 1960s was a mother and child greeting the husband and father at the door as he returns home from work. When America moved into the 1960s and beyond, the family dynamic changed, as more women entered the work force.

© H. Armstrong Roberts/Corbis. Reproduced by permission.

In a progress report to the President in August 1962, the Commission's Chairman, Eleanor Roosevelt, said: "A rapidly rising national output is the strongest weapon against substandard jobs, poverty-stricken homes, and barren lives."

In the same vein, Secretary of Labor W. Willard Wirtz has warned: "There is not going to be much in the way of expanding opportunities for women unless we are ready and able to assure the jobs which the economy as a whole requires."

Growth and Opportunity

Unless the economy grows at a substantially faster rate than at present, oncoming generations will not find work **commensurate** with their skills. The number of new **entrants** of all ages into the labor force was about 2 million a year in 1960. By 1970, it will be 3 million.

Much of the work offered by a modern economy demands types of skill requiring levels of education that only a nation with abundant resources can supply; if such skills, when acquired, are not used because the economy is lagging, the resulting **human frustrations**...are very costly indeed.

Economic expansion is of particular significance to women. One of the **ironies** of history is that war has brought American women their greatest economic opportunities. In establishing this Commission, the President noted: "In every period of national emergency, women have served with distinction in widely varied capacities but thereafter have been subject to treatment as a **marginal group** whose skills have been inadequately utilized."

Comparable opportunity—and far more varied choice—could be provided by full employment in a period without war.

The Council of Economic Advisers has estimated that between 1958 and 1962 the country's productive capacity exceeded its actual output by some $170 billion, or almost $1,000 per person in the United States. Had this potential been realized, lower rates of unemployment and an impressive supply of additional goods and services would have contributed to national well-being. The currently unused resources of the American economy include much work that could be done by women.

Higher Expectations

But while freedom of choice for many American women, as for men, is limited by economic considerations, one of the most **pervasive limitations** is the social climate in which women choose what they prepare themselves to do. Too many plans recommended to young women reaching maturity are only partially suited to the second half of the twentieth century. Such advice is correspondingly confusing to them.

Even the role most generally approved by counselors, parents, and friends—the making of a home, the rearing of children, and the transmission to them in their earliest years of the values of the

Commensurate: Equal with; proportionate.

Entrants: Workers.

Human frustrations: In this case, meaning the disappointment felt by not being able to find work proportionate to one's skills.

Ironies: Unexpected results, or incongruous from expected results, from an event.

Marginal group: An unimportant social group.

Comparable opportunity: In this case, meaning similar employment opportunities for men and women.

Pervasive limitations: Widespread barriers.

For women who worked outside the home in the 1960s and prior, the positions they occupied generally fell into the areas of teaching, nursing, and social work. © Bettmann/Corbis. Reproduced by permission.

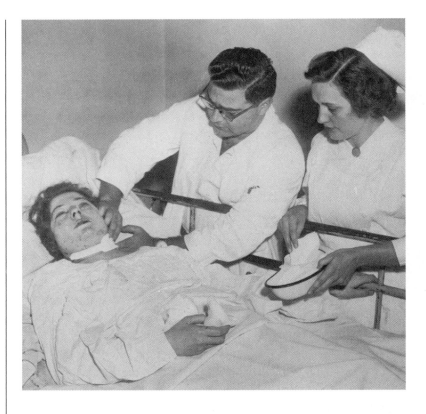

American heritage—is frequently presented as it is thought to have been in an earlier and simpler society. Women's ancient function of providing love and nurture stands. But for entry into modern life, today's children need a preparation far more **diversified** than that of their **predecessors**.

Similarly, women's participation in such traditional occupations as teaching, nursing, and social work is generally approved, with current shortages underscoring the nation's need for such **personnel**. But means for keeping up to date the skills of women who continue in such professions are few. So, too, are those for bringing up to date the skills of women who withdraw in order to raise families but return after their families are grown.

Commendation of women's entry into certain other occupations is less general, even though some of them are equally in need of trained people. Girls hearing that most women find mathematics and science difficult, or that engineering and architecture are unusual occupations for a woman, are not led to test their interest by activity in these fields.

Diversified: Varied.

Predecessors: Ancestors, or those who have lived before oneself.

Personnel: Workers.

Commendation: Recommendation as worthy or desired.

Because too little is expected of them, many girls who graduate from high school intellectually able to do good college work do not go to college. Both they as individuals and the nation as a society are thereby made losers.

*The subtle limitations imposed by custom are, upon occasion, reinforced by specific barriers. In the course of the twentieth century many **bars** against women that were firmly in place in 1900 have been lowered or dropped. But certain restrictions remain.*

Discriminations and Disadvantages

*Some of these discriminatory provisions are contained in the common law. Some are written into statute. Some are upheld by court decisions. Others take the form of practices of industrial, labor, professional, or governmental organizations that **discriminate** against women in **apprenticeship**, training, hiring, wages, and promotion. We have identified a number of outmoded and **prejudicial attitudes and practices**.*

*Throughout its **deliberations**, the Commission has kept in mind certain women who have special disadvantages. Among heads of families in the United States, 1 in 10 is a woman. At least half of them are carrying responsibility for both earning the family's living and making the family's home. Their problems are correspondingly greater; their resources are usually less.*

Seven million nonwhite women and girls belong to minority racial groups. Discrimination based on color is morally wrong and a source of national weakness. Such discrimination currently places an oppressive dual burden on millions of Negro women. The consultation held by the Commission on the situation of Negro women emphasized that in too many families lack of opportunity for men as well as women, linked to racial discrimination, has forced the women to assume too large a share of the family responsibility. Such women are twice as likely as other women to have to seek employment while they have preschool children at home; they are just beginning to gain entrance to the expanding fields of clerical and commercial employment; except for the few who can qualify as teachers or other professionals, they are forced into low-paid service occupations.

Hundreds of thousands of other women face somewhat similar situations: American Indians, for instance, and Spanish-Americans, many of whom live in urban centers but are new to urban life and burdened with language problems.

Bars: Limits.

Discriminate: In this case, meaning bar or deny.

Apprenticeship: A type of job training in which an inexperienced person learns by working for a period of time with an experienced worker.

Prejudicial attitudes and practices: Detrimental beliefs and actions.

Deliberations: Research into and consideration of a topic.

*While there are highly skilled members of all these groups, in many of the families of these women the unbroken cycle of **deprivation and retardation** repeats itself from generation to generation, compounding its individual cost in human **indignity** and unhappiness and its social cost in capacity and **delinquency**. This cycle must be broken, swiftly and at as many points as possible. The Commission strongly urges that in the carrying out of its recommendations, special attention be given to difficulties that are wholly or largely the products of this kind of discrimination.*

Lengthening Life Spans

*The Commission has also been impressed with the extent to which lengthening life spans are causing changes in women's occupations and preoccupations from decade to decade of their adult experience. The **life expectancy** of a girl baby is now 73 years; it was 48 years in 1900. In comparison with her own grandmother, today's young woman has a quarter century of additional life with abundant new choices to plan for. It is essential that the counseling of girls enable them to foresee the later as well as the earlier phases of their adulthood.*

Eight out of 10 women are in paid employment outside the home at some time during their lives, and many of these, and others as well, engage in unpaid work as volunteers.

*The population contains 13 million single girls and women 14 and over. A 20-year-old girl, if she remains single, will spend some 40 years in the labor force. If after working for a few years, she marries and has a family, and then goes back into the labor force at 30, she is likely to work for some 23 years. Particularly during the years when her children are in school but have not yet left home permanently, the work she seeks is apt to be part-time. **Inflexibility** with regard to part-time employment in most current hiring systems, alike in government and in private enterprise, excludes the use of much able and available trained woman power; practices should be altered to permit it.*

*Women's greater **longevity** as compared with men makes them the predominant group in the final age brackets. There are almost 800,000 more women than men 75 and over. The number of such women grew from slightly over 2 million in 1950 to more than 3 million in 1960. To most, this is a period of **economic dependency** which often ends in a need for terminal care.*

Deprivation and retardation: The withholding of education and opportunity and the preventing or hindering of social advancement.

Indignity: Humiliating treatment.

Delinquency: A social debt to these mistreated individuals on which payment is overdue.

Life expectancy: The average life span of an individual.

Inflexibility: Unwillingness to change.

Longevity: Length of life.

Economic dependency: A person's need to be financially supported, either by the government or by family.

What happened next...

The President's Commission on the Status of Women presented an analysis of women's lives that assumed that any person who did not have full access to the opportunities available to white, adult males was in some way handicapped and should be helped. The commission was careful to outline the differences between the lives of women and men, suggesting programs to equalize their opportunities over time. For example, women caring for young children early in life might need more access to part-time employment and adult education programs after their children had grown.

As the commission puzzled over the opportunities needed for women to balance work and homemaking, it discussed the difference between a job and a career, noting the first is merely a task done for money while the second is a labor pursued for intellectual as well as monetary fulfillment. The idea that women should have access to intellectual stimulation and the freedom to pursue any occupation of their choosing became the theme of the feminist movement, which broke U.S. cultural reliance on motherhood and wifehood as the only measures of feminine achievement. But the struggles involved for women who tried to be both good wives and mothers and to be dedicated business women, scholars, artists, or other professionals caused heated debates that continued into the early 2000s.

Did you know...

- The space race that started between the United States and the Soviet Union in 1957 helped the women's liberation movement by increasing the need for a skilled, educated workforce. Suddenly the U.S. government became concerned with finding the best and the brightest minds, no matter their gender.

- The commission opposed the Equal Rights Amendment to the Constitution (which had been discussed by politicians since 1923) in favor of a number of legislative bills targeting specific grievances affecting women.

- Working independently during the time of the commission, Betty Friedan wrote *The Feminine Mystique,* published in 1963, which described many of the limitations in women's lives that the commission reported and which became a best-selling book with more than three million copies sold.

- By 1967 every state had established a commission on the status of women.

- By 1965 thirty-five states had enacted equal pay laws.

- By 1965 four states had rewritten jury service provisions to stop discrimination against women jurors.

Consider the following...

- How did the commission's report describe American women's lives?

- In what ways have women's lives changed since the commission's report in 1963?

- How could women have brought the difficulties in their lives to the attention of the U.S. government without the study of the Commission of the Status of Women?

For More Information

Books

Hurley, Jennifer A., ed. *Women's Rights*. San Diego, CA: Greenhaven, 2002.

Mead, Margaret, and Frances Balgley Kaplan, eds. *American Women: The Report of the President's Commission on the Status of Women and Other Publications of the Commission*. New York: Charles Scribner's Sons, 1965.

Treanor, Nick, ed. *The Feminist Movement*. San Diego, CA: Greenhaven, 2002.

Betty Friedan

Excerpt from The Feminine Mystique
Originally published in 1963; excerpt taken from 1997 reprint.

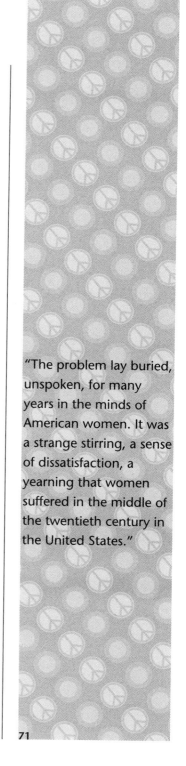

Betty Friedan gave voice to the suffering of many American women in her book *The Feminine Mystique,* in which she documented the damage American society did to women by insisting that the acceptable roles for them were limited to wives and mothers. Betty Friedan was born Betty Naomi Goldstein on February 4, 1921, in Peoria, Illinois, to Harry (a jeweler) and Miriam (Horowitz) Goldstein. Miriam Goldstein, who had worked as a newspaper editor but left her job to raise her family, encouraged her daughter to pursue her education and work as a journalist. Friedan graduated summa cum laude, which in Latin means with highest praise, from Smith College with a bachelor's degree in psychology and went on to study at the University of California, Berkeley; University of Iowa; and Esalen Institute. She worked as a newspaper journalist in 1943 but gave up her job to a returning veteran after World War II (1939–45) to take another job at a labor union newspaper. She married Carl Friedan (a theater producer) in June of 1947. Friedan continued to work for the newspaper while the couple started a family. She took a one-year maternity leave for the birth of her first child but was fired when

"The problem lay buried, unspoken, for many years in the minds of American women. It was a strange stirring, a sense of dissatisfaction, a yearning that women suffered in the middle of the twentieth century in the United States."

Betty Friedan pictured in 1970. © *Bettmann/Corbis. Reproduced by permission.*

she asked for a second maternity leave in 1949. The couple had a third child together, while Friedan remained a housewife.

Friedan soon became dissatisfied with simply being a wife and mother. She began working as a freelance journalist, a writer who is hired for a writing task rather than working full- or part-time for a company, while continuing to raise her children. In order to figure out whether she was alone in her thinking about domestic life, she conducted interviews with other housewives and sent out surveys to her former college classmates. Her research proved she was not alone. When no magazines would publish her findings, she put together all the interviews and surveys of housewives she received from across the country to create her first book, *The Feminine Mystique.*

Her study reported the dissatisfaction of housewives and mothers, no matter their education level. Her book expressed the feelings of many women and became a best-seller soon after its publication in 1963. Her book exposed the myth, or widely held but unrealistic belief, that said women were happy homemakers who were content to care for their husbands and families without regard for their own interests. Labeling this myth "the feminine mystique," Friedan analyzed how this "ideal" denied women complex, interesting lives. The popularity of *The Feminine Mystique* launched Friedan into the center of the women's liberation movement. By 1966 she had become one of the founding members of the National Organization for Women (NOW). Through her political activism, Friedan worked hard for such causes as the passage of the Equal Rights Amendment, which stated that women and men are equal and must be treated equally by law, and the legalization of abortion, a medical procedure to end a pregnancy.

Things to remember while reading the excerpt from *The Feminine Mystique*:

- It took Betty Friedan five years to turn her original magazine article into *The Feminine Mystique*.

- As a solution to the discontent felt by so many housewives, Friedan suggested that women continue to support their families and begin to develop other interests through employment, a profession, volunteer work, or further education.

- Betty Friedan participated in the government's special committee to investigate the portrayal of women in the media that contributed to the President's Commission on the Status of Women's report, *American Women*.

- As influential as the government *American Women* report was, the government only distributed 83,000 copies before its publication in 1965 by Charles Scribner's Sons. But *The Feminine Mystique* sold five million copies by 1970, reaching far more people.

- Friedan's description of suburban homes as "comfortable concentration camps" struck a chord with readers.

Excerpt from The Feminine Mystique

Chapter 1: The Problem That Has No Name

The problem lay buried, unspoken, for many years in the minds of American women. It was a strange stirring, a sense of dissatisfaction, a yearning that women suffered in the middle of the twentieth century in the United States. Each suburban wife struggled with it alone. As she made the beds, shopped for groceries, matched slipcover material, ate peanut butter sandwiches with her children, chauffeured Cub Scouts and Brownies, lay beside her husband at night—she was afraid to ask even of herself the silent question—"Is this all?"

For over fifteen years there was no word of this yearning in the millions of words written about women, for women, in all the columns, books and articles by experts telling women their role was

A stereotypical image of the 1950s housewife, content only with taking care of the home and family. Betty Friedan openly discussed many women's frustration with this scenario in *The Feminine Mystique.* © H. Armstrong Roberts/Corbis. Reproduced by permission.

| **The Sixties in America: Primary Sources**

Freudian sophistication: This expression refers to an educated familiarity with belief in the theories about human behavior developed by Sigmund Freud (1856–1939), the founder of psychoanalysis.

to seek fulfillment as wives and mothers. Over and over women heard in voices of tradition and of **Freudian sophistication** that they could desire—no greater destiny than to glory in their own femininity. Experts told them how to catch a man and keep him, how to breastfeed children and handle their toilet training, how to cope with sibling rivalry and adolescent rebellion; how to buy a dishwasher, bake bread, cook gourmet snails, and build a swimming pool with their own hands; how to dress, look, and act more feminine and *make marriage more exciting; how to keep their husbands from dying young and their sons from growing into delinquents. They were taught to pity the neurotic, unfeminine, unhappy women who wanted to be poets or physicists or presidents. They learned that truly feminine women do not want careers, higher education, political rights—the independence and the opportunities that the old-fashioned feminists fought for. Some women, in their forties and fifties, still remembered painfully giving up those dreams, but most of the younger women no longer even thought about them. A thousand expert voices applauded their femininity, their adjustment, their new maturity. All they had to do was devote their lives from earliest girlhood to finding a husband and bearing children.*

By the end of the nineteen-fifties, the average marriage age of women in America dropped to 20, and was still dropping, into the teens. Fourteen million girls were engaged by 17. The proportion of women attending college in comparison with men dropped from 47 per cent in 1920 to 35 per cent in 1958. A century earlier, women had fought for higher education; now girls went to college to get a husband. By the mid-fifties, 60 per cent dropped out of college to marry, or because they were afraid too much education would be a marriage bar. Colleges built dormitories for "married students," but the students were almost always the husbands. A new degree was instituted for the wives—"Ph.T." (Putting Husband Through).

Then American girls began getting married in high school. And the women's magazines, deploring the unhappy statistics about these young marriages, urged that courses on marriage, and marriage counselors, be installed in the high schools. Girls started going steady at twelve and thirteen, in junior high. Manufacturers put out brassieres with false bosoms of foam rubber for little girls of ten. And one advertisement for a child's dress, sizes 3-6x, in the New York Times *in the fall of 1960, said: "She Too Can Join the Man-Trap Set."*

By the end of the fifties, the United States birthrate was overtaking India's.... **Statisticians** *were especially astounded at the fantastic increase in the number of babies among college women. Where once they had two children, now they had four, five, six. Women who had once wanted careers were now making careers out of having babies. So rejoiced* Life *magazine in a 1956* **paean** *to the movement of American women back to the home....*

Interior decorators were designing kitchens with mosaic murals and original paintings, for kitchens were once again the center of

Statisticians: Persons engaged in the analysis and interpretation of data.

Paean: Strong expression of praise.

An idealized image of the young, happy housewife. In her book, Betty Friedan asked women to challenge this image and determine for themselves what makes them happy.

© Bettmann/Corbis. Reproduced by permission.

Sociological phenomenon: A societal change.

Mortgage: House payments; a lien against a property.

Science fellowship: Monies awarded to pursue scientific study.

women's lives. Home sewing became a million-dollar industry. Many women no longer left their homes, except to shop, chauffeur their children, or attend a social engagement with their husbands. Girls were growing up in America without ever having jobs outside the home. In the late fifties, a **sociological phenomenon** was suddenly remarked: a third of American women now worked, but most were no longer young and very few were pursuing careers. They were married women who held part-time jobs, selling or secretarial, to put their husbands through school, their sons through college, or to help pay the **mortgage**. Or they were widows supporting families. Fewer and fewer women were entering professional work. The shortages in the nursing, social work, and teaching professions caused crises in almost every American city. Concerned over the Soviet Union's lead in the space race, scientists noted that America's greatest source of unused brain-power was women. But girls would not study physics: it was "unfeminine." A girl refused a **science fellowship** at **Johns Hopkins** to take a job in a real-estate office. All she wanted, she said, was what every other American girl wanted—to get married, have four children and live in a nice house in a nice suburb.

The suburban housewife—she was the dream image of the young American women and the envy, it was said, of women all over the world. The American housewife—freed by science and **labor-saving appliances** from the **drudgery**, the dangers of childbirth and the illnesses of her grandmother. She was healthy, beautiful, educated, concerned only about her husband, her children, her home. She had found true feminine fulfillment. As a housewife and mother, she was respected as a full and equal partner to man in his world. She was free to choose automobiles, clothes, appliances, supermarkets; she had everything that women ever dreamed of.

In the fifteen years after World War II, this **mystique of feminine fulfillment** became the cherished and self-perpetuating core of contemporary American culture. Millions of women lived their lives in the image of those pretty pictures of the American suburban house-wife, kissing their husbands goodbye in front of the picture window, depositing their stationwagonsful of children at school, and smiling as they ran the new electric waxer over the spotless kitchen floor. They baked their own bread, sewed their own and their children's clothes, kept their new washing machines and dryers running all day. They changed the sheets on the beds twice a week instead of once, took the rug-hooking class in adult education, and pitied their poor frustrated mothers, who had dreamed of having a career. Their only dream was to be perfect wives and mothers; their highest ambition to have five children and a beautiful house, their only fight to get and keep their husbands. They had no thought for the unfeminine problems of the world outside the home; they wanted the men to make the major decisions. They gloried in their role as women, and wrote proudly on the census blank: "Occupation: housewife."

For over fifteen years, the words written for women, and the words women used when they talked to each other, while their husbands sat on the other side of the room and talked shop or politics or septic tanks, were about problems with their children, or how to keep their husbands happy, or improve their children's school, or cook chicken or make slipcovers. Nobody argued whether women were inferior or superior to men; they were simply different. Words like **"emancipation"** and "career" sounded strange and embarrassing; no one had used them for years. When a Frenchwoman named **Simone de Beauvoir** wrote a book called The Second Sex, an American critic commented that she obviously "didn't know what life was all about," and besides, she was talking about French women. The "woman problem" in America no longer existed.

If a woman had a problem in the 1950's and 1960's, she knew that something must be wrong with her marriage, or with herself. Other women were satisfied with their lives, she thought. What kind of a woman was she if she did not feel this mysterious fulfillment waxing the kitchen floor? She was so ashamed to admit her dissatisfaction that she never knew how many other women shared it. If she tried to tell her husband, he didn't understand what she was talking about. She did not really understand it herself. For over fifteen years women in America found it harder to talk about the problem than about sex. Even the **psychoanalysts** had no name for it. When a woman went to a **psychiatrist** for help, as many women did, she would say, "I'm so ashamed," or "I must be hopelessly neurotic." "I don't know what's wrong with women today," a suburban psychiatrist said uneasily. "I only know something is wrong because

Johns Hopkins: Johns Hopkins University, a respected institution of higher learning.

Labor-saving appliances: Devices, such as washing machines and electric mixers, that reduce the amount of physical labor needed to do a particular job.

Drudgery: Dull, tiring work.

Mystique of feminine fulfillment: The widespread belief that women were content to be only housewives and mothers.

Emancipation: Freedom from constraints.

Simone de Beauvoir (1908–1986): An influential feminist author.

Psychoanalyst: A professional therapist who has studied emotional and mental disorders and helps clients usually by encouraging them to speak freely about their problems.

Psychiatrist: A medical professional who deals with mental, emotional, or behavioral disorders, and who has the licensing to prescribe medications.

most of my patients happen to be women. And their problem isn't sexual." Most women with this problem did not go to see a psychoanalyst, however. "There's nothing wrong really," they kept telling themselves, "There isn't any problem."

But on an April morning in 1959, I heard a mother of four, having coffee with four other mothers in a suburban development fifteen miles from New York, say in a tone of quiet desperation, "the problem." And the others knew, without words, that she was not talking about a problem with her husband, or her children, or her home. Suddenly they realized they all shared the same problem, the problem that has no name. They began, hesitantly, to talk about it. Later, after they had picked up their children at nursery school and taken them home to nap, two of the women cried, in sheer relief, just to know they were not alone.

Gradually I came to realize that the problem that has no name was shared by countless women in America. As a magazine writer I often interviewed women about problems with their children, or their marriages, or their houses, or their communities. But after a while I began to recognize the telltale signs of this other problem. I saw the same signs in suburban ranch houses and split-levels on Long Island and in New Jersey and Westchester County; in colonial houses in a small Massachusetts town; on patios in Memphis; in suburban and city apartments; in living rooms in the Midwest. Sometimes I sensed the problem, not as a reporter, but as a suburban housewife, for during this time I was also bringing up my own three children in Rockland County, New York. I heard echoes of the problem in college dormitories and **semiprivate maternity wards**, *at PTA meetings and luncheons of the League of Women Voters, at suburban cocktail parties, in station wagons waiting for trains, and in snatches of conversation overheard at* **Schrafft's**. *The groping words I heard from other women, on quiet afternoons when children were at school or on quiet evenings when husbands worked late, I think I understood first as a woman long before I understood their larger* **social and psychological implications**.

Just what was this problem that has no name? What were the words women used when they tried to express it? Sometimes a woman would say "I feel empty somehow...incomplete." Or she would say, "I feel as if I don't exist." Sometimes she blotted out the feeling with a tranquilizer. Sometimes she thought the problem was with her husband or her children, or that what she really needed was to redecorate her house, or move to a better neighborhood, or

Semiprivate maternity wards: A two-bed hospital room in which women stay after giving birth.

Schrafft's: A popular candy store.

Social and psychological implications: The effects on society and on the minds of people.

have an affair, or another baby. Sometimes, she went to a doctor with symptoms she could hardly describe: "A tired feeling…I get so angry with the children it scares me…I feel like crying without any reason." (A Cleveland doctor called it "the housewife's syndrome.") A number of women told me about great bleeding blisters that break out on their hands and arms. "I call it the house wife's blight," said a family doctor in Pennsylvania. "I see it so often lately in these young women with four, five and six children who bury themselves in their dishpans. But it isn't caused by detergent and it isn't cured by cortisone."

Sometimes a woman would tell me that the feeling gets so strong she runs out of the house and walks through the streets. Or she stays inside her house and cries. Or her children tell her a joke, and she doesn't laugh because she doesn't hear it. I talked to women who had spent years on the analyst's couch, working out their "adjustment to the feminine role," their **blocks** to "fulfillment as a wife and mother." But the desperate tone in these women's voices, and the look in their eyes, was the same as the tone and the look of other women, who were sure they had no problem, even though they did have a strange feeling of desperation.…

In 1960, the problem that has no name **burst like a boil** through the image of the happy American housewife. In the television commercials the pretty housewives still beamed over their foaming dishpans and Time's cover story on "The Suburban Wife, an American Phenomenon" protested: "Having too good a time…to believe that they should be unhappy." But the actual unhappiness of the American housewife was suddenly being reported—from the New York Times and Newsweek to Good Housekeeping and CBS Television ("The Trapped Housewife"), although almost everybody who talked about it found some superficial reason to dismiss it. It was attributed to incompetent appliance repairmen (New York Times), or the distances children must be chauffeured in the suburbs (Time), or too much PTA (Redbook). Some said it was the old problem—education: more and more women had education, which naturally made them unhappy in their role as housewives.…

Home economists suggested more realistic preparation for housewives, such as high-school workshops in home appliances. College educators suggested more discussion groups on home management and the family, to prepare women for the adjustment to domestic life. A **spate** of articles appeared in the mass magazines offering "Fifty-eight Ways to Make Your Marriage More Exciting." No

Blocks: In this case, meaning mental obstacles.

Burst like a boil: Literally, this is an eruption of an infected skin gland. In this case, it means to "expose the ugly truth."

Home economists: Persons engaged in the study of homemaking.

Spate: A large number.

*month went by without a new book by a psychiatrist or **sexologist** offering technical advice on finding greater fulfillment through sex....*

A number of educators suggested seriously that women no longer be admitted to the four-year colleges and universities: in the growing college crisis, the education which girls could not use as housewives was more urgently needed than ever by boys to do the work of the atomic age....

The problem was dismissed by telling the housewife she doesn't realize how lucky she is—her own boss, no time clock, no junior executive gunning for her job. What if she isn't happy—does she think men are happy in this world? Does she really, secretly, still want to be a man? Doesn't she know yet how lucky she is to be a woman?

The problem was also, and finally, dismissed by shrugging that there are no solutions: this is what being a woman means, and what is wrong with American women that they can't accept their role gracefully? As Newsweek *put it (March 7, 1960):*

> *She is dissatisfied with a lot that women of other lands can only dream of. Her discontent is deep, pervasive, and impervious to the superficial remedies which are offered at every hand....An army of professional explorers have already charted the major sources of trouble....From the beginning of time, the female cycle has defined and confined woman's role. As Freud was credited with saying: "Anatomy is destiny." Though no group of women has ever pushed these natural restrictions as far as the American wife, it seems that she still cannot accept them with good grace....A young mother with a beautiful family, charm, talent and brains is apt to dismiss her role apologetically. "What do I do?" you hear her say. "Why nothing. I'm just a housewife." A good education, it seems, has given this **paragon** among women an understanding of the value of everything except her own worth....*

And so she must accept the fact that "American women's unhappiness is merely the most recently won of women's rights," and adjust and say with the happy housewife found by Newsweek: *"We ought to salute the wonderful freedom we all have and be proud of our lives today. I have had college and I've worked, but being a housewife is the most rewarding and satisfying role....My mother was never included in my father's business affairs...she couldn't get out of the house and away from us children. But I am an equal to my husband; I can go along with him on business trips and to social business affairs."*

The alternative offered was a choice that few women would contemplate. In the sympathetic words of the New York Times: *"All admit to*

Sexologist: A therapist who specializes in the study of sex.

Paragon: A model of perfection.

The Sixties in America: Primary Sources

being deeply frustrated at times by the lack of privacy, the physical burden, the routine of family life, the confinement of it. However, none would give up her home and family if she had the choice to make again." Redbook commented: "Few women would want to thumb their noses at husbands, children and community and go off on their own. Those who do may be talented individuals, but they rarely are successful women."

The year American women's discontent boiled over, it was also reported (Look) that the more than 21,000,000 American women who are single, widowed, or divorced do not cease even after fifty their **frenzied**, desperate search for a man. And the search begins early—for seventy per cent of all American women now marry before they are twenty-four. A pretty twenty-five-year-old secretary took thirty-five different jobs in six months in the futile hope of finding a husband. Women were moving from one political club to another, taking evening courses in accounting or sailing, learning to play golf or ski, joining a number of churches in succession, going to bars alone, in their ceaseless search for a man.

Of the growing thousands of women currently getting private psychiatric help in the United States, the married ones were reported dissatisfied with their marriages, the unmarried ones suffering from anxiety and, finally, depression. Strangely, a number of psychiatrists stated that, in their experience, unmarried women patients were happier than married ones. So the door of all those pretty suburban houses opened a crack to permit a glimpse of uncounted thousands of American housewives who suffered alone from a problem that suddenly everyone was talking about, and beginning to take for granted, as one of those unreal problems in American life that can never be solved—like the **hydrogen bomb**. By 1962 the plight of the trapped American housewife had become a national parlor game. Whole issues of magazines, newspaper columns, books learned and frivolous, educational conferences and television panels were devoted to the problem.

Even so, most men, and some women, still did not know that this problem was real....Most adjusted to their role and suffered or ignored the problem that has no name. It can be less painful for a woman, not to hear the strange, dissatisfied voice stirring within her.

It is no longer possible to ignore that voice, to dismiss the desperation of so many American women. This is not what being a woman means, no matter what the experts say. For human suffering there is a reason; perhaps the reason has not been found because the right questions have not been asked, or pressed far enough. I do not accept

Frenzied: Intense or compulsive.

Hydrogen bomb: When Betty Friedan wrote *The Feminine Mystique* in the 1960s, people felt threatened by the potential world devastation that would be caused if either the United States or the Soviet Union should ever launch a hydrogen bomb at the other during the Cold War (1945–91).

the answer that there is no problem because American women have luxuries that women in other times and lands never dreamed of; part of the strange newness of the problem is that it cannot be understood in terms of the age-old material problems of man: poverty, sickness, hunger, cold. The women who suffer this problem have a hunger that food cannot fill. It persists in women whose husbands are struggling internes [sic] and law clerks, or prosperous doctors and lawyers; in wives of workers and executives who make $5,000 a year or $50,000. It is not caused by lack of material advantages; it may not even be felt by women preoccupied with desperate problems of hunger, poverty or illness. And women who think it will be solved by more money, a bigger house, a second car, moving to a better suburb, often discover it gets worse....

The fact is that no one today is muttering angrily about "women's rights," even though more and more women have gone to college. In a recent study of all the classes that have graduated from Barnard College [a women's liberal arts college in New York], a significant minority of earlier graduates blamed their education for making them want "rights," later classes blamed their education for giving them career dreams, but recent graduates blamed the college for making them feel it was not enough simply to be a housewife and mother; they did not want to feel guilty if they did not read books or take part in community activities. But if education is not the cause of the problem, the fact that education somehow festers in these women may be a clue....

...I became aware of a growing body of evidence, much of which has not been reported publicly because it does not fit current modes of thought about women—evidence which throws into question the standards of feminine normality, feminine adjustment, feminine fulfillment, and feminine maturity by which most women are still trying to live.

I began to see in a strange new light the American return to early marriage and the large families that are causing the **population explosion**; the recent movement to **natural childbirth** and breastfeeding; suburban conformity, and the new **neuroses**, character **pathologies** and sexual problems being reported by the doctors. I began to see new dimensions to old problems that have long been taken for granted among women: **menstrual difficulties**, **sexual frigidity**, promiscuity, pregnancy fears, childbirth depression, the high incidence of emotional breakdown and suicide among women in their twenties and thirties, the menopause crises, the so-called passivity

Population explosion: The birth of record numbers of children after World War II, known as the baby boom.

Natural childbirth: The process of giving birth without pain medications or anesthesia.

Neuroses: Mental or emotional disorders.

Pathologies: Diseases.

Menstrual difficulties: Troubles with regular, monthly menstruation cycles.

Sexual frigidity: An indifference to or repulsion from sexual relations.

Betty Friedan, president of the National Organization for Women, is interviewed at the Women's Equality March on August 26, 1970, commemorating the 50th anniversary of the passage of the Nineteenth Amendment, which granted women the right to vote.
© JP Laffont/Sygma/Corbis. Reproduced by permission.

and immaturity of American men, the discrepancy between women's tested intellectual abilities in childhood and their adult achievement, the changing incidence of adult *sexual orgasm* in American women, and persistent problems in psychotherapy and in women's education.

If I am right, the problem that has no name stirring in the minds of so many American women today is not a matter of loss of femininity or too much education, or the demands of **domesticity**. It is far more important than anyone recognizes. It is the key to these other new and old problems which have been torturing women and their husbands and children, and puzzling their doctors and educators for years. It may well be the key to our future as a nation and a culture. We can no longer ignore that voice within women that says: "I want something more than my husband and my children and my home."

Sexual orgasm: The release of neuromuscular tensions at the height of sexual arousal.

Domesticity: Household affairs.

What happened next...

Betty Friedan's *The Feminine Mystique* reinforced the issues documented in the President's Commission on the Status of Women's report published the same year. But rather than calling on bureaucratic decision makers to reshape laws and set up governmental programs to help women, Friedan's book called on women to help themselves. Friedan went further in her own life, devoting herself to the betterment of others.

On October 29, 1966, Friedan and other women founded the National Organization for Women (NOW), a lobbying group committed to pushing for women's rights. Friedan was elected president and co-wrote the organization's Statement of Purpose, which outlined women's rights to develop to their fullest human potential. Successes NOW had under Friedan's leadership included getting employers to stop listing jobs under the headings of "men" and "women" in the classifieds; getting more companies to let women apply for traditionally male jobs; and insisting that President Lyndon B. Johnson issue a presidential order outlawing sex discrimination by the government. Her last act as president of NOW was organizing a simultaneous Women's Strike for Equality in several American cities in 1970 on the fiftieth anniversary of women's gaining the right to vote. She organized demonstrations, marches, and speeches in forty major cities and led a parade of over ten thousand down Fifth Avenue in New York City.

Friedan also organized the National Abortion Rights Action League (NARAL) in 1969. NARAL persuaded the New York legislature to pass laws giving women the right to choose to have an abortion. To help change public policy, she became a founding member of the National Women's Political Caucus in 1971. In 1975 Friedan went on to found the First Women's Bank & Trust Company in order to offer women discrimination-free access to credit, mortgages, and loans. As her political career developed, Friedan continued to write, publishing several books about the women's movement and other topics.

Did you know...

- The Civil Rights Act of 1964 made sexual discrimination in employment illegal.

- Sometimes people refer to the law that made sexual discrimination illegal as Title VII. Title VII is the section of the Civil Rights Act of 1964 that details the law against sexual discrimination in employment. The Civil Rights Act contains eleven titles.

- Women's issues such as childcare, abortion rights, and maternity leave all became important topics of political debate in the 1960s and 1970s.

- Although women's presence in the workforce increased into the 1970s, most women continued to retain primary responsibility for household chores and childcare.

- Feminists gained attention for the women's liberation movement by protesting against the Miss America Pageant in Atlantic City, New Jersey, in 1968, which they felt treated women as sexual objects and not as people.

- The first national women's liberation conference was held in Chicago in 1968.

Demonstrators from the National Women's Liberation Party picket in protest of the Miss America Pageant, September 7, 1968. *AP/Wide World Photos. Reproduced by permission.*

- More women than men entered college for the first time in history in 1978.

Consider the following...

- Do you think Betty Friedan's book would have been as popular if it had encouraged women to leave their families to pursue a career?

- Describe some of the difficulties women following Friedan's advice might have encountered in the 1960s.

- Some women did not consider Friedan to be a feminist. Explain why you agree or disagree.

For More Information

Books

Friedan, Betty. *The Feminine Mystique.* New York: Norton, 1963; 1997 reprint.

Hurley, Jennifer A. *The 1960s.* San Diego, CA: Greenhaven, 2000.

Skrentny, John D. *The Minority Rights Revolution.* Cambridge, MA: Belknap Press, 2002.

Stearman, Katy. *Women's Rights: Changing Attitudes, 1900–2000.* Austin, TX: Raintree, Steck-Vaughn, 2000.

National Organization for Women

Complete text of "Bill of Rights for Women in 1968"
Originally issued at NOW convention, 1968.

Reprinted from *"Takin' It to the Streets:" A Sixties Reader,* **2003;**
also available online at http://coursesa.matrix.msu.edu/
~hst203/documents/nowrights.html

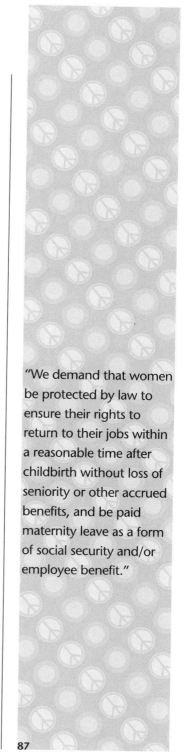

"We demand that women be protected by law to ensure their rights to return to their jobs within a reasonable time after childbirth without loss of seniority or other accrued benefits, and be paid maternity leave as a form of social security and/or employee benefit."

The National Organization for Women (NOW) was founded on June 30, 1966, in Washington, D.C., by twenty-eight participants in the Third National Conference of the Commission on the Status of Women who were angered by the conference's dismissal of equal rights issues. The Equal Employment Opportunity Commission (EEOC) had been established to enforce Title VII of the 1964 Civil Rights Act. Title VII made it illegal for employers to discriminate against people based on their gender. Within its first five years, it received fifty thousand sex discrimination complaints, but at the conference it became known that the EEOC had done little to address these complaints.

NOW was formed to push the government to enforce the protections it had established for women, and more. Betty Friedan (1921–), author of *The Feminine Mystique* (1963), was elected NOW's first president. The organization dedicated itself to making legal, political, social, and economic change in order to eliminate sexism or stereotyping people according to sex roles and to eliminate other forms of inequality that deny rights or privileges to certain groups.

National Organization for Women (NOW) leaders Betty Friedan, right, and Dr. Kathryn Clarenbach announce that NOW has adopted a "Bill of Rights for Women in 1968," November 20, 1967.

NOW worked toward its goals by organizing marches, rallies, pickets, counter-demonstrations, and nonviolent civil disobedience protests. (Civil disobedience is the peaceful expression of objection to certain laws by refusing to obey them.) NOW also developed political lobbying efforts and litigation, including class-action lawsuits, which are lawsuits brought by a group of people who have been harmed in a similar way. To get one of its points across to the public, the group popularized the slogan, "Every Mother Is a Working Mother."

Friedan and Rev. Pauli Murray, the first African-American woman Episcopal priest, co-authored NOW's original Statement of Purpose which begins: "The purpose of NOW is to take action to bring women into full participation in the mainstream of American society now, exercising all privileges and responsibilities thereof in truly equal partnership with men." At its national conference in 1967 NOW adopted a "Bill of Rights for Women in 1968" that listed the group's goals for Congress and society. The "Bill of Rights for Women in 1968" highlights how different life was for women in the 1960s than it was in the early 2000s.

Things to remember while reading the National Organization for Women's "Bill of Rights for Women in 1968":

- NOW was formed as the women's liberation movement and civil rights movement were reaching their peaks.

- In *Bowe v. Colgate-Palmolive Company,* in 1969, the Seventh Circuit Court of Appeals ruled that women who met the necessary physical requirements could work in jobs once open only to men.

- In the 1971 ruling in *Phillips v. Martin Marietta Corporation* the U.S. Supreme Court prohibited private employers from refusing to hire women with preschool children.

National Organization for Women Bill of Rights in 1968

(Adopted at the 1967 National Conference)

I. Equal Rights Constitutional Amendment

II. Enforce Law Banning Sex Discrimination in Employment

III. Maternity Leave Rights in Employment and in Social Security Benefits

IV. Tax Deduction for Home and Child Care Expenses for Working Parents

V. Child Day Care Centers

VI. Equal and Unsegregated Education

VII. Equal Job Training Opportunities and Allowances for Women in Poverty

VIII. The Right of Women to Control their Reproductive Lives

WE DEMAND:

National Organization for Women members demonstrate outside the White House in 1969 asking for passage of the Equal Rights Amendment, as stated in Section I of the "Bill of Rights for Women in 1968."
© Bettmann/Corbis. Reproduced by permission.

I. That the U.S. Congress immediately pass the Equal Rights Amendment to the Constitution to provide that "Equality of rights under the law shall not be denied or abridged by the United States or by any State on account of sex" and that such then be immediately ratified by the several States.

*II. That equal employment opportunity be guaranteed to all women, as well as men, by insisting that the Equal Employment Opportunity Commission enforces the **prohibitions** against sex discrimination in employment under Title VII of the Civil Rights Act of 1964 with the same vigor as it enforces the prohibitions against racial discrimination.*

III. That women be protected by law to ensure their rights to return to their jobs within a reasonable time after childbirth without loss of seniority or other accrued benefits, and be paid maternity leave as a form of social security and/or employee benefit.

IV. Immediate revision of tax laws to permit the deduction of home and child-care expenses for working parents.

Prohibitions: Restrictions.

The Sixties in America: Primary Sources

V. That child-care facilities be established by law on the same basis as parks, libraries, and public schools, adequate to the needs of children, from the pre-school years through adolescence, as a community resource to be used by all citizens from all income levels.

*VI. That the right of women to be educated to their full potential equally with men be secured by Federal and State legislation, eliminating all discrimination and **segregation** by sex, written and unwritten, at all levels of education including college, graduate and professional schools, loans and fellowships and Federal and State training programs, such as the Job Corps.*

VII. The right of women in poverty to secure job training, housing, and family allowances on equal terms with men, but without prejudice to a parent's right to remain at home to care for his or her children; revision of welfare legislation and poverty programs which deny women dignity, privacy and self-respect.

*VIII. The right of women to control their own reproductive lives by removing from **penal codes** the laws limiting access to contraceptive information and devices, and by repealing penal laws governing abortion.*

What happened next...

Once formed, the National Organization for Women grew at a quick rate. Using political strategies that resembled those used by civil rights groups, NOW campaigned for equal rights for women in education, employment, and politics. The tactics ultimately worked for many of NOW's demands. The Equal Rights Amendment that stated that "men and women shall have equal rights throughout the United States and in every place subject to its jurisdiction," was first proposed in 1923, just after women were granted the right to vote. Although the amendment had been presented to Congress for twenty years, it was the political pressure of the women's liberation movement in the late 1960s and early 1970s that finally passed the amendment through Congress in 1972. By 1973 thirty states had ratified the amendment, and only eight more were needed. Even though Congress extended the ratification

Segregation: Separation.

Penal codes: Laws relating to crime and their offenses.

deadline until 1982, the amendment never gained the votes needed. Although the Equal Rights Amendment ultimately was not added to the Constitution, the political efforts of NOW and other women's groups had brought the social and political inequality of women, children, blacks, and other groups to the public's attention. By the end of the 1970s, court decisions and laws granted women more equality and society began to accept the idea that women were more than mothers and wives.

By 2004 NOW continued to be the largest women's political activist organization. NOW remained focused on its goals and helped push several influential legislative bills through Congress and brought many class-action suits to court that resulted in more freedoms for women and others.

Did you know...

- In 1967 NOW became the first national organization to work toward the legalization of abortion and for the repeal of all anti-abortion laws.

- NOW launched a nationwide campaign to pass an Equal Rights Amendment (ERA) to the U.S. Constitution in the 1970s.

- As part of the campaign, NOW distributed buttons reading "59¢" to draw attention to the figure that represented the median wage then paid to women for every dollar paid to men.

- NOW, in 1971, became the first major national women's organization to support lesbian rights (the social and legal rights of homosexual women for equal treatment).

- In the 1973 decisions of *Roe v. Wade* and *Doe v. Bolton,* the U.S. Supreme Court made abortion legal in the United States.

- NOW grew to become a network of more than five hundred thousand grassroots activists with members in each of the fifty states.

Consider the following...

- NOW placed an Equal Rights Amendment to the Constitution high on its list of priorities in 1968. Some people, including the executive vice chairman of the President's Commission on the Status of Women, Esther Peterson, thought an Equal Rights Amendment would do more harm to women than good. Describe your opinion.

- Although the Equal Rights Amendment to the Constitution ultimately failed to be ratified by enough states, NOW succeeded in securing many of the ERA's objectives for women in various separate laws. Some people think these separate laws are more powerful securities for women than a sweeping amendment to the Constitution. What do you think?

- Women, gays, and racial minorities worked together to change laws in the 1960s and 1970s. How would they have had to change their strategies to succeed without each other's help?

For More Information

Books

Blau, Justine. *Betty Friedan*. New York: Chelsea House, 1990.

Hurley, Jennifer A. *The 1960s*. San Diego, CA: Greenhaven, 2000.

Web sites

National Organization for Women. http://www.now.org/history/history.html (accessed on August 1, 2004).

Helen Gurley Brown

Excerpt from Sex and the Single Girl
Published in 1962.

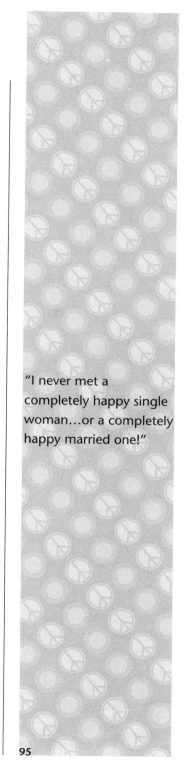

"I never met a completely happy single woman…or a completely happy married one!"

At a time when American society made it very clear that women should aspire to be wives and mothers, Helen Gurley Brown lived happily as a single, working woman. Recognizing that some women felt torn between society's expectations of them to marry and a drive to pursue careers, Brown wrote *Sex and the Single Girl* as a guide for others to enjoy the kind of life she had discovered for herself. In it she detailed how to get a satisfying job and earn pay raises, dress for success in business, eat right, and exercise. While no book had ever before offered women such useful career advice, the book became a sensation for its explicit discussion of sex between unmarried people. Brown described how to flirt, "be sexy," find available men, and have an affair. "The single woman," Brown wrote, was "far from being a creature to be pitied and patronized," but instead was "emerging as the newest glamour girl of our times."

Helen Gurley Brown was born on February 18, 1922, in Green Forest, Arkansas, the second daughter of Ira and Cleo (Sisco) Gurley. Both parents had worked as schoolteachers, but Cleo quit teaching to raise her two children. Ira Gur-

Helen Gurley Brown, pictured in 1965.

© Bettmann/Corbis. Reproduced by permission.

ley moved his young family to Little Rock when he was elected to a seat in the state legislature. When Helen was ten years old, tragedy struck when her father was killed in an elevator accident, leaving her mother to support her daughters during the Great Depression (1929–41), a period of high unemployment. Cleo moved to Los Angeles. But her oldest daughter, Mary, contracted polio there, and large medical bills strained the family's finances. (Polio is a disease that causes paralysis.) Helen did well in high school and worked to put herself through college while helping to support her mother and sister.

After a succession of seventeen different secretarial jobs, Brown landed an executive secretary position at an advertising agency. She worked hard at her job and impressed her boss with the funny letters she wrote when traveling. But when she wrote an essay which won *Glamour* magazine's "Girls of Taste" contest, her boss offered her the opportunity to write advertising copy. She quickly displayed talent for the task and became an award-winning copywriter. By the late 1950s, Brown had become the top-paid female copywriter on the West Coast.

In 1959, when she was thirty-seven, Brown married film executive David Brown. Her husband encouraged her to write a book about her experiences as a single woman. Her book *Sex and the Single Girl* was published in 1962 and became an immediate best-seller. Never before had the sex life of single women been so openly discussed. The following excerpt is taken from the final chapter of the book. It sums up Brown's advice for women, encouraging them to accept that neither single life nor married life is always blissful. She invites single women to ignore society's pressure to marry and to embrace the opportunities of the single life without guilt.

Things to remember while reading the excerpt from *Sex and the Single Girl*:

- At the time *Sex and the Single Girl* was published, it was acceptable for single men to have sex, but not single women. Brown's book was the first popular book to address the concept that single women have sexual desires just as men do. This was one of the key ideas of the sexual revolution of the 1960s, a movement that encouraged people to reconsider many traditional beliefs about sexuality.

- The introduction in 1960 of the first oral contraceptive (birth control pill), commonly called the Pill, helped raise the debate about sexuality because it enabled women to separate sex from procreation.

- By 1965, five million women were taking the Pill.

Excerpt from **Sex and the Single Girl**

Chapter 13: The Rich, Full Life

I never met a completely happy single woman…or a completely happy married one!

A single woman admittedly has a special set of problems, but I think her worst one is not the lack of someone to belong to officially but the pippy-poo, day-to-day annoyances that plague her. For example, she has purchased a secondhand TV set from a private owner, and the 400-pound bargain is waiting in the trunk of her car to be brought upstairs and hooked up. She hasn't a date until next weekend—and anyway she outweighs him by ten pounds!

Or she has called a taxi to take her to the airport for a 6 A.M. departure. The taxi is now thirty minutes late, and she must be on that plane to keep an important business appointment in another city. A married woman could simply wake up a husband. That's what I did once in such a predicament. I woke up a husband next door (and his wife, unfortunately, or I might have had more luck) and asked if he would mind driving me to a central part of town where I could find a cab. He was anything but thrilled with the idea, considering his wife's admonitions which I could hear from the bed-

room, and I can't say I really blamed her. Mercifully, my taxi arrived while he was probably wondering how to say no.

These are the frustrating little experiences that **vex** and humiliate a single woman from time to time; however, they are not so frequent as to make life unendurable. I've jotted down a few suggestions for coping with them.

And for a finale I can't resist adding a few last thoughts on how I think a single woman can have a happier life.

Be Brazen When Helpless

If there's anything you can't lift, lug, tote, tug or tow alone, you'll just have to get help; and it will mean imposing on your friends as well as total strangers. You'll have to speak up, too. Nobody's going to know you need a before-work ride to the doctor for a **basal metabolism** if you don't say so.

You'll find ways to repay. You'll help move them to their new apartment when the time comes, or bake a cake or send a valentine. You can even offer money tactfully, though you'll probably be refused.

Even wives have to be brazen sometimes. I know one married to a mechanical incompetent; for weeks she has been hunting for somebody able to get the hard-top off her convertible....

Don't Compare Yourself to Married Couples

Your apartment, though charming, is not meant to compete with leading architects' houses photographed in Better Homes and Gardens. Your entertaining, often hostless, can't be like a couple's. Your guests, though highly amusing, could be considered a little off-beat in Married-landia. Your investment program can't begin to compare with a top executive's. But whose college education are you planning?

Married couples go places in neat little twos, fours, and sixes—which seems so orderly. Naturally they do! There are two of each, so they multiply for social outings in twos like themselves. But you are not one of Noah's aardvarks, and it is all right to move in threes and fives occasionally. Hearing **Dixieland** with a good friend and her beau is not the worst kind of evening when all you'd planned was to go to bed early. Having dinner with two delightful men can be sensational. Unmarried people's parties are often livelier because of the non-pairings.

Vex: Bother.

Basal metabolism: A calculation of the minimum calorific requirement needed to sustain a person's life.

Dixieland: A style of jazz music associated with the South.

The married usually go places on Saturday night, which seems so normal and American! Saturday is the logical night for parents to hire a baby sitter, do the whole bit and sleep late the next morning. What if your next big date is on a Tuesday? The food, the wine, the music and the chatter are just as sweet and the atmosphere is better for being less crowded.

Don't Fold Up over What You Read—or Don't Read

Many publications deal with the problems of single women in the same vein as their articles on fall-out. I read a newspaper editorial last night which stated among other philosophies: "The bachelor is only half-man or half-woman. They are to be pitied." Now really!

Still other publications—most others for that matter—ignore the existence of single women entirely!...

You see enough picture stories in national publications about couples and families to make you feel like the sole occupant of a life raft. To further depress you, the couples and families are always blueberry-pie normal, as industrious as gophers, and as much at home in the world as an egg in custard.

We know the married state is the normal one in our culture, and anybody who deviates from "normal" has a price to pay in **nonacceptance and nonglorification**. There is no one universal "normal" time, however, for participating in the normal state of marriage. Furthermore, part of what you are at the moment, missing in marriage may be well worth missing!

Ernest Havemann, writing on love and marriage in the September 29, 1961, issue of Life, says:

> Married love is not a constant round of candy, flowers and birthday presents. It is more likely to be a long series of sacrifices in which the fishing trip gives way to a down payment on a washer and the new party dress gives way to an appendectomy, and where even the weekly night out at the movies may have to give way to new shoes for the kids. It is not a guarantee of living happily ever after, for every marriage involves struggle, boredom, illness, financial problems and worry over the children....
>
> The love nest in the suburbs has a leaky roof, crabgrass, a mortgage that burns up every second paycheck and mice which the bride has to catch and dispose of single-handed because the husband has an annoying way of being on a business trip during every crisis.
>
> The groom, alas, is not quite so brilliant as promised. His job prospects fade. He never earns that million dollars. He loses

Nonacceptance and nonglorification: Social discomfort and disregard.

*his hair and his teeth. His wife loses her figure. The babies are not the dimpled darlings of the ads, but **imperious tyrants** who have to be bottled, burped, bathed and changed...."*

Are you really *a great deal worse off than a wife?*

[...]

Put Your Guilt Away

*Would it surprise you to know that your most wicked and base thoughts—secret fantasies—even leanings to homosexuality, are not unusual, and should not alarm you? You may share your desire to make love to an African lion with the vicar's wife—or even the vicar! Far from making you a depraved monster, your thinking is probably not even original. This is the **consensus** of psychiatrists. Doing something about these thoughts and not merely thinking them is what makes you cuckoo!*

*Perhaps you will reconsider the idea that sex without marriage is dirty. This is not a plea to get you into bed—your moral code is your business—but if you are already involved you might remember that sex was here a long time before marriage. You inherited your **proclivity** for it. It isn't some random piece of mischief you dreamed up because you're a bad, wicked girl.*

*The psychiatrist I mentioned before frequently shows sexually guilt-ridden patients pictures from an **entomology** book. All the patients can figure out at first look is that they are seeing some kind of bug. "And do you know what the bugs are doing?" the doctor asks. No, they don't know. Well, the bugs, according to the text, are Mediterranean fruit flies engaged in the act of mating. "Okay, so what?" asks the patient. And the doctor explains that, by the patient's own concept of sex, he is looking at some very dirty pictures, indeed!*

The point is, you may be much harder on yourself than you are on other creatures of nature who are less deserving of your tolerance. When you accept yourself, with all your foibles, you will be able to accept other people too. And you and they will be happier to be near you. (Big order, but you can fill it.)

Use the Time

The single years are very precious years because that's when you have the time and personal freedom for adventure.

Of course, maddeningly, the least appealing time to do anything is *when you already aren't doing something.*

Imperious tyrants: Demanding rulers.

Consensus: General agreement.

Proclivity: Inclination toward something.

Entomology: The scientific study of insects.

*If you can forget the **stultifying** concept that there are appropriate years for certain endeavors (like getting married) and appropriate days for being gay and merry (like Saturday nights) and use these times without embarrassment or self-pity to do something creative and constructive (what an assignment!), I believe half your single-girl battle is over....*

*But if you are worried about being single, or, more importantly, uneasy about being you all your life (as I was and still am), **intermittent forays** into dressing, cooking, looking, flirting, and flattering better can help you rout the trembles.*

One last thought: When you do start new projects, don't tell anyone. Once you've talked and bragged about your I'm-doing-me-over plans, you won't do them!

Finally

*You may marry or you may not. In today's world that is no longer the big question for women. Those who **glom on** to men so that they can collapse with relief, spend the rest of their days shining up their status symbol and figure they never have to reach, stretch, learn, grow, face dragons or make a living again are the ones to be pitied. They, in my opinion, are the unfulfilled ones.*

You, my friend, if you work at it, can be envied the rich, full life possible for the single woman today. It's a good show...enjoy it from wherever you are....

The End

What happened next...

Helen Gurley Brown maintained her media presence with a syndicated newspaper advice column, albums, and radio shows, but her second book, *Sex and the Office* (1964), failed to interest audiences as much as her first. In 1965 the Hearst magazine corporation offered Brown the chance to recreate *Cosmopolitan* magazine as editor in chief.

Brown immediately made the formerly conservative magazine the female equivalent to the men's magazine, *Playboy*. Brown quickly won a large audience for the magazine by

Stultifying: Absurd, foolish, or ridiculous.

Intermittent forays: Occasional attempts to do something new or out of the ordinary.

Glom on: To grab hold of.

introducing sexier cover models and controversial topics. By the time Brown "retired" as editor in chief of *Cosmopolitan* in 1996, she had transformed it into one of Hearst's most successful magazines.

Brown's celebration of an independent life for women was published a year before Betty Friedan's *The Feminine Mystique,* which offered married women suggestions to make their married life more fulfilling. The two books' differing views of women's lives sparked lively debates about women's place in society. Indeed, the books also initiated discussion about the definition of feminism. Despite much controversy, both Brown and Friedan considered themselves feminists.

Did you know...

- Warner Brothers purchased the rights to *Sex and the Single Girl* for what was then the highest price ever paid for a nonfiction title. They made a film of the same name in 1964 starring Natalie Wood (as Helen Gurley Brown) and Tony Curtis.

- *Sex and the Single Girl* sparked debates about whether women put themselves in lesser positions to men when they dress or act in ways that appeal to men.

- Brown's book shocked many people for its open discussion of sexuality.

Consider the following...

- If *Sex and the Single Girl* were published today, how would public reaction to it differ from that of the 1960s?

- How do you think a single mother's opinion of single life would have differed from Helen Gurley Brown's in the 1960s?

- In what ways does Brown's advice to single women still apply today?

For More Information

Books

Brown, Helen Gurley. *Sex and the Single Girl*. New York: Bernard Geis Associates, 1962.

Escoffier, Jeffrey, ed. *Sexual Revolution.* New York: Thunder's Mouth Press, 2003.

Williams, Mary E., ed. *The Sexual Revolution.* San Diego, CA: Greenhaven Press, 2002.

The War in Vietnam

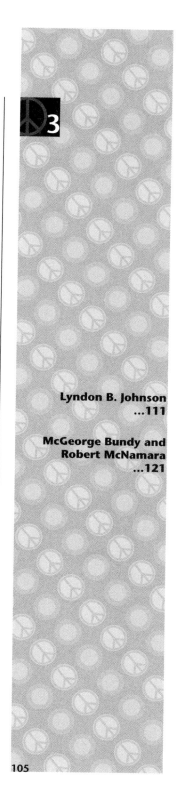

At the beginning of the 1960s, few Americans could have identified Vietnam on a map or explained why the United States might be involved in the small southeast Asian nation that lay halfway around the world. But by the end of the decade, U.S. involvement in Vietnam had cost thousands of American lives and embroiled the nation in a furious and sometimes violent debate over U.S. foreign policy. A growing antiwar movement in the United States drew public attention to its arguments with public protests and campaigns to change policy. By 1968 these protests had helped drive President Lyndon B. Johnson (1908–1973; served 1963–69) from office.

The roots of the conflict in Vietnam stretched back to the nineteenth century, when French colonizers took control of an area they called French Indochina, which included the modern countries of Vietnam, Cambodia, Laos, and other portions of Asia. Early in World War II (1939–45), as the Japanese attempted to gain control of trade in the Far East, they evicted French forces from Indochina. Like the French, the Japanese were more interested in extracting riches from the area than they were in providing effective government. When native political forces rose up to combat Japanese rule, the United States was happy to help, for it too was fighting the Japanese in World War II. The United States provided arms and advice to Vietnamese patriots, called Vietminh, who were led by a man named Ho Chi Minh (1890?–1969). When the Japanese were defeated in 1945, Ho Chi Minh came to power. He quoted the American Declaration of Independence as he asserted Vietnam's right to be a free and self-governing nation. Many hoped that the United States, who fought the Revolutionary War (1775–83) with England in order to become independent, would support this new nation.

Cold War pressures

The appealing idea of supporting people who have been held down soon came into conflict with the larger driving force of American foreign policy in the years following World War II: the Cold War (1945–91). Soon after World War II ended, the United States and its Western allies, led by France, Great Britain, and West Germany, began to compete with the Soviet Union, China, and their allies for leadership of the world. The opposing sides did not engage in open armed conflict, but rather in a struggle to see which ideological system—capitalist democracy (a system of government and economics characterized by private ownership of property and free-market competition, such as that of the United States) or state-controlled communism (a system of government and economics characterized by state ownership of property and state control of economic decisions, such as that of the Soviet Union)—would control world trade and politics. From the moment World War II ended, both sides competed to attain influence over smaller nations around the world. This struggle to gain allies took place in Eastern Europe, Africa, and, most violently, in Vietnam. This Cold War struggle for supremacy pushed both sides into actions that were incredibly destructive and contrary to the very ideals they claimed to support.

Within the context of the Cold War competition, the United States was slowly drawn into the conflict in Vietnam. Following the collapse of Japanese control in French Indochina in 1945, the United States helped its longtime ally, France, reassert control over the area. Critics claimed that the United States had abandoned its ideological allies, the Vietminh, in order to enrich the French colonizers. But American politicians justified their support of France by claiming that the Vietminh were communist and that America needed to help prevent the spread of communism in the area. When the Vietminh went to war to evict the French from Vietnam, America provided great amounts of money, arms, and advice to the French (and ignored the pleas of the Vietminh for assistance). By 1954, the war had killed 95,000 French soldiers, 300,000 Vietnamese soldiers, and as many as a million Vietnamese civilians. In that year France withdrew from the area by negotiating a peace treaty that split Vietnam in half and granted Cambodia and Laos independence. North Vietnam was controlled by communists led by Ho Chi Minh, and South Vietnam, backed by the United States, was ruled by a corrupt government led by Ngo Dinh Diem (1901–1963). Neither side was satisfied with the divided country.

Between 1954 and 1964, America provided support to South Vietnam in the form of economic assistance, arms, and military training. Over the years, however, U.S. support for the Diem regime in South Vietnam became a source of embarrassment as Diem ruled in ways that violated American values. Diem enjoyed little support in his own country, and he ruled by oppressing, even torturing and killing, those who opposed him. More and more of the common people in South Vietnam supported the North Vietnamese and wished to see the two countries unite under communist rule. These people were known as the Vietcong; the "cong" part of the name meant "commies" because they supported the communist North. They mounted their own attacks against the Diem forces, supporting the growing civil war between South and North Vietnam. In 1960 alone the Vietcong killed more than 2,500 government officials.

The pull of war in Vietnam

This difficult situation greeted President John F. Kennedy (1917–1963; served 1961–63) when he took office in 1961. Kennedy had campaigned as a dedicated anticommunist, and he was determined to support the capitalist South Vietnam. Slowly, he increased the amount of American monetary aid, which reached half a billion dollars in 1962. More importantly, he increased the number of American military advisors stationed in South Vietnam, from 1,400 in 1961 to 11,300 in 1962. (Under American law, the president could not send soldiers to fight in a foreign war without authorization from Congress, so all soldiers sent to Vietnam were considered advisors.) He hoped that with more money and more military advice, the United States could help the South Vietnamese army defeat the Vietcong. Initial American military aid was not meant to fund attacks on the North, but only to support the government in the South. Yet as the failure of the Diem government became more obvious and the North continued to gain supporters in the South, the United States was drawn further and further into the conflict.

When Kennedy was assassinated late in 1963, President Lyndon Johnson (1909–1973; served 1963–69) inherited a miserable political situation. Some advisors urged him to withdraw from Vietnam while he still could. They pointed to the example of the French and argued that further involvement would cost many American lives. But those advocating withdrawal were in the minority. A majority of advisors urged Johnson to increase American involvement, arguing that to lose Vietnam to the communists would only encourage communists to attempt to take control of other small countries. They argued that it was vital to maintain a South Vietnamese government that was friendly to the United States, and they advised Johnson to send fighting troops and to use American forces to bomb North Vietnam. Johnson, believing that he had to send a strong signal to the Soviet Union, decided to increase American involvement even further, short of going to war. By the summer of 1964, Johnson increased the number of American soldiers and advisors in South Vietnam to 20,000. It was a significant step on the road to all-out American involvement in the war in Vietnam.

The long first stage to full-fledged American engagement in the conflict in Vietnam ended in August of 1964, when a minor military clash led President Johnson to ask Congress for full authority to commit American troops to the war. Once that authority was granted, American military goals—and the number of American troops involved—

increased sharply. The documents included in this chapter explain why the United States got involved in the war and how it expected to win. President **Lyndon B. Johnson**'s Message to Congress, in which Johnson asked for support for the war, and the congressional resolution offering that support are two important documents related to the Vietnam War. Also presented here are excerpts from documents written by two key military advisors to President Johnson, **McGeorge Bundy** (1919–1996) and **Robert McNamara** (1916–). These documents urged Johnson to continue to escalate the war, suggesting ways that increased military resources might win the war.

Lyndon B. Johnson

Excerpt from "Message to Congress, August 5, 1964"
Reprinted from *Department of State Bulletin,* **August 24, 1964**

Excerpt from "House Joint Resolution 1145, August 7, 1964"
Reprinted from *Department of State Bulletin,* **August 24, 1964**

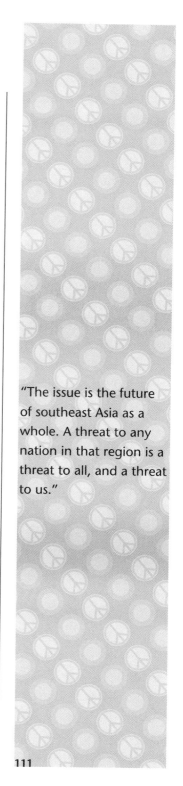

The pressure of America's commitment to stop the spread of communism in Southeast Asia grew especially intense in the spring and summer of 1964. President Lyndon B. Johnson had inherited from his Democratic predecessor, John F. Kennedy, the policy of providing military advisors and weapons to support the government of South Vietnam. But pressures in Vietnam and at home soon pushed Johnson to look for a different policy. In Vietnam, North Vietnamese troops, supported by their Vietcong supporters in South Vietnam, increased their attacks on South Vietnam. The South Vietnamese army was disintegrating under this pressure, especially following the assassination of brutal South Vietnamese leader Ngo Dinh Diem in 1963.

Back in the United States, 1964 was an election year. Johnson's Republican opponents, especially Republican presidential nominee Barry Goldwater (1909–1998), accused Johnson of not getting tough with the North Vietnamese and thus of encouraging the spread of communism. These combined pressures pushed Johnson to look for a way to change American policy.

"The issue is the future of southeast Asia as a whole. A threat to any nation in that region is a threat to all, and a threat to us."

Johnson and the majority of his advisors believed that the only way to support the government of South Vietnam would be to provide massive support from the United States. Johnson authorized a number of undercover operations against North Vietnam, including DeSoto missions, which were intelligence-gathering missions performed by specially equipped Navy ships called destroyers off the coast of North Vietnam. On the morning of August 2, 1964, U.S. destroyer *Maddox* reported that the North Vietnamese had fired torpedoes at it while the ship was patrolling in the Gulf of Tonkin off North Vietnam. Wanting to prove American strength and resolve, Johnson ordered the *Maddox* to resume its offshore patrol accompanied by another destroyer, the *C. Turner Joy*. On August 4, both destroyers reported torpedo attacks, although the commander of the *Maddox* later conceded that this incident might in fact have resulted from the combined effects of bad weather and nervous radar and sonar operators.

The alleged torpedo attacks gave Johnson the opening he was looking for. He immediately authorized air strikes against North Vietnamese targets, and he appeared on the three major television networks to tell the American people that North Vietnam had openly attacked the United States. On August 5, he submitted to Congress a resolution that would authorize him to take "all necessary measures to repel any armed attacks against the forces of the United States and to prevent further aggression." In his message to Congress, President Johnson asked for approval of a joint resolution authorizing him to use military force in Southeast Asia; the resolution giving him that approval is also included here.

Things to remember while reading President Johnson's "Message to Congress" and the "Joint Resolution of Congress":

- The United States Constitution specifies the rights of Congress and the president as they relate to waging war. According to the Article I, Section 8, only Congress has the power to declare war. According to Article II, Section 2, the president "shall be Commander in Chief of the Army and Navy of the United States," an authorization that is extended to all military forces. This statement means that the president has the responsibility of determining how American military forces will be used once Congress has authorized war.

- President Johnson refers frequently to Laos, a small country located just west of North Vietnam and South Vietnam. In 1962, several countries signed a treaty called the Geneva Convention of 1962 that guaranteed the neutrality of Laos. However, soldiers from both North and South Vietnam sometimes ventured into Laotian territory when conducting missions against their enemy. Laos and Cambodia, another country just to the south of Laos, eventually were caught up in the war in Vietnam.

- President Johnson refers to SEATO, which stands for the Southeast Asian Treaty Organization, a military alliance of eight nations—Great Britain, France, the Philippine Republic, Thailand, Pakistan, Australia, New Zealand, and the United States—that pledged to protect each other against communist aggression. American participation in this organization was authorized in 1955 by the Southeast Asia Collective Defense Treaty. The organization disbanded in 1977.

President Lyndon Johnson and the majority of his advisors believed that the only way to support the government of South Vietnam was to provide massive support from the United States.
AP/Wide World Photos. Reproduced by permission.

Excerpt from "Message to Congress, August 5, 1964"

To the Congress of the United States:

*Last night I announced to the American people that the North Vietnamese **regime** had conducted further **deliberate** attacks*

Regime: A form of government.

Deliberate: On purpose; planned.

against U.S. naval vessels operating in international waters, and I had therefore directed air action against gunboats and supporting facilities used in these hostile operations. This air action has now been carried out with substantial damage to the boats and facilities. Two U.S. aircraft were lost in the action.

After consultation with the leaders of both parties in the Congress, I further announced a decision to ask the Congress for a resolution expressing the unity and determination of the United States in supporting freedom and in protecting peace in southeast Asia.

*These latest actions of the North Vietnamese regime has given a new and **grave** turn to the already serious situation in southeast Asia. Our commitments in that area are well known to the Congress. They were first made in 1954 by **President Eisenhower**. They were further defined in the Southeast Asia Collective Defense Treaty approved by the Senate in February 1955.*

*This treaty with its accompanying **protocol** obligates the United States and other members to act in accordance with their constitutional processes to meet Communist aggression against any of the parties or protocol states.*

Our policy in southeast Asia has been consistent and unchanged since 1954. I summarized it on June 2 in four simple propositions:

1. America keeps her word. *Here as elsewhere, we must and shall honor our commitments.*

2. The issue is the future of southeast Asia as a whole. *A threat to any nation in that region is a threat to all, and a threat to us.*

3. Our purpose is peace. *We have no military, political, or territorial ambitions in the area.*

4. This is not just a jungle war, but a struggle for freedom on every front of human activity. *Our military and economic assistance to South Vietnam and Laos in particular has the purpose of helping these countries to repel aggression and strengthen their independence.*

*The threat to the free nations of southeast Asia has long been clear. The North Vietnamese regime has constantly sought to take over South Vietnam and Laos. This Communist regime has violated the **Geneva accords** for Vietnam. It has systematically conducted a campaign of **subversion**, which includes the direction, training, and supply of personnel and arms for the conduct of **guerrilla warfare** in South Vietnamese territory. In Laos, the North Viet-*

Grave: Extremely serious.

President Eisenhower: U.S. president Dwight D. Eisenhower, 1890–1969; served 1953–61.

Protocol: A record or draft of an agreement.

Geneva accords: A treaty signed in 1954 that forbid North Vietnam from attacking South Vietnam.

Subversion: An attempt to undermine or overthrow the government of a country.

Guerrilla warfare: Warfare that is conducted by loosely organized bands of fighters instead of uniformed armies, and that consists of harassment and small-scale attacks.

The Sixties in America: Primary Sources

namese regime has maintained military forces, used Laotian territory for **infiltration** into South Vietnam, and most recently carried out combat operations—all in direct violation of the Geneva Agreements of 1962.

In recent months, the actions of the North Vietnamese regime have become steadily more threatening.... [Johnson gives the details of incident in which North Vietnamese forces fired on an American airplane.]

As President of the United States I have concluded that I should now ask the Congress, on its part, to join in affirming the national determination that all such attacks will be met, and that the United States will continue in its basic policy of assisting the free nations of the area to defend their freedom.

As I have repeatedly made clear, the United States intends no rashness, and seeks no wider war. We must make it clear to all that the United States is united in its determination to bring about the end of Communist subversion and aggression in the area. We seek the full and effective restoration of the international agreements signed in Geneva in 1954, with respect to South Vietnam, and again in Geneva in 1962, with respect to Laos.

I recommend a resolution expressing the support of the Congress for all necessary action to protect our Armed Forces and to assist nations covered by the SEATO treaty. At the same time, I assure Congress that we shall continue readily to explore any avenues of political solution that will effectively guarantee the removal of Communist subversion and the preservation of the independence of the nations of the area....

The events of this week would in any event have made the passage of a congressional resolution essential. But there is an additional reason for doing so at a time when we are entering on 3 months of political campaigning. Hostile nations must understand that in such a period the United States will continue to protect its national interests, and that in these matters there is no division among us.

Infiltration: Sending troops behind enemy lines.

Lyndon Johnson speaking at a pro-Johnson rally in 1966. As the Vietnam War dragged on throughout the 1960s, pro-Johnson sentiment grew less and less.

Lyndon Baines Johnson Library.

Excerpt of "House Joint Resolution 1145, August 7, 1964"

...Resolved by the Senate and House of Representatives of the United States of America in Congress assembled, *That the Congress approves and supports the determination of the President, as Commander in Chief, to take all necessary measures to repel* any armed attack against the forces of the United States and to prevent further aggression.

Sec. 2. The United States regards as vital to its national interest and to world peace the maintenance of international peace and security in southeast Asia. **Consonant** with the Constitution of the United States and the Charter of the United Nations and in accordance with its obligations under the Southeast Asia Collective Defense Treaty, the United States is, therefore, prepared, as the President determines, to take all necessary steps, including the use of armed force, to assist any member or protocol state of the Southeast Asia Collective Defense Treaty requesting assistance in defense of its freedom.

Sec. 3. This resolution shall expire when the President shall determine that the peace and security of the area is reasonably assured by international conditions created by action of the United Nations or otherwise, except that it may be terminated earlier by concurrent resolution of the Congress.

What happened next...

Johnson's request for the power to wage war against North Vietnam was greeted with great enthusiasm in Congress. It was approved unanimously in the House of Representatives and passed 88-2 in the Senate. The American people also supported Johnson's strength in the face of the North Vietnamese "aggression." The results of the congressional resolution granting President Johnson the authority to "prevent further aggression" were slow in coming, however. Johnson's political advisors warned him against sending American soldiers to fight in Vietnam before the election in November, for they felt such a move would cost him votes. Instead, they hoped that the North Vietnamese, led by attention-getting leader Ho Chi Minh, would change their ways and quit their efforts to destabilize the government in South Vietnam.

North Vietnam did not cooperate with American plans. Beginning in the fall of 1964, it stepped up its efforts to defeat South Vietnam and reunite the country. Where once

Repel: Drive back or keep away.

Consonant: In accordance or agreement with.

North Vietnam had avoided killing U.S. military advisors, now the U.S. forces became fair game. In a series of secretive strikes, the North Vietnamese and their allies in the South, the Vietcong, proved their military skills. The Americans conducted several bombing raids over North Vietnam, but Johnson's military advisors increasingly warned that the only way to protect South Vietnam was to send in a massive military force. By the spring of 1965, Johnson faced this choice: withdraw from the conflict or increase the number of troops, thus increasing the American commitment. As the following excerpts show, Johnson received advice to increase U.S. involvement.

Looking back on the Vietnam War from the perspective of the early 2000s, most people believed that getting involved in the Vietnam War was a tragic mistake on the part of the United States. So why did it seem to make so much sense at the time? First, people inside the Johnson administration truly believed that once the United States declared war, the North Vietnamese would back off and leave South Vietnam alone. These individuals anticipated that in response to U.S. strikes on North Vietnam, the war would end, leaving America the champion of freedom in Southeast Asia. Second, most Americans knew little about the politics or history of Vietnam. They accepted the Johnson administration's claims that the United States was simply protecting the interests of the legitimate South Vietnamese government. The American public and media had not yet grown to question claims made by government officials, though they would by war's end. Finally, the Cold War attitude of most American politicians assumed that communism must be kept from spreading so that it did not threaten democratic forms of government. By painting the North Vietnamese as communist aggressors, Johnson avoided any criticism. He could do almost anything he wanted under the banner of anti-communism. Sadly, none of these justifications for becoming more deeply involved in the war in Vietnam could protect the United States from the disaster that unfolded over the following several years.

Did you know...

- One of the main arguments for going to war in Vietnam was known as the "domino theory." The domino theory held that if one small country was allowed to fall into communist hands, then all the other countries would follow—like a string of dominoes is knocked over in sequence after the first one falls. President Dwight D. Eisenhower (1890–1969; served 1953–61) first explained the domino theory in 1954 when he told the press: "The loss of Indochina [the original name for Vietnam] will cause the fall of Southeast Asia like a set of dominoes."

- The leader of the North Vietnamese government during most of the Vietnam War was Ho Chi Minh (1890–1969). Ho was born in Vietnam, but during his youth he traveled widely, spending time in Paris, London, and New York, and learning many different languages. Ho led his people in their victory over the Japanese in 1945, in their long war against French colonizers from 1945 to 1954, and in the long civil war that began in 1954 and lasted until after his death in 1969. When Vietnam was finally reunified in 1975, the nation's capital, Saigon, was renamed Ho Chi Minh City.

Consider the following...

- In what ways was the "domino theory" a valid theory for structuring U.S. foreign policy? Can you create an argument against the validity of the theory? Try to create a better theory to guide the policies of the U.S. government during this time of conflict.

- President Johnson wanted to avoid the criticism that he was carelessly leading the nation into war, so he gave several explanations for why war was necessary. Can you identify several of those pressing reasons that Johnson gives?

- Knowing what you do about the way the war went in Vietnam, do you think President Johnson's reasons for going to war were valid? Do you think later U.S. actions were consistent with his stated reasons for going to war?

- Compare President Johnson's reasons for going to war with those offered by other presidents, such as President George W. Bush (1946–) when he asked for authorization to send troops to Iraq in 2003. What are the similarities and differences between the requests?

For More Information

Books

Barr, Roger. *The Vietnam War.* San Diego, CA: Lucent Books, 1991.

Department of State Bulletin, Volume LI, No. 1312. Washington, D.C., The Library of Congress, August 24, 1964.

Farber, David. *The Age of Great Dreams: America in the 1960s.* New York: Hill and Wang, 1994.

Levy, Debbie. *Lyndon B. Johnson.* Minneapolis, MN: Lerner Publications, 2003.

Wormser, Richard. *Three Faces of Vietnam.* New York: F. Watts, 1993.

Wright, David K. *Causes and Consequences of the Vietnam War.* Austin, TX: Raintree Steck-Vaughn, 1996.

Wright, David K. *War in Vietnam.* 4 vols. Chicago, IL: Children's Press, 1989.

Web sites

Battlefield: Vietnam. www.pbs.org/battlefieldvietnam/index.html (accessed on August 1, 2004).

"Sixties Project: Primary Document Archive," *The Sixties Project.* http://lists.village.virginia.edu/sixties/HTML_docs/Resources/Primary.html (accessed on August 1, 2004).

Vietnam Online. www.pbs.org/wgbh/amex/vietnam/whos/index.html (accessed on August 1, 2004).

McGeorge Bundy and Robert McNamara

Excerpt from "A Policy of Sustained Reprisal"

Memorandum to President Lyndon B. Johnson written by McGeorge Bundy, February 7, 1965

Reprinted from *The Pentagon Papers*.

Published in 1971.

Excerpt from "Recommendations of Additional Deployments to Vietnam"

Memorandum to President Lyndon B. Johnson written by Robert McNamara, July 20, 1965.

Reprinted from *Our Nation's Archive*.

Published in 1999.

When President Lyndon Johnson asked Congress to authorize his use of force in North Vietnam in August of 1964, he declared that the United States "seeks no wider war" (see "Message to Congress" excerpt, page 113). In fact, he hoped that the mere threat of American military force would convince North Vietnam to stop its efforts to topple the government of South Vietnam and reunite the country under communist leadership. Instead, North Vietnam stepped up its attacks in late 1964 and early 1965, creating further instability in a country where a majority of the population opposed the American-backed government. Having very publicly pledged the United States to preserving a non-communist government in South Vietnam, the United States could not now stand by and watch the South Vietnamese government collapse. But what could it do?

Some both within and outside the Johnson administration argued that the right thing to do was withdraw right away, while there was still an intact government in South Vietnam. These people, nicknamed "doves" because they preferred peace, felt that any further involvement would cost

"Our object in Vietnam is to create conditions for a favorable outcome by demonstrating to the VC/DRV that the odds are against their winning. We want to create these conditions, if possible, without causing the war to expand into one with China or the Soviet Union and in a way which preserves support of the American people and, hopefully, of our allies and friends."

numerous American lives with little chance of real gain. One dove, George Ball, had suggested as early as 1961 that it would take 300,000 American soldiers to prop up an independent government in South Vietnam. His estimate—which would later come true—was laughed off. At the other extreme were the "hawks," so-called because they preferred military aggression, who argued that the only way to achieve American goals in Vietnam was to send an overwhelming military force. Senator Barry Goldwater even suggested that the United States drop an atomic bomb on North Vietnam.

In the end, the policy that emerged in 1965 was somewhere between these two extremes. The United States, policy makers explained, did not want to conquer North Vietnam or even topple the North Vietnamese government. All it really wanted was to preserve what it described as the legitimate government in South Vietnam (though many doubted that the South Vietnamese government was legitimate at all). To achieve this goal, the United States began a series of incremental increases in its engagement in Vietnam. The two documents excerpted in this section spell out how those increases would work. The first was written by McGeorge Bundy (1919–1996), a foreign policy advisor in both the Kennedy and Johnson administrations. It was the most elaborate explanation of the policy known as "sustained reprisal." The second document was authored by secretary of defense Robert McNamara (1916–). He gives specific advice about how to increase the U.S. military presence in Vietnam and suggests the likely results of such increases. These documents explain the gradual way the United States entered into all-out war in Vietnam.

Things to remember while reading the excerpts of "A Policy of Sustained Reprisal" and "Recommendation of Additional Deployments":

- The Pleiku incident of February 7, 1965, mentioned by Bundy was a Vietcong attack on a U.S. helicopter base in the South Vietnamese city of Pleiku. The attack killed eight Americans and destroyed ten aircraft—and prompted the United States to consider more violent attacks of its own.

- The U. S. and South Vietnamese armies were fighting against two different though very closely linked forces: the North Vietnamese Army, the official fighting forces of the Republic of Vietnam; and the Vietcong, an unofficial army composed of South Vietnamese supporters of the communist north.

- Both authors use acronyms, or initials, to refer to key players in the conflict. VC stands for Vietcong. NLF stands for National Liberation Front. DRV stands for the Democratic Republic of Vietnam, or North Vietnam. PAVN stands for the People's Army of Vietnam, or the North Vietnamese Army. GVN stands for the Government of Vietnam, or South Vietnam. ARVN stands for the Army of the Republic of Vietnam, or the South Vietnamese Army. VNAF stands for (South) Vietnamese Air Force.

McGeorge Bundy, an advisor to President Lyndon Johnson, pictured in 1965. *AP/Wide World Photos. Reproduced by permission.*

A Policy of Sustained Reprisal

I. INTRODUCTORY

*We believe that the best available way of increasing our chance of success in Vietnam is the development and execution of a policy of sustained **reprisal** against North Vietnam—a policy in which air and naval action against the North is justified by and related to the whole Vietcong campaign of violence and terror in the South.*

While we believe that the risks of such a policy are acceptable, we emphasize that its costs are real. It implies significant U.S. air losses even if no full air war is joined, and it seems likely that it would eventually require an extensive and costly effort against the

Reprisal: An act of retaliation or revenge.

McGeorge Bundy's policy of "sustained reprisal" called for retaliation against North Vietnam for each act of violence committed against South Vietnam. *AP/Wide World Photos. Reproduced by permission.*

VC: Vietcong, the communist-backed army that fought within South Vietnam.

Pleiku incident: A 1965 Vietcong attack on American forces.

Hamlet: A small village.

Saigon: The capital of South Vietnam.

whole air defense system of North Vietnam. U.S. casualties would be higher—and more visible to American feelings—than those sustained in the struggle in South Vietnam.

Yet measured against the costs of defeat in Vietnam, this program seems cheap. And even if it fails to turn the tide—as it may—the value of the effort seems to us to exceed its cost.

II. OUTLINE OF THE POLICY

*1. In partnership with the Government of Vietnam, we should develop and exercise the option to retaliate against any **VC** act of violence to persons or property.*

*2. In practice, we may wish at the outset to relate our reprisals to those acts of relatively high visibility such as the **Pleiku incident**. Later, we might retaliate against the assassination of a province chief, but not necessarily the murder of a **hamlet** official; we might retaliate against a grenade thrown into a crowded cafe in **Saigon** , but not necessarily to a shot fired into a small shop in the countryside.*

The Sixties in America: Primary Sources

3. Once a program of reprisals is clearly underway, it should not be necessary to connect each specific act against North Vietnam to a particular outrage in the South. It should be possible, for example, to publish weekly lists of outrages in the South and to have it clearly understood that these outrages are the cause of such action against the North as may be occurring in the current period....We must keep it clear at every stage both to **Hanoi** and to the world, that our reprisals will be reduced or stopped when outrages in the South are reduced or stopped—and that we are not attempting to destroy or conquer North Vietnam.

4. In the early stages of such a course, we should take the appropriate occasion to make clear our firm intent to undertake reprisals on any further acts, major or minor, that appear to us and the **GVN** as indicating Hanoi's support. We would announce that our two governments have been patient and forbearing in the hope that Hanoi would come to its senses without the necessity of our having to take further action; but the outrages continue and now we must react against those who are responsible; we will not provoke; we will not use our force indiscriminately; but we can no longer sit by in the face of repeated acts of terror and violence for which the **DRV** is responsible.

5. Having once made this announcement, we should execute our reprisal policy with as low a level of public noise as possible. It is to our interest that our acts should be seen—but we do not wish to boast about them in ways that make it hard for Hanoi to shift its ground. We should instead direct maximum attention to the continuing acts of violence which are the cause of our continuing reprisals.

6. This reprisal policy should begin at a low level. Its level of force and pressure should be increased only gradually—and as indicated above it should be decreased if VC terror visibly decreases. The object would not be to "win" an air war against Hanoi, but rather to influence the course of the struggle in the South.

7. At the same time it should be recognized that in order to maintain the power of reprisal without risk of excessive loss, an "air war" may in fact be necessary....

III. EXPECTED EFFECT OF SUSTAINED REPRISAL POLICY

1. We emphasize that our primary target in advocating a reprisal policy is the improvement of the situation in South Vietnam. Action against the North is usually urged as a means of affecting the will of Hanoi to direct and support the VC. We consider this an

Hanoi: The capital of North Vietnam.

GVN: Government of South Vietnam.

DRV: Democratic Republic of Vietnam, or North Vietnam.

*important but longer-range purpose. The immediate and critical targets are in the South—in the minds of the South Vietnamese and in the minds of the Vietcong **cadres** ....*

*8. We cannot assert that a policy of sustained reprisal will succeed in changing the course of the contest in Vietnam. It may fail, and we cannot estimate the odds of success with any accuracy— they may be somewhere between 25% and 75%. What we can say is that even if it fails, the policy will be worth it. At a minimum it will damp down the charge that we did not do all that we could have done, and this charge will be important in many countries, including our own. Beyond that, a reprisal policy—to the extent that it demonstrates U.S. willingness to employ this new norm in **counter-insurgency** —will set a higher price for the future upon all adventures of guerrilla warfare, and it should therefore somewhat increase our ability to deter such adventures. We must recognize, however, that that ability will be gravely weakened if there is failure for any reason in Vietnam.*

[...]

Excerpt of "Recommendations of additional deployments to Vietnam"

THE SECRETARY OF DEFENSE

WASHINGTON

20 July 1965

MEMORANDUM FOR THE PRESIDENT

SUBJECT: Recommendations of additional deployments to Vietnam

1. Introduction. Our object in Vietnam is to create conditions for a favorable outcome by demonstrating to the VC/DRV that the odds are against their winning. We want to create these conditions, if possible, without causing the war to expand into one with China or the Soviet Union and in a way which preserves support of the American people and, hopefully, of our allies and friends. The following assessments...are my own and are addressed to the achievement of that object....

Cadres: Small groups of communist leaders.

Counter-insurgency: Military efforts to put down a revolt against a government.

Quiescent: Quiet; causing no trouble.

PAVN: People's Army of Vietnam, the North Vietnamese army.

Infiltrators: North Vietnamese guerrillas who had entered South Vietnam.

NLF: National Liberation Front, the political branch of the Vietcong.

AID: Agency for International Development, an international aid agency.

UN: United Nations.

Stalemate: A condition of deadlock in which neither side can gain an advantage.

2. Favorable outcome. In my view, a favorable "outcome" for purposes of these assessments and recommendations has nine fundamental elements:

(a) VC stop attacks and drastically reduce incidents of terror and sabotage.

(b) DRV reduces infiltration to a trickle, with some reasonably reliable method of our obtaining confirmation of this fact.

(c) US/GVN stop bombing of North Vietnam.

(d) GVN stays independent (hopefully pro-US, but possibly genuinely neutral).

(e) GVN exercises governmental functions over substantially all of South Vietnam.

(f) Communists remain **quiescent** *in Laos and Thailand.*

(g) DRV withdraws **PAVN** *forces and other North Vietnamese* **infiltrators** *... from South Vietnam.*

*(h) VC/***NLF** *transform from a military to a purely political organization.*

(i) US combat forces (not advisors or **AID***) withdraw.*

A favorable outcome could also include arrangements regarding elections, relations between North and South Vietnam, participation in peace-keeping by international forces, membership for North and South Vietnam in the **UN***, and so on....*

3. Estimate of the situation. The situation in South Vietnam is worse than a year ago (when it was worse than a year before that). After a few months of **stalemate** *, the tempo of the war has quickened. A hard VC push is now on to* **dismember** *the nation and to maul the army. The initiative and, with large attacks (some in* **regimental** *strength) are hurting* **ARVN** *forces badly....US combat troops deployments and US/VNAF strikes against the North have put to rest most South Vietnamese fears that the United States will forsake them, and US/VNAF air strikes in-country have probably shaken VC morale somewhat. Yet the government is able to provide security to*

Dismember: Tear apart or destroy.

Regimental: Relating to a regiment, a military unit of between 500 and 1000 soldiers.

ARVN: South Vietnamese Army.

fewer and fewer people in less and less territory as terrorism increases. Cities and towns are being isolated as fewer and fewer roads and railroads are usable and power and communications lines are cut.

The economy is deteriorating—the war is disrupting rubber production, rice distribution…vegetable production, and coastal fishing industry, causing the loss of jobs and income, displacement of people and frequent breakdown or suspension of vital means of transportation and communication; foreign exchange earnings have fallen; and severe inflation is threatened.

*The odds are less than even that the **Ky government** will last out the year. Ky is "executive agent" for a **directorate of generals**. His government is youthful and inexperienced, but dedicated to a "revolutionary" program. His tenure depends upon the unity of the armed forces behind him….*

The Government-to-VC ratio over-all is now only a little better than 3-to-1, and in combat battalions little better than 1.5-to-1. Some ARVN units have been mauled; many are under strength and therefore "conservative." Desertions are at a high rate, and the force build-up has slipped badly. The VC, who are undoubtedly suffering badly too (their losses are very high), now control a South Vietnamese manpower pool of 500,000 to 1 million fighting-age men and reportedly are trying to double their combat strength, largely by forced draft (down to 15-year-olds) in the increasing areas they control. They seem to be more than able to replace their losses.

*There are no signs that we have **throttled** the inflow of supplies for the VC or can throttle the flow while their material needs are as low as they are; indeed more and better weapons have been observed in VC hands, and it is probable that there has been further build-up of North Vietnamese regular units in the I and II Corps areas, with at least three full regiments (all of the 325th Division) there. Nor have our air strikes in North Vietnam produced tangible evidence of willingness on the part of Hanoi to come to the conference table in a reasonable mood. The DRV/VC seem to believe that South Vietnam is on the run and near collapse; they show no signs of settling for less than a complete take-over.*

4. Options open to us. We must choose among three courses of action with respect to Vietnam all of which involve different probabilities, outcomes, and costs:

(a) Cut our losses and withdraw under the best conditions that can be arranged—almost certainly conditions humiliating the Unit-

Ky government: The government of South Vietnam from 1965 to 1967, led by Marshal Nguyen Cao Ky.

Directorate of generals: A group of generals acting as a board of directors.

Throttled: Cut off, stopped.

Robert McNamara believed that increasing the number of U.S. troops in Vietnam would help bring about a quicker, more "favorable," end to the conflict.
National Archives.

ed States and very damaging to our future effectiveness on the world scene.

(b) Continue at about the present level, with the US forces limited to say 75,000, holding on and playing for the breaks—a course of action which, because our position would grow weaker, almost certainly would confront us later with a choice between withdrawal and an emergency expansion of forces, perhaps too late to do any good.

(c) Expand promptly and substantially the US military pressure against the Vietcong in the South and maintain the military pressure against the North Vietnamese in the North while launching a vigorous effort on the political side to lay the groundwork for a favorable outcome by clarifying our objectives and establishing channels of communication. This alternative would **stave off** defeat in the short run and offer a good chance of producing a favorable settlement in the longer run; at the same time it would imply a commitment to see a fighting war clear through at considerable cost in casualties and material and would make any later decision to with-

Stave off: Hold off.

draw even more difficult and even more costly than would be the case today.

My recommendations in paragraph 5 below are based on the choice of the third alternative (Option c) as the course of action involving the best odds of the best outcome with the most acceptable cost to the United States.

5. Military recommendations. There are now 15 US (and 1 Australian) combat battalion in Vietnam; they, together with other combat personnel and non-combat personnel, bring the total US personnel in Vietnam to approximately 75,000.

I recommend that the deployment of US ground troops in Vietnam be increased by October to 34 maneuver battalions (or, if the Koreans fail to provide the expected 9 battalions promptly, to 43 battalions). The battalions—together with increases in helicopter lift, air squadrons, naval units, air defense, combat support and miscellaneous log support and advisory personnel which I also recommend—would bring the total US personnel in Vietnam to approximately 175,000 (200,000 if we must make up for the Korean failure). It should be understood that the deployment of more men (perhaps 100,000) may be necessary in early 1966, and that the deployment of additional forces thereafter is possible but will depend on developments.

I recommend the Congress be requested to authorize the call-up of approximately 235,000 men in the Reserve and National Guard. This number—approximately 125,000 Army, 75,000 Marines, 25,000 Air Force and 10,000 Navy—would provide approximately 36 maneuver battalions by the end of this year. The call-up would be for a two-year period; but the intention would be to release them after one year, by which time they could be relieved by regular forces if conditions permitted.

I recommend that the regular armed forces be increased by approximately 375,000 men (approximately 250,000 Army, 75,000 Marines, 25,000 Air Force and 25,000 Navy). This would provide approximately 27 additional maneuver battalions by the middle of 1966. The increases would be accomplished by increasing recruitment, increasing the draft and extending tours of duty of men already in the service....

7. Actions against North Vietnam. We should continue the program of bombing military targets in North Vietnam. While avoiding striking population and industrial targets not closely related to the

DRV's supply of war material to the VC, we should announce to Hanoi and carry out actions to destroy such supplies and to **interdict** their flow. The number of strike **sorties** against North Vietnam—should increase slowly from the present level of 2,500 a month to 4,000 or more a month. We should be prepared at any time to carry out a severe reprisal should the VC or DRV commit a particularly damaging or horrendous act (e.g., VC interdiction of the Saigon river could call for a quarantine of DRV harbors, or VC assassination of a high-ranking US official could call for a destruction of all the major power plants in North Vietnam)....

9. *Expanded political moves.* Together with the above military moves, we should take political initiatives in order to lay a groundwork for a favorable political settlement by clarifying our objectives and establishing channels of communications. At the same time as we are taking steps to turn the tide in South Vietnam, we should make quiet moves through diplomatic channels (a) to open a dialogue with **Moscow** and Hanoi, and perhaps the VC, looking first toward **disabusing** them of any misconceptions as to our goals and second toward laying the groundwork for a settlement when the time is ripe; (b) to keep the Soviet Union from deepening its military involvement and support of North Vietnam and from generating crises elsewhere in the world until the time when settlement can be achieved; and (c) to cement support for US policy by the US public, allies and friends, and to keep international opposition at a manageable level. Our efforts may be unproductive until the tide begins to turn, but nevertheless they should be made....

11. *Communist reaction to the expanded program.* The Soviets can be expected to continue material assistance to North Vietnam and to lodge verbal complaints, but not to intervene otherwise. The Chinese—at least so long as we do not invade North Vietnam, do not sink a Chinese ship and, most important, do not strike China—will probably not send regular ground forces or aircraft into the war. The DRV, on the other hand, may well send up to several divisions of regular forces in South Vietnam to assist the VC if they see the tide turning and victory, once so near, being snatched away. This possible DRV action is the most ominous one, since it would lead to increased pressure on us to "counter-invade" North Vietnam and to extend air strikes to population targets in the North; acceding to these pressures could bring the Soviets and the Chinese in. The Vietcong, especially if they continue to take high losses, can be expected to depend increasingly upon the PAVN forces as the war moves into a more conventional phase; but they may find ways to contin-

Interdict: To destroy, damage, or cut off by force.

Sorties: Single-plane attacks.

Moscow: The capital of the Soviet Union.

Disabusing: Freeing from error.

ue almost indefinitely their present intensive military, guerrilla and terror activities, particularly if reinforced by some regular PAVN units. A key question on the military side is whether POL, ammunition, and cadres can be cut off and, if they are cut off, whether this really renders the Vietcong impotent.

12. Evaluation. ARVN overall is not capable of successfully resisting the VC initiatives with more active assistance from more US/third-country ground forces than those thus far committed....The success of the program from the military point of view turns on whether the Vietnamese hold their own in terms of numbers and fighting spirit, and on whether the US forces can be effective in a quick-reaction reserve role in which they are only being tested. The number of US troops is too small to make a significant difference in the traditional 10-1 government-guerrilla formula, but it is not too small to make a significant difference in the kind of war which seems to be evolving in Vietnam—a "Third Stage" or conventional war in which it is easier to identify, locate, and attack the enemy.

The plan is such that the risk of escalation into war with China or the Soviet Union can be kept small. US and South Vietnamese casualties will increase—just how much cannot be predicted with confidence, but the US killed-in-action might be in the vicinity of 500 a month by the end of the year. The South Vietnamese under one government or another will probably see the thing through and the United States public will support the course of action because it is a sensible and courageous military-political program designed and likely to bring about a success in Vietnam....

The overall evaluation is that the course of action recommended in this memorandum—if the military and political moves are properly integrated and executed with continuing vigor and visible determination—stands a good chance of achieving an acceptable outcome within a reasonable time in Vietnam.

Robert S. McNamara

What happened next...

In the end, both Bundy's and McNamara's policies were adopted as the guide to increasing U.S. military involve-

ment in the conflict in Vietnam. Following Bundy's advice, U.S. forces reacted to North Vietnamese and Vietcong attacks with attacks of their own. And following McNamara's advice, President Johnson ordered a steady increase in the number of American troops stationed in Vietnam. In 1964 there was a total of 23,300 troops in Vietnam, most classified as military advisors. But in March of 1965 the first contingent of 3,500 combat troops arrived. By the end of 1965 the numbers had risen dramatically, to 184,300 troops. A year later the number had nearly doubled, to 385,300. American troop strength in Vietnam topped out at 536,100 in 1968.

Most U.S. political and military strategists believed that following these policies would quickly lead to the desired outcomes in Vietnam. General William Westmoreland (1914–), the American military commander in Vietnam, boasted that powerful American forces would soon achieve the objectives that had seemed impossible to the South Vietnamese army. As quoted in David Farber's *The Age of Great*

American troops search for Vietcong soldiers in a South Vietnamese village, 1966. Because the Vietcong lived among the South Vietnamese population, it was often impossible to tell soldiers from civilians, thus allowing the Vietcong to ambush U.S. troops much of the time. © *Corbis. Reproduced by permission.*

Dreams: America in the 1960s, Westmoreland said in 1965: "We're going to out-guerrilla the guerilla and out-ambush the ambush...because we're smarter, we have greater mobility and firepower; we have endurance and more to fight for...and we've got more guts."

Though the United States implemented its policies as planned, the results were hardly what had been intended. American troops went after the enemy—and could not find him. The Vietcong were an elusive enemy, organizing in small bands and disappearing into the jungle when confronted by units of American soldiers. Because the Vietcong lived among the South Vietnamese population, it was often impossible to tell soldiers from civilians. In 1968, the Central Intelligence Agency estimated that only one in ten American combat patrols actually located the enemy. When they found the enemy and met in conventional battles, the Americans dominated. But most of the time Vietcong and North Vietnamese patrols caught Americans by surprise and slowly drove higher the death toll among Americans.

The Americans did not achieve the successes they had hoped for, and so they tried harder. They increased the number of bombs they dropped, hoping to knock out enemy targets in North Vietnam and South Vietnam. Soon they dropped bombs on Vietcong positions in the neighboring countries on Cambodia and Laos. By war's end they had dropped over seven million tons of bombs—five million more than they had dropped during all of World War II (1939–45)—and had destroyed nearly every important target. Yet the enemy kept on fighting, sending lightly armed soldiers scurrying into the jungle to launch guerrilla raids on unsuspecting targets.

The United States found itself in a war unlike any it had known before, and it did not know how to get out. Eventually, politicians and generals would realize that they were supporting a South Vietnamese government that was so unpopular that its own people turned against it in massive numbers. They also realized that they were fighting an enemy who was willing to endure any cost, in property and in human life, to achieve its ultimate goal: the reunification of Vietnam under communist rule. By the end of the 1960s, pressured by military defeat and by intense political pressure at home, U.S. leaders were looking for any reasonable way out of Vietnam.

Did you know...

- Between 1964 and 1975, the United States spent $140 billion fighting the Vietnam War.

- According to the *Columbia Guide to America in the 1960s,* the total number of U.S. combat deaths in Vietnam was 45,941. The total number of South Vietnamese combat deaths was estimated at 223,750, while the North Vietnamese and Vietcong combat deaths topped 830,000. Altogether, it is estimated that nearly 500,000 Vietnamese civilians also lost their lives, most of these in the South.

- From 1962 to 1970, it is estimated that over 5,100,000 acres of land in Vietnam were defoliated, or stripped of all vegetable matter, by bombs and herbicides dropped by U.S. and South Vietnamese forces. The defoliation agents were later found to be responsible for thousands of birth defects among the Vietnamese living in combat areas.

- Robert McNamara, one of the principal architects of early American policy in Vietnam, came to believe after 1966 that the United States should work for a peaceful solution to the conflict.

Consider the following...

- Imagine that you are President Johnson and that your top military advisors are urging you to commit more troops to the war in Vietnam. What are some of the factors you will consider in making your decision? You might break your list down into economic, political, and economic factors.

- Pretend that you are one of President Johnson's advisors in 1965. What advice would you give the president? Would you have agreed with Bundy and McNamara, or would you have argued for a different plan?

- The documents that you have just read did not become public until the early 1970s. Would it have made a difference if the private governmental debate for going to war and increasing troops was made public in 1965? Explain your reasoning.

For More Information

Books
Barr, Roger. *The Vietnam War.* San Diego, CA: Lucent Books, 1991.

Bruun, Erik, and Jay Crosby, eds. *Our Nation's Archive: The History of the United States in Documents.* New York: Black Dog & Leventhal, 1999.

Farber, David. *The Age of Great Dreams: America in the 1960s.* New York: Hill and Wang, 1994.

Kutler, Stanley, I. *Encyclopedia of the Vietnam War.* New York: Charles Scribner's Sons, 1996.

McNamara, Robert S. *In Retrospect: The Tragedy and Lessons of Vietnam.* New York: Vintage Books, 1996.

The Pentagon Papers. New York: Quadrangle Books, 1971.

Wormser, Richard. *Three Faces of Vietnam.* New York: F. Watts, 1993.

Wright, David K. *Causes and Consequences of the Vietnam War.* Austin, TX: Raintree Steck-Vaughn, 1996.

Wright, David K. *War in Vietnam.* 4 vols. Chicago, IL: Children's Press, 1989.

Web sites

Battlefield: Vietnam. www.pbs.org/battlefieldvietnam/index.html (accessed on August 1, 2004).

"Sixties Project: Primary Document Archive," *The Sixties Project.* http://lists.village.virginia.edu/sixties/HTML_docs/Resources/Primary.html (accessed on August 1, 2004).

Vietnam Online. www.pbs.org/wgbh/amex/vietnam/whos/index.html (accessed on August 1, 2004).

The Antiwar Movement

4

L ike the American involvement in the Vietnam War (1954–75), the movement to protest that war started slowly. Before President Lyndon B. Johnson (1908–1973; served 1963–69) asked Congress for authorization to broaden American involvement in Vietnam in August of 1964, most Americans did not even realize that the United States had a stake in the small country in Southeast Asia. But those few political activists who knew Vietnam and its history as a French colony perceived it to be a small, impoverished country that wished to shake off the yoke of French domination and practice self-government—much like the United States had done when it freed itself from British rule two hundred years earlier. These activists hoped that the United States would help North and South Vietnam unite under a policy of self-rule. When it became obvious that the United States would rather support a corrupt but capitalistic government in South Vietnam than a popular but communist government in North Vietnam, these activists launched a campaign to criticize American involvement. (A capitalist government, like the one in the United States, is characterized by private ownership of property and free-market competition whereas a communist government, like the Soviet Union had in the 1960s, is characterized by state ownership of property and state control of economic decisions.)

The first national protest against American policy in Vietnam was led by a small group of college students calling itself Students for a Democratic Society (SDS). In April of 1965, SDS organized a group of fifteen thousand people at the Washington Monument in the nation's capital, and SDS president Paul Potter gave an impassioned speech. He argued that America was doing a poor job of guaranteeing justice and equality at home, and he criticized the government for fighting against a popular movement for self-government overseas. "What kind of a system is it," he asked, as quoted in Farber's *The Age of Great Dreams*, "that disenfranchises people in the South, leaves millions upon millions of people throughout the country impoverished and excluded from the mainstream and promise of American society, that creates faceless and terrible bureaucracies and makes those the place where people spend their lives and do their work, that consistently puts material values before human values—and still persists in calling itself free and still persists in finding itself fit to police the world?" Potter's words set the tone for an antiwar movement that grew in size and intensity in the years that followed.

The fledgling antiwar movement expanded along with the war. As more and more soldiers were shipped overseas to fight on foreign soil and as more and more of the taxpayers' dollars were spent on the war—total war costs mounted to $140 billion between 1964 and 1975—a sizable and growing minority of Americans rose up in opposition to the war. At first, protestors merely wanted to see American troops out of Vietnam. But as media reports revealed that military and political leaders had misled the American public about the number of American soldiers being killed and underestimated the difficulties of fighting the war, the goals of the protests changed. The antiwar protestors questioned all areas of American foreign policy. They demanded to know why their money could be spent to solve problems abroad, but not at home. They began to doubt that politicians ever told the truth about difficult issues. Antiwar protests thus began to draw supporters from a variety of other social movements and groups, including the civil rights movement, the women's movement, and a variety of youth organizations.

By 1967 and 1968, the antiwar movement was a significant political force in America. Protests raged on college campuses and in major cities. Many young men began to resist the draft, the system by which they were selected to join the military forces. Some of these people burned their draft registration cards and defied the government to force them into military service. Civil rights leaders such as Malcolm X (1925–1965) and Martin Luther King Jr. (1929–1968) spoke out against the war, as did a number of prominent intellectuals and celebrities. Together, these people exerted a real influence on American policy. President Lyndon Johnson was jeered by antiwar protestors at nearly all of his public appearances, and he eventually decided not to run for re-election in 1968.

The growth of the antiwar movement is one of the most dramatic stories of the 1960s. The primary sources that follow present arguments made by some of the antiwar protestors. The first document presented is the position paper issued in 1968 by the **Student Nonviolent Coordinating Committee** (SNCC), a prominent student-led civil rights group. This position paper is one of many manifestos (a public declaration of principles and goals, usually of a political nature) issued by groups that were opposed to the war. The second document is testimony given before Congress by **John Kerry**, a veteran of the U.S. armed forces who later became a U.S. senator and the 2004 Democratic presidential candidate. As head of a group calling itself Vietnam Veterans Against the War, Kerry presented the antiwar arguments of those who had actually participated in the war. The third document, presented in a sidebar, is the lyrics of one of many antiwar songs that were very popular, especially among young people, during the 1960s.

Student Nonviolent Coordinating Committee

Complete text of "Position Paper On Vietnam," January 6, 1966

Reprinted from *"Takin' It to the Streets:" A Sixties Reader,* published in 2003; also available online at http://lists.village.virginia.edu/ sixties/HTML_docs/Resources/Primary/Manifestos/SNCC_VN.html

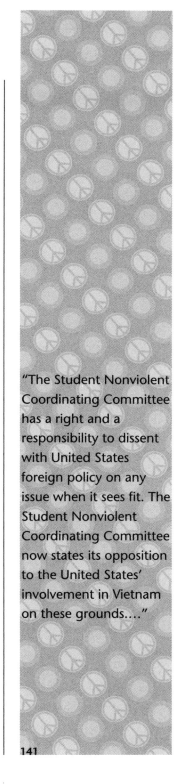

The 1960s are known for the many organized movements that worked to bring about social change. Student activists, women's rights activists, gay rights activists, and civil rights activists, among others, are a few examples of groups that organized to press for important changes they felt were needed to ensure that all Americans had access to equal rights. In the late 1950s, some college students had participated in nonviolent sit-ins to protest the separation according to race in eating facilities, pools, theaters, and other public facilities in the South. These students were deeply influenced by the teachings of the Rev. Martin Luther King Jr. (1929–1968), who advocated nonviolent civil disobedience to bring about social change. In 1960 a group of these students organized themselves into the Student Nonviolent Coordinating Committee (SNCC). SNCC (pronounced "snick") participated in the famous Freedom Rides of 1961, in which students integrated bus service in southern states, and helped organize the massive March on Washington in 1963.

Under the leadership of founder John Lewis (1940–) SNCC devoted itself to integrating facilities restricted by race and

"The Student Nonviolent Coordinating Committee has a right and a responsibility to dissent with United States foreign policy on any issue when it sees fit. The Student Nonviolent Coordinating Committee now states its opposition to the United States' involvement in Vietnam on these grounds...."

SNCC president Stokely Carmichael speaks before a crowd of college students at Florida A & M University in 1967. *AP/Wide World Photos. Reproduced by permission.*

to expanding voting rights for African Americans, but by the late 1960s the group had grown more radical. SNCC president Stokely Carmichael (1941–1998), elected in 1966, grew impatient with the group's efforts to bring about gradual change. He pushed the group to advocate for sweeping social change, and he aligned the group with the radical Black Power movement, a movement that called for militant action by armed blacks.

In the position paper reprinted below, which was first released in January of 1966, SNCC links its resistance to U.S. policy in Vietnam with America's failure to assure civil rights or equality at home. The paper charges the United States government with being hypocritical, with pretending to take a virtuous stand and with saying one thing but actually doing something very different. This charge had special significance in the 1960s, when young people especially were concerned with being "authentic" and "true to themselves," and thought that older people were willing to betray their ideals in support of the government.

Things to remember while reading the SNCC "Position Paper On Vietnam":

- SNCC's main goal was the extension of full civil rights to all Americans, including African Americans.

- Position papers served an important purpose for organizations such as SNCC, the National Association for the Advancement of Colored People (NAACP), and the Students for a Democratic Society (SDS). They announced that the group had taken an official position on the topic, and they could be given to the media and distributed to widely scattered members of the organization.

Student Nonviolent Coordinating Committee "Position Paper On Vietnam"

The Student Nonviolent Coordinating Committee has a right and a responsibility to dissent with United States foreign policy on any issue when it sees fit. The Student Nonviolent Coordinating Committee now states its opposition to the United States' involvement in Vietnam on these grounds:

We believe the United States government has been deceptive in its claims of concern for the freedom of the Vietnamese people, just as the government has been deceptive in claiming concern for the freedom of colored people in other countries [such] as the Dominican Republic, the Congo, South Africa, Rhodesia, and in the United States itself.

We, the Student Nonviolent Coordinating Committee, have been involved in the black people's struggle for liberation and self-determination in this country for the past five years. Our work, particularly in the South, has taught us that the United States government has never guaranteed the freedom of oppressed citizens, and is not yet truly determined to end the rule of terror and oppression within its own borders.

We ourselves have often been victims of violence and confinement executed by United States governmental officials. We recall the numerous persons who have been murdered in the South because of

Student Nonviolent Coordinating Committee (SNCC) demonstrators in front of the White House with a casket representing the life of slain civil rights activist Samuel Young Jr., whose picture is on the casket, January 11, 1966. Police are shown removing the casket. © Bettmann/Corbis. Reproduced by permission.

Samuel Young: A SNCC activist murdered for defending a black girl's right to drink from a water fountain.

their efforts to secure their civil and human rights, and whose murderers have been allowed to escape penalty for their crimes.

The murder of **Samuel Young** in Tuskegee, Alabama, is no different than the murder of peasants in Vietnam, for both Young and the Vietnamese sought, and are seeking, to secure the rights guaranteed them by law. In each case, the United States government bears a great part of the responsibility for these deaths.

Samuel Young was murdered because United States law is not being enforced. Vietnamese are murdered because the United States is pursuing an aggressive policy in violation of international law. The United States is no respecter of persons or law when such persons or laws run counter to its needs or desires.

We recall the indifference, suspicion and outright hostility with which our reports of violence have been met in the past by government officials.

We know that for the most part, elections in this country, in the North as well as the South, are not free. We have seen that the

1965 Voting Rights Act and the 1966 Civil Rights Act have not yet been implemented with full federal power and sincerity.

We question, then, the ability and even the desire of the United States government to guarantee free elections abroad. We maintain that our country's cry of "preserve freedom in the world" is a **hypocritical mask**, behind which it squashes liberation movements which are not bound, and refuse to be bound, by the **expediencies** of United States cold war policies.

We are in sympathy with, and support, the men in this country who are unwilling to respond to a **military draft** which would compel them to contribute their lives to United States aggression in Vietnam in the name of the "freedom" we find so false in this country.

We recoil with horror at the inconsistency of a supposedly "free" society where responsibility to freedom is equated with the responsibility to lend oneself to military aggression. We take note of the fact that 16% of the draftees from this country are Negroes called on to stifle the liberation of Vietnam, to preserve a "democracy" which does not exist for them at home.

SNCC's position paper describes the irony of black U.S. soldiers who were called on to preserve democracy in Vietnam, but who did not enjoy the same rights as white Americans in their own country. *Photo by U.S. Army/Getty Images.*

Hypocritical mask: This refers to the idea that the United States says one thing and does another.

Expediencies: Actions taken to achieve a goal, without regard for ideals.

Military draft: The system by which men between the ages of 18 and 34 were randomly selected to join the military.

We ask, where is the draft for the freedom fight in the United States?

We therefore encourage those Americans who prefer to use their energy in building democratic forms within this country. We believe that work in the civil rights movement and with other human relations organizations is a valid alternative to the draft. We urge all Americans to seek this alternative, knowing full well that it may cost them their lives—as painfully as in Vietnam.

What happened next...

Statements made by civil rights leaders and groups like SNCC had a powerful influence, for many people recognized and admired the moral position that these groups had taken. Like SNCC, civil rights leader Martin Luther King Jr. spoke out against the war. Soon after this position paper was issued, however, SNCC's influence began to decline. Like many protest groups of the era, especially those founded by young people without a great deal of experience in holding together large organizations, SNCC fell apart as its members squabbled over the direction the group should take. Certain members' struggles for power drove other members from the organization. SNCC leader Stokely Carmichael left the group in 1968 to lead California's Black Panther party, a radical black political group. James Forman took over the leadership of the organization, but it ceased to exert a major influence in the civil rights struggle and faded away in the early 1970s.

Did you know...

- African Americans served and died in the Vietnam War in disproportionate numbers. From 1961 to 1966, African Americans made up 13 percent of the American population but accounted for nearly 20 percent of combat-related deaths. In 1965 alone, African Americans accounted for nearly one-fourth of those killed in battle. Late in the war, when military leaders were made aware of this problem, they began to direct black soldiers away from frontline combat positions.

- Many of America's wealthiest and more privileged young men were able to avoid service in the Vietnam War through draft deferments, or special exemptions given to people who fit in certain categories. For example, those who were attending a four-year university or graduate school received deferments for most of the war, as did those who supervised four or more workers. Two American presidents—Bill Clinton and George W. Bush—were criticized because they sought exemptions from service during the Vietnam War years. As a result of these deferments, the makeup of the armed forces tended to be dominated by members of the working classes and minorities.

Consider the following...

- If you were a newspaper reporter writing on SNCC's position on Vietnam, how would you summarize its charges?

- Do you think that SNCC's complaints about the war in Vietnam were legitimate?

- When SNCC founder John Lewis campaigned for the U.S. Congress in 1986, his opponents took him to court claiming that his statements urging people to resist the draft disqualified him from public office. If you were the judge presiding on this case, how would you rule? Why?

For More Information

Books

Bloom, Alexander, and Wini Breines, eds. *"Takin' It to the Streets": A Sixties Reader.* New York: Oxford University Press, 2003.

Farber, David. *The Age of Great Dreams: America in the 1960s.* New York: Hill and Wang, 1994.

Super, Neil. *Vietnam War Soldiers.* New York: Twenty-First Century Books, 1993.

Tucker, Spencer C. *Encyclopedia of the Vietnam War: A Political, Social, and Military History.* 3 vols. Santa Barbara, CA: ABC-CLIO, 1998.

Westheider, James E. *Fighting on Two Fronts: African Americans and the Vietnam War.* New York: New York University Press, 1997.

Web sites

Battlefield: Vietnam. www.pbs.org/battlefieldvietnam/index.html (accessed on August 1, 2004).

"Sixties Project: Primary Document Archive," *The Sixties Project.* http://lists.village.virginia.edu/sixties/HTML_docs/Resources/Primary.html (accessed on August 1, 2004).

Vietnam Online. www.pbs.org/wgbh/amex/vietnam/whos/index.html (accessed on August 1, 2004).

John Kerry

*Excerpt from a statement on behalf of
Vietnam Veterans Against the War*

**Delivered to the Senate Committee of Foreign Relations,
April 23, 1971**

Reprinted from *"Takin' It to the Streets": A Sixties Reader,* **published in
2003; also available at http://lists.village.virginia.edu/sixties/HTML_
docs/Resources/Primary/Manifestos/VVAW_Kerry_Senate.html**

By the late 1960s there were many groups speaking out against the Vietnam War, but few did so with as much authority as a group known as Vietnam Veterans Against the War (VVAW). The group was formed in 1967 when six Vietnam veterans met while participating in a protest march in New York City. These six soon expanded their group to include hundreds and then thousands of war veterans who were interested in talking about their experiences both during the war and after their return home. They spoke out against the terrible acts they were forced to commit while waging war in Vietnam but also about the poor treatment that veterans received upon returning home. For example, veterans were often blamed for participating in the war, and they often received substandard medical care at veterans' medical facilities.

By early 1971 the VVAW determined that it needed to become more active in protesting against the Vietnam War. For three days in January, the group held hearings at which soldiers testified about the exceedingly cruel and repulsive actions they had witnessed and committed while stationed in

"We who have come here to Washington have come here because we feel we have to be winter soldiers now. We could come back to this country, we could be quiet, we could hold our silence, we could not tell what went on in Vietnam, but we feel because of what threatens this country...that we have to speak out...."

Vietnam veterans throw their Purple Hearts, Bronze Stars, and other ribbons and medals earned during the Vietnam War on the steps of the U.S. Capitol as an antiwar protest, April 23, 1971. *AP/Wide World Photos. Reproduced by permission.*

Vietnam. These hearings, held in a Detroit, Michigan, motel, were called the Winter Soldier Investigation. They helped the soldiers realize that they shared the belief that the war in Vietnam was unjust and against their higher ideals as Americans.

In April 1971 the VVAW organized a week-long demonstration in Washington, D.C., that the group called Operation Dewey Canyon III, named after an actual military operation held in Vietnam earlier that year. The protest began with a mass march of veterans and mothers of fallen soldiers to Arlington National Cemetery. During the week, veterans staged street theater performances, simulating attacks on civilians played by actors. Approximately sixty men tried to surrender themselves to the Pentagon, the headquarters of the U.S. military in Washington, D.C., for committing war crimes. On the final day of the protest, two actions occurred: seven hundred veterans threw their medals and ribbons, military honors received for service in the war that the soldiers were protesting against, over a barricade onto the Capitol steps, and twenty-seven-year-old Navy lieutenant John Kerry (1944–) delivered a powerful testimony before the Senate Foreign Relations Committee.

John Kerry had enlisted in the U.S. Navy when he was a senior at Yale University in 1966. Over the course of his sixteen months of active duty in Vietnam, Kerry was injured three times and received three Purple Hearts, a Silver Star, and a Bronze Star. He was, by all accounts, an excellent soldier and leader, committed to the safety of the soldiers under his command. He was also an articulate spokesman for the concerns of the VVAW, as is evident in this testimony that he delivered before the Senate Foreign Relations Committee on April 23, 1971.

Things to remember while reading the excerpt of John Kerry's statement of behalf of the Vietnam Veterans Against the War:

- One of the biggest problems facing American soldiers in Vietnam was the difficulty in identifying the enemy. The principal enemy group, the Vietcong, contained South Vietnamese who supported the efforts of North Vietnam. They looked no different than South Vietnamese civilians. American soldiers were often ordered to kill everyone in a village just because that village was suspected of aiding the Vietcong.

- Before the Vietnam War, the United States had never had a group of veterans who spoke out publicly about their resistance to the war. These veterans felt very strongly that their government had lied to the American people about the reasons the United States was fighting the war and about American troops having success in that war. They felt compelled to speak out against the horror and injustice of the war.

Excerpt of John Kerry's statement on behalf of Vietnam Veterans Against the War

I would like to talk on behalf of all those veterans and say that several months ago in Detroit we had an investigation at which over 150 honorably discharged, and many very highly decorated, veterans testified to war crimes committed in Southeast Asia. These were not isolated incidents but crimes committed on a day-to-day basis with the full awareness of officers at all levels of command.

It is impossible to describe to you exactly what did happen in Detroit—the emotions in the room and the feelings of the men who were reliving their experiences in Vietnam. They relived the absolute horror of what this country, in a sense, made them do.

*They told stories that at times they had personally raped, cut off ears, cut off heads, taped wires from portable telephones to human genitals and turned up the power, cut off limbs, blown up bodies, randomly shot at civilians, **razed** villages in fashion reminiscent of **Genghis Khan**, shot cattle and dogs for fun, poisoned food stocks, and generally ravaged the countryside of South Vietnam in addition to the normal ravage of war and the normal and very particular ravaging which is done by the applied bombing power of this country.*

*We call this investigation the Winter Soldier Investigation. The term Winter Soldier is a play on words of **Thomas Paine**'s in 1776 when he spoke of the Sunshine Patriots and summertime soldiers who deserted at **Valley Forge** because the going was rough.*

*We who have come here to Washington have come here because we feel we have to be winter soldiers now. We could come back to this country, we could be quiet, we could hold our silence, we could not tell what went on in Vietnam, but we feel because of what threatens this country, not the **reds**, but the crimes which we are committing that threaten it, that we have to speak out....*

Razed: Destroyed.

Genghis Khan: A medieval Mongolian warlord known for his brutality.

Thomas Paine: 1737–1809; American writer who wrote and published works in favor of the American Revolution.

Valley Forge: The site of a famous battle in the American Revolutionary War (1775–83).

Reds: A slang term for communists.

Hypocrisy: The act of pretending to be something other than what you are, as in the false appearance of virtue.

John Kerry testifying before the Senate Committee on Foreign Relations, April 23, 1971. *AP/Wide World Photos. Reproduced by permission.*

*In our opinion and from our experience, there is nothing in South Vietnam which could happen that realistically threatens the United States of America. And to attempt to justify the loss of one American life in Vietnam, Cambodia or Laos by linking such loss to the preservation of freedom, which those misfits supposedly abuse, is to us the height of criminal **hypocrisy**, and it is that kind of hypocrisy which we feel has torn this country apart.*

*We found that not only was it a civil war, an effort by a people who had for years been seeking their liberation from any **colonial influence** whatsoever, but also we found that the Vietnamese whom we had enthusiastically molded after our own image were hard put to take up the fight against the threat we were supposedly saving them from.*

*We found most people didn't even know the difference between communism and democracy. They only wanted to work in rice paddies without helicopters **strafing** them and bombs with **napalm** burning their villages and tearing their country apart. They wanted everything*

Colonial influence: Kerry is referring to the Vietnamese attempt to free themselves from the influence of the French, who had once ruled Vietnam as a colony.

Strafing: Raking with gunfire at close range.

Napalm: An explosive liquid bomb used to burn villages and surrounding foliage.

The Ultimate Antiwar Song

The Vietnam War came at a time when rock 'n' roll music was going through an energizing process of change and adjustment. The first visit of the rock band the Beatles to the United States in 1964, the merging of folk and rock music in the work of singers Bob Dylan and Joan Baez, the rekindling of blues traditions in American rock, and the growth of FM radio all made rock music a steady accompaniment in young people's lives in the 1960s. As America became involved in the Vietnam War, many rock and folk musicians began to pen songs that offered their protest of the war.

Arguably the best-known and most pointed of all the antiwar songs of the 1960s and early 1970s was the "I-Feel-Like-I'm-Fixin'-to-Die Rag," first released in 1967 by a band called Country Joe and the Fish. Country Joe was Joe McDonald (1942–), a singer-songwriter who had made a career singing folk songs in the San Francisco, California, area. The song made it to Number 32 on the Billboard Charts (a listing of the most popular songs played on the radio). Other popular antiwar songs of the era were: "Turn, Turn, Turn," by The Byrds; "Where Have All the Flowers Gone," by Peter, Paul, and Mary; "Eve of Destruction," by Barry McGuire; "Ohio," by Crosby, Stills, Nash, and Young; and "Masters of War" and "Blowin' in the Wind," by Bob Dylan.

"I-Feel-Like-I'm-Fixin'-to-Die Rag" (music and lyrics by Joe McDonald)

Come on all of you big strong men,
Uncle Sam needs your help again.
He's got himself in a terrible jam
Way down yonder in Vietnam
So put down your books and pick up a gun,
We're gonna have a whole lotta fun.

Chorus:

And it's one, two, three,
What are we fighting for?
Don't ask me, I don't give a damn,
Next stop is Vietnam;
And it's five, six, seven,
Open up the pearly gates,
Well there ain't no time to wonder why,
Whoopee! we're all gonna die.

Come on generals, let's move fast;
Your big chance has come at last.
Gotta go out and get those reds—
The only good commie is the one that's dead
You know that peace can only be won
When we've blown'em all to kingdom come.

[Chorus]

Come on Wall Street, don't move slow,
Why man, this is war a-go-go.
There's plenty good money to be made
Supplying the Army with the tools of the trade,
Just hope and pray that if they drop the bomb,
They drop it on the Vietcong.

[Chorus]

Come on mothers throughout the land,
Pack your boys off to Vietnam.
Come on fathers, don't hesitate,
Send your sons off before it's too late.
You can be the first one on your block
To have your boy come home in a box.

to do with the war, particularly with this foreign presence of the United States of America, to leave them alone in peace, and they practiced the art of survival by siding with whichever military force was present at a particular time, be it Vietcong, North Vietnamese or American.

We found also that all too often American men were dying in those rice paddies for want of support from their allies. We saw first hand how monies from American taxes were used for a **corrupt dictatorial regime.** We saw that many people in this country had a one-sided idea of who was kept free by the flag, and blacks provided the highest percentage of casualties. We saw Vietnam ravaged equally by American bombs and **search and destroy missions,** as well as by Vietcong terrorism—and yet we listened while this country tried to blame all of the havoc on the Vietcong.

We **rationalized** destroying villages in order to save them. We saw America lose her sense of morality as she accepted very coolly a **My Lai** and refused to give up the image of American soldiers who hand out chocolate bars and chewing gum.

A U.S. soldier dumps out perfectly good rice while raiding a Vietnamese village on a search and destroy mission.
National Archives.

Corrupt dictatorial regime: Kerry is referring to the government of South Vietnam.

Search and destroy missions: Military missions in which soldiers were sent out to find and kill any enemies they encountered, and/or raid and destroy the villages.

Rationalized: Provided rational reasons for actions that were questionable on moral grounds.

My Lai: The site of a U.S. massacre of innocent civilians that came to stand as a symbol of military excesses in Vietnam.

Free fire zones: Areas in which soldiers shot anything that moved.

Orientals: A term formerly used to refer to people from Asia, now little used.

Falsification of body counts: Kerry is referring to the Army's practice of exaggerating the number of enemy soldiers killed, to justify a battle.

Platoon: A unit of soldiers, usually consisting of two squads.

Hamburger Hills and Khe Sanhs and Hill 81s and Fire Base 6s: Names of Vietnam War battles that are notorious for the loss of American lives and poor leadership by American generals.

Vietnamizing: Vietnamization was the term that President Nixon used to describe his policy of turning over responsibility for conducting the war to the Vietnamese, while withdrawing U.S. troops.

Washes her hands: Kerry is using a metaphor to describe the way the United States was abandoning its early commitment to defend South Vietnam.

McNamara, Rostow, Bundy, Gilpatrick: American military planners Robert McNamara (1916–), Walt Rostow (1916–2003), McGeorge Bundy (1919–1996), and Roswell Gilpatrick (1906–).

*We learned the meaning of **free fire zones**, shooting anything that moves, and we watched while America placed a cheapness on the lives of **orientals** .*

*We watched the United States **falsification of body counts**, in fact the glorification of body counts. We listened while month after month we were told the back of the enemy was about to break. We fought using weapons against "oriental human beings." We fought using weapons against those people which I do not believe this country would dream of using were we fighting in the European theater. We watched while men charged up hills because a general said that hill has to be taken, and after losing one **platoon** or two platoons they marched away to leave the hill for reoccupation by the North Vietnamese. We watched pride allow the most unimportant battles to be blown into extravaganzas, because we couldn't lose, and we couldn't retreat, and because it didn't matter how many American bodies were lost to prove that point, and so there were **Hamburger Hills and Khe Sanhs and Hill 81s and Fire Base 6s**, and so many others.*

*Now we are told that the men who fought there must watch quietly while American lives are lost so that we can exercise the incredible arrogance of **Vietnamizing** the Vietnamese.*

*Each day to facilitate the process by which the United States **washes her hands** of Vietnam someone has to give up his life so that the United States doesn't have to admit something that the entire world already knows, so that we can't say that we have made a mistake. Someone has to die so that President Nixon won't be, and these are his words, "the first President to lose a war."*

We are asking Americans to think about that because how do you ask a man to be the last man to die in Vietnam? How do you ask a man to be the last man to die for a mistake?....

*We are here to ask, and we are here to ask vehemently, where are the leaders of our country? Where is the leadership? We're here to ask where are **McNamara, Rostow, Bundy, Gilpatrick**, and so many others? Where are they now that we, the men they sent off to war, have returned? These are the commanders who have deserted their troops. And there is no more serious crime in the laws of war. The Army says they never leave their wounded. The marines say they never even leave their dead. These men have left all the casualties and retreated behind a pious shield of public rectitude. They've left the real stuff of their reputations bleaching behind them in the sun in this country....*

We wish that a merciful God could wipe away our own memories of that service as easily as this administration has wiped away their memories of us. But all that they have done and all that they can do by this denial is to make more clear than ever our own determination to undertake one last mission—to search out and destroy the last vestige of this barbaric war, to pacify our own hearts, to conquer the hate and fear that have driven this country these last ten years and more. And more. And so when thirty years from now our brothers go down the street without a leg, without an arm, or a face, and small boys ask why, we will be able to say "Vietnam" and not mean a desert, not a filthy obscene memory, but mean instead where America **finally turned** and where soldiers like us helped it in the turning.

Vietnam Veterans Against the War (VVAW) members gather near the Peace Monument in Washington, D.C., to protest American involvement in Vietnam, December 1971. © Bettmann/Corbis. Reproduced by permission.

Finally turned: Kerry is referring to his hope that the United States will change its policies to better reflect its ideals of freedom and democracy.

What happened next...

The VVAW was at its peak of influence in 1971 and 1972. It had grown from eight thousand to fifty thousand members during that period, and many of its actions attracted national media attention. In December 1971 VVAW members occupied the Betsy Ross House in Philadelphia and the Statue of Liberty in New York to protest the bombing of North Vietnam. In the summer of 1972, they demonstrated at the Republican National Convention in Miami. The group peaked at the very time that the antiwar movement as a whole had attained its greatest influence. Protests, rallies, and demonstrations by a variety of groups convinced American politicians that the American public no longer supported the war.

The VVAW's influence declined after 1972, but its most notable spokesman, John Kerry, went on to enjoy a distinguished political career. He was elected lieutenant governor of Massachusetts in 1982 and won a seat in the United States Senate in 1984. Kerry served in the Senate from 1984 into the early 2000s and was, as of mid-2004, the Democratic presidential nominee. In his 2004 campaign, Kerry pointed proudly to both his illustrious war record and his statements in 1971 as the co-founder of the VVAW.

Did you know...

- The withdrawal of American troops from Vietnam began slowly then picked up pace as American politicians looked for a way out. Troop levels declined from a high of 536,100 troops in 1968 to 450,200 in 1969; 334,600 in 1970; 156,800 in 1971; 24,200 in 1972; 50 in 1973 and 1974, and finally zero in 1975.

- As troop numbers declined in the late 1960s and early 1970s, the United States waged war from the air, with massive bombing campaigns. By war's end the United States had dropped over seven million tons of bombs— five million more than it had dropped during all of World War II—and had destroyed nearly every important target in North Vietnam.

- The last Americans evacuated the capital of South Vietnam on April 30, 1975. North and South Vietnam were soon reunited to form the Socialist Republic of Vietnam, and all relations with the United States were severed until 1995.

Consider the following...

• The participation of war veterans in antiwar protests caused great controversy in the United States. Do you think soldiers have the right to criticize the actions of their government?

• John Kerry raised the question of whether there are limits to the actions that soldiers should be asked to carry out to wage war. Are there just and unjust actions in war? Or does being at war remove all rules of conduct? Explain how military leaders should explain these issues to soldiers preparing to go into battle.

• The antiwar movement in the 1960s raised the issue of whether public opinion should influence a president's decisions relating to the waging of war. Is public opinion a legitimate factor for a president to consider when making decisions about war? Do some citizens' opinions—such as those of veterans—carry more weight than others? Explain your position.

For More Information

Books

Bloom, Alexander, and Wini Breines, eds. *"Takin' It to the Streets": A Sixties Reader.* New York: Oxford University Press, 2003.

Dolan, Edward F. *America after Vietnam: Legacies of a Hated War.* New York: F. Watts, 1989.

Farber, David. *The Age of Great Dreams: America in the 1960s.* New York: Hill and Wang, 1994.

Hunt, Andrew. *The Turning: A History of Vietnam Veterans Against the War.* New York: New York University Press, 1999.

Nicosia, Gerald. *Home to War: A History of the Vietnam Veterans' Movement.* New York: Crown, 2001.

Stacewicz, Richard. *Winter Soldiers: An Oral History of the Vietnam Veterans Against the War.* New York: Twayne, 1997.

Wormser, Richard. *Three Faces of Vietnam.* New York: F. Watts, 1993.

Wright, David K. *Causes and Consequences of the Vietnam War.* Austin, TX: Raintree Steck-Vaughn, 1996.

Web sites

Battlefield: Vietnam. www.pbs.org/battlefieldvietnam/index.html (accessed on August 1, 2004).

"Sixties Project: Primary Document Archive," *The Sixties Project.* http://lists.village.virginia.edu/sixties/HTML_docs/Resources/Primary.html (accessed on August 1, 2004).

Vietnam Online. www.pbs.org/wgbh/amex/vietnam/whos/index.html (accessed on August 1, 2004).

Vietnam Veterans Against the War. www.vvaw.org (accessed on August 2, 2004).

"The Times They Are a Changin'": Radicals on the Left and Right

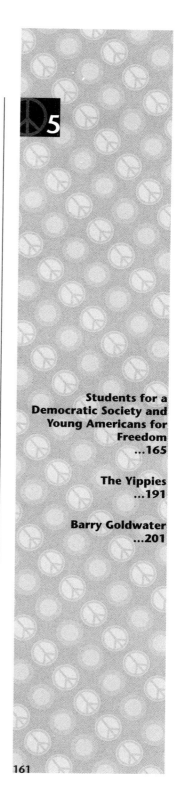

The United States in the 1960s was an immensely powerful and wealthy country. The dominant world power at the end of World War II (1939–45), the United States had developed the strongest military in the world during the 1950s. The military buildup was a product of the Cold War (1945–91), a long-simmering conflict between the United States and the Soviet Union that prompted both countries to maintain large armies and develop powerful arsenals of weapons. The United States was also the world's economic giant. Well-off in the 1950s, the nation became even more prosperous in the 1960s. For example, the country experienced economic growth during every month between 1961 and 1969. This American affluence was widespread, bringing such goods as televisions, automobiles, and electric appliances within reach of a large segment of the American population.

Yet all this wealth and power did not necessarily mean that the United States was at peace with itself. Indeed, in the 1960s Americans confronted a number of issues that had simmered beneath the surface of American social and political life since well before the Great Depression (1929–41)

Students for a Democratic Society and Young Americans for Freedom ...165

The Yippies ...191

Barry Goldwater ...201
Students for a Democratic Society and Young Americans for Freedom ...165

The Yippies ...191

Barry Goldwater ...201

and World War II. The widespread denial of civil rights to African Americans in the South, women's unequal access to jobs and educational opportunities, and the wide gulf between the rich and poor were just a few of the pressing issues that drew national attention in the 1960s. In a speech that he gave at the University of Michigan in April of 1964, President Lyndon Johnson (1908–1973; served 1963–69) wondered whether the nation had the "wisdom to use...[its] wealth to enrich and elevate our national life, and to advance the equality of our American civilization." In fact, many Americans were unwilling to wait for government leaders to gain the wisdom to elevate national life. They joined together, in movements large and small, to push for social change. Their efforts gave the 1960s much of its distinct character.

The calls for social and political change in the 1960s came from both the "left" and the "right," terms used by political scientists to describe political positions as they compare to a theoretically neutral and balanced "center." In the United States, in the early 2000s and in the 1960s, the center was defined by the political practices of the two mainstream parties, the Democrats and the Republicans. Although these two parties had different political programs that they favored, they both agreed that social change should come about slowly and in small increments, as government adjusted to the peaceful demands of its citizens. This basic agreement was known as the "liberal consensus" or just "liberalism."

By the early 1960s, this liberal consensus faced pressures from both sides. Those on the left, as it is known, were growing impatient with the slow pace of change allowed by American liberalism. They wanted more dramatic or radical changes, and they wanted them to happen quickly. For example, those on the left wanted segregation by race ended in the South right away, and they believed that African Americans and women should be granted equal rights enjoyed by white American men. They also called for an end to the war in Vietnam (1954–75). Those on the right, known as conservatives, felt that the government was already allowing social change to move too quickly and had caved in to demands from the left. They were uncomfortable with the role that government played in changing race and gender relations. They also wanted to commit the United States to an all-out war on communism (the system of government characterized by state-owned property and authority imposed from the top, and followed by the Soviet Union, America's enemy in the Cold War [1945–91]).

The demands from the left and the right were, in fact, far more complicated than just wanting change to go faster or slower. The best way to understand the complexity of the changes being demanded in the 1960s is to read some of the most important documents created by "radicals" on the left and right. This chapter presents four documents advocating political change. The first two—the Port Huron Statement, issued by the **Students for a Democratic Society** (SDS) in 1962, and the Sharon Statement, issued by a conservative group called **Young Americans for Freedom** (YAF) in 1960—were the expressions of young idealists, college students who dreamed of a better world than the one currently ruled by their parents. The chapter also presents the Yippie Manifesto, a flyer issued by a loosely organized group called **the Yippies** just before the presidential election in 1968. The Yippies were one of the most extreme variations of left political protest, and their proposals border on the absurd. Finally, presented here is a speech given in 1964 by Republican presidential candidate **Barry Goldwater** (1909–1998). Goldwater was supported by the YAF, but many Americans were scared by his political extremism.

Students for a Democratic Society and Young Americans for Freedom

Excerpt from "The Port Huron Statement," 1962

Originally published as *The Port Huron Statement*, New York, 1964. Reprinted from *"Takin' It to the Streets:" A Sixties Reader*, 2003. Also available online at *The Sixties Project: Primary Document Archive*, http://lists.village.virginia.edu/sixties/HTML_docs/Resources/ Primary/Manifestos/SDS_Port_Huron.html.

Complete text of "The Sharon Statement," 1960

Originally published in *National Review*, September 24, 1960, pp. 172-173. Reprinted from *"Takin' It to the Streets:" A Sixties Reader*, 2003. Also available online at www.yaf.com/sharon.html.

College students had never played a very large role in American politics before the 1960s. First, there were not many of them: only two million people were enrolled in American colleges in 1950. Second, most were not old enough to vote: until 1971, the voting age in federal elections was set at twenty-one. Beginning in the late 1950s and early 1960s, however, college students began to play a larger role in politics. College enrollments surged, reaching seven million by 1968. And though most still could not vote, college students became increasingly active in advocating for social change.

There were a variety of reasons that college students became more interested and engaged in politics in the late 1950s and early 1960s. There was, in this period, a real emphasis in the United States on the importance of higher education as a means of preparing the nation to compete in the world economy. College students were told again and again how important they were to the nation's future, and they became more interested in the role that they would play in that future. Second, the greatest social movement of the 1960s—

"We are people of this generation, bred in at least modest comfort, housed now in universities, looking uncomfortably to the world we inherit."

Students in the 1960s became increasingly active in advocating for social change. Here, New York City plainclothes police officers drop a student protestor on the ground after he and others holding a sit-in at a Columbia University building were removed, April 30, 1968. *AP/Wide World Photos. Reproduced by permission.*

the civil rights movement—showed what could happen when people worked together to support a cause that they believed in. Idealistic young people were strong supporters of the civil rights movement, and they applied the lessons they learned from that movement to their own experience.

The experience of college students in the late 1950s and early 1960s was very different than it was in the early 2000s. Many universities had strict dress codes and rules that determined all kinds of aspects of students' lives, as for example when lights were turned off in dorms. Male students were required to serve two years in the Reserve Officers Training Corps (ROTC) at most state universities. Committees of adults had the right to control the content of student publications. For the first time, universities began to assign students identification numbers to help keep track of them. Students on both the left and right resisted these restrictions. They argued that, as adults, they had the right to independence and were responsible for their own behavior.

These experiences, along with many other influences, led many college students to participate actively in politics. Two of the most influential groups of the period were the Students for a Democratic Society (SDS) and the Young Americans for Freedom (YAF).

Students for a Democratic Society

In 1960, the Students for a Democratic Society was a tiny group of some three hundred college students with no influence. Within a few years, the group became one of the most important voices for change in the United States and its events would draw many thousands of participants. SDS emerged from a group known as the Student League for Industrial Democracy, which had sponsored discussion groups on college campuses. Energized by the civil rights sit-ins of the late 1950s and by the writings of leftist intellectuals like C. Wright Mills and Herbert Marcuse, a number of students at the University of Michigan and several other universities began to talk about increasing the activities of the SDS. In June of 1962 the group held a national convention in Port Huron, Michigan. Following several days of discussing civil rights, nuclear disarmament (a call for nations to stop their production and stockpiling of nuclear weapons and begin reducing the number of them), and political participation, the SDS issued the "Port Huron Statement," a lengthy declaration of political principles primarily authored by University of Michigan student Tom Hayden (1939–).

The "Port Huron Statement" nearly single-handedly created a political movement known as the New Left. This group was called the New Left because its members rejected many of the political principles of the Old Left, the term given to those who had embraced communism and socialism in the 1920s and 1930s. Though the New Left platform was never spelled out precisely, it was founded on the idea of participatory democracy, the idea that if the majority of people actively supported the issues that were important to them, then the federal government would become more responsive to these issues, such as the needs of working-class, antiwar voters.

The "Port Huron Statement" was issued by a student group, but many people outside of universities identified

The University of Michigan chapter of Students for a Democratic Society march through Ann Arbor, Michigan, calling for a student strike to protest the Vietnam War, November 1968. © Bettmann/Corbis. Reproduced by permission.

with the issues it raised. The SDS became a major force in American politics by the mid-1960s, especially when it made opposition to the Vietnam War (1954–75) a major part of its activities. But at the time the "Port Huron Statement" was issued, the SDS was still a quite new organization searching for a purpose.

Young Americans for Freedom

The Young Americans for Freedom (YAF) came into being in September of 1960, when some ninety students from forty-four colleges in twenty-four states gathered at the Sharon, Connecticut, estate of conservative spokesman William F. Buckley Jr. (1925–). They elected Douglas Caddy (1938–) as their national director and admitted members between the ages of eighteen and thirty-five. More important, they set about to define a set of principles that could guide a still-fledgling (new or inexperienced) conservative political movement. That set of principles became known as the "Sharon Statement."

Like the SDS, the Young Americans for Freedom formed as a way of announcing its members' opposition to the values of an earlier generation. Before 1960, American conservatism had not been well defined. American conservatives had been primarily concerned with generating profits for business and keeping the government from exercising too much control over the free exercise of businesses. YAF members believed that American conservatism could be much more. In the words of William F. Buckley Jr., writing to the subscribers of the *National Review* in 1960, as quoted in *Conservatism in America since 1930,* the YAF would go well beyond the idea that "conservatism was merely a highbrow word for the profit system": it would offer a statement that covered "the moral aspect of freedom; of transcendent values; of the nature of man. All this together with a tough-as-nails statement of political and economic convictions...."

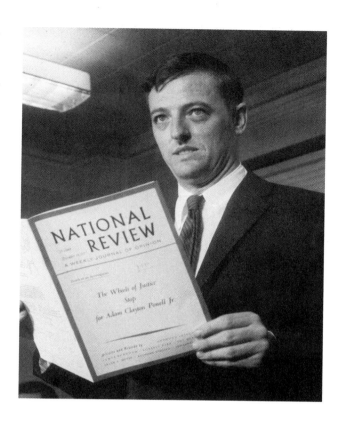

William F. Buckley Jr., a founding member of the Young Americans for Freedom, pictured in 1958.
© *Bettmann/Corbis. Reproduced by permission.*

Like the "Port Huron Statement," the "Sharon Statement" was a call to action, and it spurred the creation of a substantial conservative political movement in the United States. The YAF soon published its own magazine, called *New Guard,* and it backed a political candidate, Barry Goldwater (1909–1998), who would go on to win the Republican presidential nomination in 1964.

Things to remember while reading the excerpt of the "Port Huron Statement" and the "Sharon Statement":

- Political organizing in the 1960s was quite a bit different than it was in the early 2000s, when the Internet allowed documents to be made instantaneously available to people all over the country. Both the "Port Huron Statement" and the "Sharon Statement" were likely photocopied and circulated among close followers of the new movements, then reproduced in magazines that did not reach subscribers until days or weeks later.

- Beginning in 1957, professors in universities who received grants from the federal government were forced to sign an oath of loyalty to the U.S. government. This oath became a source of controversy on college campuses. Students who supported the oath found that they had much in common, and many joined to help found YAF. Students who protested the oath also discovered shared political leanings, and many of them later joined SDS.

- Tom Hayden was the primary author of the "Port Huron Statement," but he received input from the many participants at the SDS conference in Port Huron.

- College enrollment in 1960 was 3,216,000; by 1970, enrollment had more than doubled, to 7,136,000.

- SDS is seen by many as the founding organization of the New Left, and many view YAF as the founder of the New Right.

Excerpt of "The Port Huron Statement"

Introduction: Agenda for a Generation

We are people of this generation, bred in at least modest comfort, housed now in universities, looking uncomfortably to the world we inherit.

*When we were kids the United States was the wealthiest and strongest country in the world; the only one with the atom bomb, the least scarred by modern war, an initiator of the United Nations that we thought would distribute Western influence throughout the world. Freedom and equality for each individual, government of, by, and for the people—these American values we found good, principles by which we could live as men. Many of us began maturing in **complacency**.*

Complacency: Self-satisfaction combined with an unawareness of actual dangers or deficiencies.

Southern struggle against racial bigotry: This phrase is a reference to the civil rights movement.

Cold War: The long conflict for world supremacy between the United States and the Soviet Union.

Bomb: The Bomb is a generic term referring to nuclear weapons held by the U.S. and Russia in the Cold War.

Rankled: Irritated.

Paradoxes: Things that are opposed to common sense or opinion, yet true.

Status quo: A Latin phrase meaning the existing state of affairs.

Incurred: Brought upon.

Superfluous: Excess; beyond what is needed.

As we grew, however, our comfort was penetrated by events too troubling to dismiss. First, the permeating and victimizing fact of human degradation, symbolized by the **Southern struggle against racial bigotry**, compelled most of us from silence to activism. Second, the enclosing fact of the **Cold War**, symbolized by the presence of the **Bomb**, brought awareness that we ourselves, and our friends, and millions of abstract "others" we knew more directly because of our common peril, might die at any time. We might deliberately ignore, or avoid, or fail to feel all other human problems, but not these two, for these were too immediate and crushing in their impact, too challenging in the demand that we as individuals take the responsibility for encounter and resolution.

While these and other problems either directly oppressed us or **rankled** our consciences and became our own subjective concerns, we began to see complicated and disturbing **paradoxes** in our surrounding America. The declaration "all men are created equal..." rang hollow before the facts of Negro life in the South and the big cities of the North. The proclaimed peaceful intentions of the United States contradicted its economic and military investments in the Cold War **status quo**.

We witnessed, and continue to witness, other paradoxes. With nuclear energy whole cities can easily be powered, yet the dominant nation-states seem more likely to unleash destruction greater than that **incurred** in all wars of human history. Although our own technology is destroying old and creating new forms of social organization, men still tolerate meaningless work and idleness. While two-thirds of mankind suffers under nourishment, our own upper classes revel amidst **superfluous** abundance. Although world population is expected to double in forty years, the nations still tolerate **anarchy** as a major principle of international conduct and uncontrolled **exploitation** governs the sapping of the earth's physical resources. Although mankind desperately needs revolutionary leadership, America rests in national **stalemate**, its goals ambiguous and tradition-bound instead

Tom Hayden was the primary author of the "Port Huron Statement." *AP/Wide World Photos. Reproduced by permission.*

Anarchy: The absence of government or other established order.

Exploitation: Use without regard for consequences.

Stalemate: The position in a contest in which no movement is possible.

Apathetic: Showing little or no feeling or emotion.

Hypocrisy: The false appearance of virtue, or the contradiction between what one does and what one says.

American Golden Age: The 1950s were often referred to as a golden age, for the United States had won a war and returned to economic prosperity.

Colonialism and imperialism: Systems by which powerful countries exert control and influence over less powerful colonies or independent countries.

Entrenchment of totalitarian states: This phrase refers to the establishment of nations where autocratic leaders exert complete control, for example the Soviet Union.

Tenacity: Persistence.

Equilibriums: States of balance.

Imbued: Permeated or filled with.

Viable: Capable of working.

Utopias: Places of perfection, especially in law or government.

Chaos: A state of utter confusion or disarray.

Dissipate: To break up or scatter.

Expectancies: Hopes or expectations.

of informed and clear, its democratic system **apathetic** and manipulated rather than "of, by, and for the people."

Not only did tarnish appear on our image of American virtue, not only did disillusion occur when the **hypocrisy** of American ideals was discovered, but we began to sense that what we had originally seen as the **American Golden Age** was actually the decline of an era. The worldwide outbreak of revolution against **colonialism and imperialism**, the **entrenchment of totalitarian states**, the menace of war, overpopulation, international disorder, supertechnology—these trends were testing the **tenacity** of our own commitment to democracy and freedom and our abilities to visualize their application to a world in upheaval.

Our work is guided by the sense that we may be the last generation in the experiment with living. But we are a minority—the vast majority of our people regard the temporary **equilibriums** of our society and world as eternally functional parts. In this is perhaps the outstanding paradox; we ourselves are **imbued** with urgency, yet the message of our society is that there is no **viable** alternative to the present. Beneath the reassuring tones of the politicians, beneath the common opinion that America will "muddle through," beneath the stagnation of those who have closed their minds to the future, is the pervading feeling that there simply are no alternatives, that our times have witnessed the exhaustion not only of **Utopias**, but of any new departures as well. Feeling the press of complexity upon the emptiness of life, people are fearful of the thought that at any moment things might be thrust out of control. They fear change itself, since change might smash whatever invisible framework seems to hold back **chaos** for them now. For most Americans, all crusades are suspect, threatening. The fact that each individual sees apathy in his fellows perpetuates the common reluctance to organize for change. The dominant institutions are complex enough to blunt the minds of their potential critics, and entrenched enough to swiftly **dissipate** or entirely repel the energies of protest and reform, thus limiting human **expectancies**. Then, too, we are a materially improved society, and by our own improvements we seem to have weakened the case for further change.

Some would have us believe that Americans feel contentment amidst prosperity—but might it not better be called a glaze above deeply felt anxieties about their role in the new world? And if these anxieties produce a developed indifference to human affairs, do they not as well produce a yearning to believe that there is an alternative to the present, that something can be done to change circum-stances in the school, the workplaces, the **bureaucracies**, the gov-ernment? It is to this latter yearning, at once the spark and engine of change, that we direct our present appeal. The search for truly democratic alternatives to the present, and a commitment to social experimentation with them, is a worthy and fulfilling human enter-prise, one which moves us and, we hope, others today. On such a basis do we offer this document of our convictions and analysis: as an effort in understanding and changing the conditions of humani-ty in the late twentieth century, an effort rooted in the ancient, still unfulfilled conception of man attaining determining influence over his circumstances of life.

Values

[In the following section, the SDS clarifies its relationship to past "left" movements.]

We regard men *as infinitely precious and possessed of unful-filled capacities for reason, freedom, and love. In affirming these principles we are aware of countering perhaps the dominant con-ceptions of man in the twentieth century: that he is a thing to be manipulated, and that he is inherently incapable of directing his own affairs. We oppose the* **depersonalization** *that reduces human beings to the status of things—if anything, the brutalities of the twentieth century teach that means and ends are intimately relat-ed, that vague appeals to* **"posterity"** *cannot justify the mutilations of the present. We oppose, too, the doctrine of human incompe-tence because it rests essentially on the modern fact that men have been "competently" manipulated into incompetence—we see little reason why men cannot meet with increasing skill the complexities and responsibilities of their situation, if society is organized not for minority, but for majority, participation in decision-making.*

Men have unrealized potential for self-cultivation, self-direction, self-understanding, and creativity. It is this potential that we regard as crucial and to which we appeal, not to the human potentiality for violence, unreason, and submission to authority. The goal of man and society should be human independence: a concern not with image or popularity but with finding a meaning in life that is per-sonally **authentic**; *a quality of mind not compulsively driven by a sense of powerlessness, nor one which unthinkingly adopts* **status values**, *nor one which* **represses** *all threats to its habits, but one which has full, spontaneous access to present and past experiences,*

Bureaucracies: Large, spe-cialized organizations such as corporations or government agencies.

Depersonalization: The loss of a sense of human identity.

Posterity: Future genera-tions.

Authentic: True to one's spir-it or character. The idea of being authentic was crucial to many young people in the 1960s, who saw their parents as inauthentic.

Status values: Values that are adopted to gain status, or perceived rank, in society.

Represses: Shuts out.

one which easily unites the fragmented parts of personal history, one which openly faces problems which are troubling and unresolved; one with an intuitive awareness of possibilities, an active sense of curiosity, an ability and willingness to learn.

*This kind of independence does not mean **egotistic** individualism—the object is not to have one's way so much as it is to have a way that is one's own. Nor do we **deify** man—we merely have faith in his potential.*

Human relationships should involve fraternity and honesty. Human interdependence is contemporary fact; human brotherhood must be willed, however, as a condition of future survival and as the most appropriate form of social relations. Personal links between man and man are needed, especially to go beyond the partial and fragmentary bonds of function that bind men only as worker to worker, employer to employee, teacher to student, American to Russian.

*Loneliness, **estrangement**, isolation describe the vast distance between man and man today. These dominant tendencies cannot be overcome by better personnel management, nor by improved gadgets, but only when a love of man overcomes the **idolatrous worship of things** by man. As the individualism we affirm is not egoism, the selflessness we affirm is not **self-elimination**. On the contrary, we believe in generosity of a kind that imprints one's unique individual qualities in the relation to other men, and to all human activity. Further, to dislike isolation is not to favor the abolition of privacy; the latter differs from isolation in that it occurs or is abolished according to individual will.*

*We would replace power rooted in possession, privilege, or circumstance by power and uniqueness rooted in love, **reflectiveness**, reason, and creativity. As a social system we seek the establishment of a democracy of individual participation, governed by two central aims: that the individual share in those social decisions determining the quality and direction of his life; that society be organized to encourage independence in men and provide the media for their common participation.*

In a participatory democracy, the political life would be based in several root principles:

> *that decision-making of basic social consequence be carried on by public groupings;*

> *that politics be seen positively, as the art of collectively creating an acceptable pattern of social relations;*

Egotistic: With an exaggerated sense of self-importance.

Deify: Make godlike or divine.

Estrangement: The removal from customary feelings of love or affection.

Idolatrous worship of things: The love of material goods above human values.

Self-elimination: The removal of concern for the individual.

Reflectiveness: Self-examination.

that politics has the function of bringing people out of isolation and into community, thus being a necessary, though not sufficient, means of finding meaning in personal life;

that the political order should serve to clarify problems in a way instrumental to their solution; it should provide outlets for the expression of personal grievance and aspiration; opposing views should be organized so as to illuminate choices and facilitate the attainment of goals; channels should be commonly available to relate men to knowledge and to power so that private problems—from bad recreation facilities to personal alienation—are formulated as general issues.

The economic sphere would have as its basis the principles:

that work should involve incentives worthier than money or survival. It should be educative, not stultifying; creative, not mechanical; self-directed, not manipulated, encouraging independence, a respect for others, a sense of dignity, and a willingness to accept social responsibility, since it is this experience that has crucial influence on habits, perceptions and individual ethics;

that the economic experience is so personally decisive that the individual must share in its full determination;

that the economy itself is of such social importance that its major resources and means of production should be open to democratic participation and subject to democratic social regulation.

*Like the political and economic ones, major social institutions— cultural, educational, **rehabilitative**, and others—should be generally organized with the well-being and dignity of man as the essential measure of success.*

*In social change or interchange, we find violence to be abhorrent because it requires generally **the transformation of the target, be it a human being or a community of people, into a depersonalized object of hate**. It is imperative that the means of violence be abolished and the institutions—local, national, international—that encourage non-violence as a condition of conflict be developed.*

*These are our central values, in **skeletal form**. It remains vital to understand their denial or attainment in the context of the modern world.*

The Students

In the last few years, thousands of American students demonstrated that they at least felt the urgency of the times. They moved actively and directly against racial injustices, the threat of war, violations of individual rights of conscience, and, less frequently, against economic manipulation. They succeeded in restoring a small

Rehabilitative: This is a reference to institutions designed to rehabilitate people, or bring them back into normal society, for example prisons or mental institutions.

The transformation of the target...into a depersonalized object of hate: This phrase refers to the way that organized violence encourages people to think of their enemies as less than fully human. For example, soldiers in war often refer to the enemy in negative, nonhuman terms.

Skeletal form: Outline or basic structure.

A scene from the Students for a Democratic Society-sponsored 1968 anti-Vietnam War protest in Des Moines, Iowa.
© Bettmann/Corbis. Reproduced by permission.

McCarthy period: A period in the 1950s, associated with Wisconsin senator Joseph McCarthy, during which many who were involved with communist causes were forced out of public life and many types of work.

Inner emigration: Self-exploration.

Twist: A dance then popular among college students.

measure of controversy to the campuses after the stillness of the **McCarthy period.** *They succeeded, too, in gaining some concessions from the people and institutions they opposed, especially in the fight against racial bigotry.*

The significance of these scattered movements lies not in their success or failure in gaining objectives—at least, not yet. Nor does the significance lie in the intellectual "competence" or "maturity" of the students involved—as some pedantic elders allege. The significance is in the fact that students are breaking the crust of apathy and overcoming the inner alienation that remain the defining characteristics of American college life.

If student movements for change are still rarities on the campus scene, what is commonplace there? The real campus, the familiar campus, is a place of private people, engaged in their notorious **"inner emigration."** *It is a place of commitment to business-as-usual, getting ahead, playing it cool. It is a place of mass affirmation of the* **Twist,** *but mass reluctance toward the controversial pub-*

lic stance. Rules are accepted as "inevitable," bureaucracy as "just circumstances," irrelevance as "scholarship," selflessness as "martyrdom," politics as "just another way to make people, and an unprofitable one, too."

Almost no students value activity as citizens. Passive in public, they are hardly more idealistic in arranging their private lives: **Gallup** concludes they will settle for "low success, and won't risk high failure." There is not much willingness to take risks (not even in business), no setting of dangerous goals, no real conception of personal identity except one manufactured in the image of others, no real urge for personal fulfillment except to be almost as successful as the very successful people. Attention is being paid to social status (the quality of shirt collars, meeting people, getting wives or husbands, making solid contacts for later on); much, too, is paid to academic status (grades, honors, the med school rat race). But neglected generally is real intellectual status, the personal cultivation of the mind.

"Students don't even give a damn about the apathy," one has said. Apathy toward apathy begets a privately constructed universe, a place of systematic study schedules, two nights each week for beer, a girl or two, and early marriage; a framework infused with personality, warmth, and under control, no matter how unsatisfying otherwise.

Under these conditions university life loses all relevance to some. Four hundred thousand of our classmates leave college every year.

But apathy is not simply an attitude; it is a product of social institutions, and of the structure and organization of higher education itself. The extracurricular life is ordered according to **in loco parentis** theory, which ratifies the Administration as the moral guardian of the young.

The accompanying "let's pretend" theory of student extracurricular affairs validates student government as a training center for those who want to live their lives in political pretense, and discourages initiative from the more articulate, honest, and sensitive students. The bounds and style of controversy are delimited before controversy begins. The university "prepares" the student for "citizenship" through perpetual rehearsals and, usually, through **emasculation** of what creative spirit there is in the individual.

The academic life contains reinforcing counterparts to the way in which extracurricular life is organized. The academic world is founded on a teacher-student relation analogous to the parent-child

Gallup: An organization that conducts polls or surveys to assess public opinion.

In loco parentis: A Latin term meaning "in the place of the parent."

Emasculation: Depriving of strength or spirit.

relation which characterizes in loco parentis. *Further, academia includes a radical separation of the student from the material of study. That which is studied, the social reality, is "**objectified**" to sterility, dividing the student from life—just as he is restrained in active involvement by the deans controlling student government. The specialization of function and knowledge, admittedly necessary to our complex technological and social structure, has produced an exaggerated **compartmentalization** of study and understanding. This has contributed to an overly **parochial** view, by faculty, of the role of its research and scholarship; to a discontinuous and **truncated** understanding, by students, of the surrounding social order; and to a loss of personal attachment, by nearly all, to the worth of study as a humanistic enterprise.*

[…]

The Society Beyond

*Look beyond the campus, to America itself. That student life is more intellectual, and perhaps more comfortable, does not obscure the fact that the fundamental qualities of life on the campus reflect the habits of society at large. The fraternity president is seen at the junior manager levels; the sorority queen has gone to **Grosse Pointe**; the serious poet burns for a place, any place, to work; the once-serious and never-serious poets work at the advertising agencies. The desperation of people threatened by forces about which they know little and of which they can say less; the cheerful emptiness of people "giving up" all hope of changing things; the faceless ones polled by Gallup who listed "international affairs" fourteenth on their list of "problems" but who also expected thermonuclear war in the next few years; in these and other forms, Americans are in withdrawal from public life, from any collective effort at directing their own affairs.*

*Some regard these national **doldrums** as a sign of healthy approval of the established order—but is it approval by consent or manipulated **acquiescence**? Others declare that the people are withdrawn because compelling issues are fast disappearing—perhaps there are fewer bread lines in America, but is **Jim Crow** gone, is there enough work and work more fulfilling, is world war a diminishing threat, and what of the revolutionary new peoples? Still others think the national quietude is a necessary consequence of the need for elites to resolve complex and specialized problems of modern industrial society—but then, why should business elites help de-*

Objectified: Turned into an object, without emotional value.

Compartmentalization: The separation into compartments, or disconnected areas of study.

Parochial: Narrow or limited in scope.

Truncated: Shortened or cut off.

Grosse Pointe: A wealthy suburb of Detroit, Michigan.

Doldrums: A state of inactivity or slump, in this case in the intellectual life of the nation.

Acquiescence: The act of complying passively.

Jim Crow: The nickname for social policies that limit the rights of African Americans in the South.

cide foreign policy, and who controls the elites anyway, and are they solving mankind's problems? Others, finally, shrug knowingly and announce that full democracy never worked anywhere in the past—but why lump qualitatively different civilizations together, and how can a social order work well if its best thinkers are **skeptics**, and is man really doomed forever to the domination of today?

There are no convincing apologies for the contemporary **malaise**. While the world tumbles toward the final war, while men in other nations are trying desperately to alter events, while the very **future qua future** is uncertain—America is without community impulse, without the inner momentum necessary for an age when societies cannot successfully perpetuate themselves by their military weapons, when democracy must be viable because of its quality of life, not its quantity of rockets.

The apathy here is, first, subjective—the felt powerlessness of ordinary people, the **resignation** before the enormity of events. But subjective apathy is encouraged by the objective American situation—the actual structural separation of people from power, from relevant knowledge, from **pinnacles of decision-making**. Just as the university influences the student way of life, so do major social institutions create the circumstances in which the isolated citizen will try hopelessly to understand his world and himself.

The very isolation of the individual—from power and community and ability to aspire—means the rise of a democracy without publics. With the great mass of people structurally remote and psychologically hesitant with respect to democratic institutions, those institutions themselves **attenuate** and become, in the fashion of the **vicious circle**, progressively less accessible to those few who aspire to serious participation in social affairs. The vital democratic connection between community and leadership, between the mass and the several elites, has been so wrenched and perverted that disastrous policies go unchallenged time and again....

The University and Social Change

There is perhaps little reason to be optimistic about the above analysis. True, the **Dixiecrat-GOP coalition** is the weakest point in the dominating complex of corporate, military, and political power. But the civil rights, peace, and student movements are too poor and socially slighted, and the labor movement too **quiescent**, to be counted with enthusiasm. From where else can power and vision be

Skeptics: Those who systematically criticize and question the existing order.

Malaise: A vague sense of moral despair or disease.

Future qua future: The word "qua" is Latin for "as"; in this case, the author raises the possibility that there will be no future in the future if nuclear weapons end life on earth.

Resignation: The sense that individuals cannot affect the course of events.

Pinnacles of decision-making: Those distant points, such as the presidency, at which important decisions are made.

Attenuate: Diminish in strength or value.

Vicious circle: A chain of events in which any action makes the original situation worse, requiring yet another damaging action.

Dixiecrat-GOP coalition: A political alliance between Southern Democrats and Republicans.

Quiescent: Inactive.

summoned? We believe that the universities are an overlooked seat of influence.

*First, the university is located in a permanent position of social influence. Its educational function makes it indispensable and automatically makes it a crucial institution in the formation of social attitudes. Second, in an unbelievably complicated world, it is the central institution for organizing, evaluating, and transmitting knowledge. Third, the extent to which academic resources presently are used to buttress immoral social practice is revealed, first, by the extent to which defense contracts make the universities engineers of the arms race. Too, the use of modern social science as a manipulative tool reveals itself in the "human relations" consultants to the modern corporations, who introduce trivial **sops** to give laborers feelings of "participation" or "belonging," while actually deluding them in order to further exploit their labor. And, of course, the use of motivational research is already infamous as a manipulative aspect of American politics. But these social uses of the universities' resources also demonstrate the unchangeable reliance by men of power on the men and storehouses of knowledge: this makes the university functionally tied to society in new ways, revealing new potentialities, new levers for change. Fourth, the university is the only mainstream institution that is open to participation by individuals of nearly any viewpoint.*

These, at least, are facts, no matter how dull the teaching, how paternalistic the rules, how irrelevant the research that goes on. Social relevance, the accessibility to knowledge, and internal openness—these together make the university a potential base and agency in a movement of social change.

> 1. *Any new left in America must be, in large measure, a left with real intellectual skills, committed to deliberativeness, honesty, reflection as working tools. The university permits the political life to be an adjunct to the academic one, and action to be informed by reason.*
>
> 2. *A new left must be distributed in significant social roles throughout the country. The universities are distributed in such a manner.*
>
> 3. *A new left must consist of younger people who matured in the postwar world, and partially be directed to the recruitment of younger people. The university is an obvious beginning point.*
>
> 4. *A new left must include liberals and socialists, the former for their relevance, the latter for their sense of thoroughgoing reforms in the system. The university is a more sensible*

Sops: Minor favors given to soften the blow of a negative action.

*place than a political party for these two traditions to begin to discuss their differences and look for **political synthesis**.*

5.   A new left must start controversy across the land, if national policies and national apathy are to be reversed. The ideal university is a community of controversy, within itself and in its effects on communities beyond.

*6.   A new left must transform modern complexity into issues that can be understood and felt close up by every human being. It must give form to the feelings of helplessness and indifference, so that people may see the political, social, and economic sources of their private troubles, and organize to change society. In a time of supposed prosperity, **moral complacency**, and political manipulation, a new left cannot rely on only **aching stomachs** to be the engine force of social reform. The case for change, for alternatives that will involve uncomfortable personal efforts, must be argued as never before. The university is a relevant place for all of these activities.*

But we need not indulge in illusions: the university system cannot complete a movement of ordinary people making demands for a better life. From its schools and colleges across the nation, a militant left might awaken its allies, and by beginning the process towards peace, civil rights, and labor struggles, reinsert theory and idealism where too often reign confusion and political barter. The power of students and faculty united is not only potential; it has shown its actuality in the South, and in the reform movements of the North.

The bridge to political power, though, will be built through genuine cooperation, locally, nationally, and internationally, between a new left of young people and an awakening community of allies. In each community we must look within the university and act with confidence that we can be powerful, but we must look outwards to the less exotic but more lasting struggles for justice.

To turn these mythic possibilities into realities will involve national efforts at university reform by an alliance of students and faculty. They must wrest control of the educational process from the administrative bureaucracy. They must make fraternal and functional contact with allies in labor, civil rights, and other liberal forces outside the campus. They must import major public issues into the **curriculum**—research and teaching on problems of war and peace is an outstanding example. They must make debate and controversy, not dull **pedantic cant**, the common style for educational life. They must consciously build a base for their assault upon the **loci** of power.

Political synthesis: The work of synthesizing or bringing together different political ideas to resolve differences.

Moral complacency: A unwarranted or undeserved satisfaction with one's morals.

Aching stomachs: A metaphor for poor people who might be expected to support social reform.

Curriculum: The course of study in a school.

Pedantic cant: Conventional opinions offered by boring teachers.

Loci: Sources.

As students for a democratic society, we are committed to stimulating this kind of social movement, this kind of vision and program in campus and community across the country. If we appear to seek the unattainable, as it has been said, then let it be known that we do so to avoid the unimaginable.

"The Sharon Statement"

Adopted in Conference, at Sharon, Connecticut, September 1960.

In this time of moral and political crisis, it is the responsibility of the youth of America to affirm certain eternal truths.

We, as young conservatives, believe:

*That foremost among the **transcendent** values is the individual's use of his God-given free will, whence derives his right to be free from the restrictions of **arbitrary** force;*

*That liberty is **indivisible**, and that political freedom cannot long exist without economic freedom;*

That the purposes of government are to protect those freedoms through the preservation of internal order, the provision of national defense, and the administration of justice;

That when government ventures beyond these rightful functions, it accumulates power, which tends to diminish order and liberty;

*That the Constitution of the United States is the best arrangement yet **devised** for empowering government to fulfill its proper role, while restraining it from the concentration and abuse of power;*

*That the genius of the Constitution—the division of powers—is summed up in the clause which reserves **primacy** to the several states, or to the people, in those spheres not specifically delegated to the Federal Government;*

That the market economy, allocating resources by the free play of supply and demand, is the single economic system compatible with the requirements of personal freedom and constitutional government, and that it is at the same time the most productive supplier of human needs;

Transcendent: Of supreme or enduring importance.

Arbitrary: Determined by individual preference, not by general rule or law.

Indivisible: Borrowed from the United States Pledge of Allegiance, this term implies that individuals' liberties must exist together and cannot be divided.

Devised: Created.

Primacy: First priority.

That when government interferes with the work of the market economy, it tends to reduce the moral and physical strength of the nation; that when it takes from one to bestow on another, it diminishes the incentive of the first, the integrity of the second, and the **moral autonomy** *of both.*

That we will be free only so long as the national sovereignty of the United States is secure; that history shows periods of freedom

Moral autonomy: This phrase is meant to indicate the government and the economy should operate independently of each other.

are rare, and can exist only when free citizens concertedly defend their rights against all enemies;

That the forces of international Communism are, at present, the greatest single threat to these liberties;

That the United States should stress victory over, rather than coexistence with, this menace; and

That American foreign policy must be judged by this criterion: does it serve the just interests of the United States?

What happened next...

Both the "Port Huron Statement" and the "Sharon Statement" were seminal documents: they led directly to the flowering of important political movements. Young people across the nation, both in and out of college campuses, identified with the principles announced in these documents, and membership in their respective organizations grew at a steady pace.

SDS grew slowly during the early 1960s, and it focused its efforts primarily on organizing inhabitants of inner-city housing projects around the campaign for better housing and health care for the poor. The group took a great leap forward, however, when its members decided to oppose the buildup of the war in Vietnam, which began late in 1964. On April 17, 1965, SDS staged the first large-scale, national protest against American policy in Vietnam. SDS president Paul Potter spoke to a crowd of over 15,000 people on the grounds of the Washington Monument.

"The incredible war in Vietnam has provided the razor, the terrifying sharp cutting edge that has finally severed the last vestiges of illusion that morality and democracy are the guiding principles of American foreign policy," Potter told the audience. His speech announced the SDS move toward a more radical politics than were contained in the "Port Huron Statement." From that point on, the group became more openly opposed to American policy and more inclined

Students for a Democratic Society led the widespread campus demonstrations at New York City's Columbia University in April 1968. Here, students protest the Vietnam War in front of Columbia's Low Memorial Library. Protestors inside are occupying the building by staging a sit-in. *AP/Wide World Photos. Reproduced by permission.*

to believe that political change could only be brought about with dramatic, perhaps even violent, actions. In 1968 at Columbia University and in 1969 at Harvard University, SDS chapters led violent and disruptive campus demonstrations against university ties to the military. By the middle of 1969, the group had split in two, with some members joining the Progressive Labor Party and others joining the revolutionary group that called itself the Weather Underground.

In some ways, the rise of YAF paralleled that of SDS. The strong anti-communist YAF agenda helped pack a 1962 rally in New York's Madison Square Garden and drew national attention to the budding political career of Arizona governor Barry Goldwater. The next several years were the heyday for the organization: it waged an active campaign against liberal groups like SDS, called for American companies to halt all trade with communist nations, and—most important—supported the candidacy of Goldwater.

YAF truly rose and fell with Goldwater. When Lyndon Johnson won a landslide victory over Goldwater in 1964, YAF lost credibility within Republican circles. Power struggles within the organization left it within the hands of a radical minority that promoted the war in Vietnam and harshly criticized Republican president Richard Nixon (1913–1994; served 1969–74) for opening relations with communist China. It was not until 1980 that the group regained some credibility when one of its longtime benefactors, Ronald Reagan (1911–2004; served 1981–89), was elected U.S. president. As of 2004 YAF existed both as a national organization and as a variety of state and local chapters.

Did you know...

- In 1971 the Twenty-sixth Amendment to the United States Constitution gave the right to vote to all citizens over the age of eighteen. Activists from both the left and the right had long advocated for this amendment, arguing that if people could die for their country fighting in Vietnam, they certainly ought to be allowed to vote.

- Political involvement by young people declined steadily after the 1960s, when it was first measured. According to data reported by the Center for Information and Research on Civic Learning and Engagement, the percentage of college freshmen who feel that it is important to keep up with political affairs has dropped from 60 percent in 1966 to less than 30 percent in 2001.

- "Port Huron Statement" author Tom Hayden went on to a distinguished career in politics. After working as a community organizer and activist through the 1960s and 1970s, he was elected to the California Assembly in 1982

and the California Senate in 1992, where he served until his retirement in 1999.

Consider the following...

- Now that you have read some of the most important political statements of the 1960s, can you identify elements of political philosophy that remain relevant to early-twenty-first century politics? Do you think people are still debating how involved the federal government should be in people's lives, for example?

- Assess the impact of SDS or YAF (or both). Did they achieve any of the goals they stated in their founding documents? Were these organizations a success or a failure?

- Many observers in the early 2000s felt that the great divide between conservatives and liberals that continued into the new millennium began in the 1960s. Use evi-

President Richard Nixon witnesses the 1971 passage of the Twenty-sixth Amendment to the U.S. Constitution, which gives the right to vote to all citizens over the age of eighteen; a measure that most activists on the left and the right agreed on.

© Bettmann/Corbis. Reproduced by permission.

dence from these two documents to argue for or against this position.

- Why did SDS assert that the university should be a resource for encouraging social and political change?

- The "Port Huron Statement" and the "Sharon Statement" engage issues of political philosophy that have deep traditions in American history. Can you point to other situations or times in history when Americans have questioned how to raise participation in the political process, how to balance the rights of individuals and the state against those of the federal government, and other issues raised by these documents?

For More Information

Books

Andrew, John A., III. *The Other Side of the Sixties: Young Americans for Freedom and the Rise of Conservative Politics.* New Brunswick, NJ: Rutgers University Press, 1997.

Dudley, William, ed. *The 1960s.* San Diego, CA: Greenhaven, 2000.

Farber, David. *The Age of Great Dreams: America in the 1960s.* New York: Hill and Wang, 1994.

Farber, David, and Beth Bailey, with others. *The Columbia Guide to America in the 1960s.* New York: Columbia University Press, 2001.

Gitlin, Todd. *The Sixties: Years of Hope, Days of Rage.* New York: Bantam, 1987; revised, 1993.

Miller, Jim. *Democracy Is in the Streets: From Port Huron to the Siege of Chicago.* Cambridge, MA: Harvard University Press, 1994.

Schneider, Gregory L. *Cadres for Conservatism: Young Americans for Freedom and the Rise of the Contemporary Right.* New York: New York University Press, 1999.

Schneider, Gregory L., ed. *Conservatism in America since 1930.* New York: New York University Press, 2003.

Periodicals

Young Americans for Freedom. "The Sharon Statement." *National Review* (September 24, 1960): pp. 172–73.

Web sites

Center for Information and Research on Civic Learning and Engagement. "Youth Civic Engagement: Basic Facts and Trends." www.

civicyouth.org/research/products/fact_sheets_outside2.htm (accessed on August 27, 2004).

"The Port Huron Statement." *The Sixties Project: Primary Document Archive.* http://lists.village.virginia.edu/sixties/HTML_docs/Resources/Primary/Manifestos/SDS_Port_Huron.html (accessed on August 30, 2004).

Young Americans for Freedom. www.yaf.com (accessed on August 30, 2004).

The Yippies

Complete text of *"The Yippie Manifesto"*
Issued in 1968.

Reprinted from *"Takin' It to the Streets:" A Sixties Reader,* **2003.**

One of the most striking social trends of the 1960s was the emergence of the counterculture, a minority culture that distinguished itself by being against the majority culture. American society had always had countercultures—groups of primarily young people who rejected the values of mainstream society in favor of ways of living that they found more authentic or liberating. In the 1960s, the counterculture was large, diverse, and very well publicized. The publicity came thanks to the counterculture's public engagement with political issues such as the movement against American participation in the Vietnam War (1954–75), but thanks also to the news and entertainment media, which found the often colorful and dramatic counterculture a good source of vivid news. Perhaps the most colorful counterculture subgroup of the 1960s was the hippies, a group of people known for their love of rock 'n' roll music, drug use, sexual experimentation, and communal living.

By the mid-1960s, some of the more politically oriented hippies began to look for ways to unite the free-and-easy hippie lifestyle with a radical criticism of the American

"Let's parade in the thousands to the places where the votes are counted and let murderous racists feel our power."

Yippies, famous for their political stunts, protest at the Democratic National Convention in Chicago, Illinois, with their presidential candidate, a pig named Pigasus, August 1968.
© Bettmann/Corbis. Reproduced by permission.

government. The more vocal and motivated hippies—including Timothy Leary, Allen Ginsberg, Paul Krassner, Abbie Hoffman (1936–1989), and Jerry Rubin (1938–1994)—charged that the American government had grown repressive and power-hungry, unresponsive to mild-mannered attempts to bring about change. Sometime in 1967 or early 1968, Rubin, Hoffman, and others decided to form a group called the Yippies, with the letters YIP later said to stand for Youth International Party. The goal of the Yippies, said its founders, would be to disrupt the political process and bring the values of sex, drugs, and rock 'n' roll to the attention of the nation.

The Yippies were not a typical political party: they did not have a president or rules or even a list of members. In fact, they were not so much a party as a vehicle for creating chaos. They did not have political theories; they had actions. Groups of self-identified Yippies pulled off guerrilla theater (outdoor dramatic events concerning controversial political or social issues) actions such as burning money in public, scattering money on the floor of the New York Stock Exchange and laughing while stockbrokers scrambled after it, or nominating a pig (named Pigasus, after the flying horse in Greek mythology, Pegasus) for president. They laughed at the idea of political programs and instead urged individuals to make their own revolutions. Asked for a political slogan, they offered the following nonsensical statement: "Rise up and abandon the creeping meatball!"

The Yippies' first major public exposure came at the Democratic presidential nominating convention in Chicago in the summer of 1968. Chicago Mayor Richard Daley (1902–1976) had publicly warned that his police would tolerate no disruptions of the peace, and he had brought in as many as fifteen thousand armed policemen to monitor the activities. Mayor Daley directed his police to use force if necessary to control unauthorized protests. Vicious police attacks on protestors, including Yippies, were televised on national television, and the entire Democratic convention was disrupted.

As the fall elections neared, the Yippies continued to draw attention to their cause. In the fall of 1968 they issued a Yippie Manifesto, which called people to participate on the day of the presidential election, November 5, in a widespread revolt against politics-as-usual.

Things to remember while reading the Yippie Manifesto…

- By 1968, authorities had come to believe that counterculture groups like the Yippies were a real danger to domestic peace. Law enforcement agencies such as the FBI and CIA infiltrated many branches of the protest move-

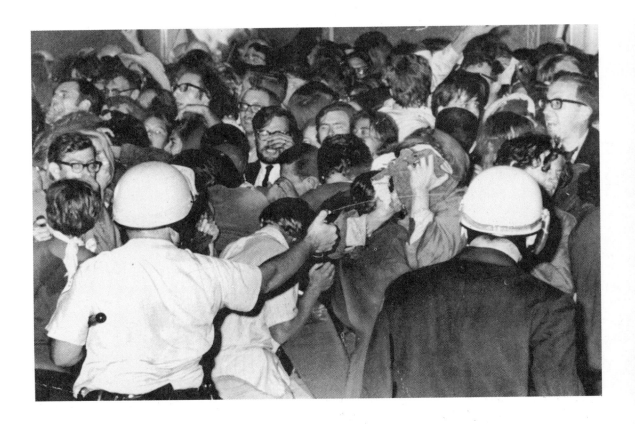

Police try to control a crowd of antiwar demonstrators outside of the Democratic National Convention, Chicago, Illinois, August 29, 1968. *AP/Wide World Photos. Reproduced by permission.*

ment in order to disrupt their efforts to organize and find reasons to prosecute movement leaders. As of the early 2000s, it had not been determined if law enforcement infiltrated the Yippies.

- The nominees for president in 1968 were Democratic vice president Hubert Humphrey and Republican Richard M. Nixon. The previous favorite for the Democratic nomination, Robert Kennedy, had been assassinated earlier in the year.

- The Yippies' nominee for president was Pigasus, a six-month-old, two-hundred-pound pig purchased for twenty-five dollars.

- The Yippie Manifesto was never published in conventional form. Instead, it circulated among members of the counterculture and was reproduced for posting on walls and lampposts. It was the most widely circulated printed statement of Yippie ideas.

- Yippie spokesmen Abbie Hoffman and Jerry Rubin had years of experience in leftist politics and had grown tired of the gradual, peaceful approach adopted by more mainstream groups.

"Yippie Manifesto"

Come into the streets on Nov. 5, election day. Vote with your feet. Rise up and abandon the creeping meatball! Demand the bars be open. Make music and dance at every red light. A festival of life in the streets and parks throughout the world. The American election represents death, and we are alive.

Come all you rebels, youth spirits, rock minstrels, bomb throwers, bank robbers, peacock freaks, toe worshippers, poets, street folk, liberated women, professors and body snatchers: it is election day and we are everywhere.

*Don't vote in a **jackass-elephant-cracker circus**. Let's vote for ourselves. Me for President. We are the revolution. We will strike and boycott the election and create our own reality.*

Can you dig it: in every metropolis and hamlet of America boycotts, strikes, sit-ins, pickets, lie-ins, pray-ins, feel-ins, piss-ins at the polling places.

Nobody goes to work. Nobody goes to school. Nobody votes. Everyone becomes a life actor of the street doing his thing, making the revolution by freeing himself and [messing] up the system.

*Ministers dragged away from polling places. Free chicken and ice cream in the streets. Thousands of kazoos, drums, tambourines, triangles, pots and pans, trumpets, street fairs, firecrackers—a symphony of life on a day of death. **LSD** in the drinking water.*

Let's parade in the thousands to the places where the votes are counted and let murderous racists feel our power.

*Force the National Guard to protect every polling place in the country. Brush your teeth in the streets. Organize a sack race. Join the rifle club of your choice. Freak out the **pigs** with exhibitions of snake dancing and karate at the nearest **pig pen**.*

Manifesto: A public declaration of principles and goals, especially of a political nature.

Jackass-elephant-cracker circus: The Yippies are referring to the donkey and the elephant because they are the traditional symbols of political parties, with the jackass representing Democrat Hubert Humphrey and the elephant representing Republican Richard Nixon. The cracker is a derogatory term for a poor southern white man, representing independent candidate George Wallace.

LSD: Lysergic acid diethylamide, a powerful drug that causes hallucinations; also known as acid.

Pigs: A negative slang term for the police.

Pig pen: A negative slang term for a police station.

Release a Black Panther in the Justice Department. Hold motorcycle races a hundred yards from the polling places. Fly an American flag out of every house so confused voters can't find the polling places. Wear costumes. Take a burning draft card to **Spiro Agnew.**

Stall for hours in the polling places trying to decide between Nixon and Humphrey and Wallace. Take your clothes off. Put wall posters up all over the city. Hold block parties. Release hundreds of greased pigs in pig uniforms downtown.

Check it out in Europe and throughout the world thousands of students will march on the USA embassies demanding to vote in the election cause Uncle Pig controls the world. No domination without representation.

Let's make 2-300 **Chicago's** on election day.

On election day let's pay tribute to rioters, anarchists, Commies, runaways, draft dodgers, acid freaks, snipers, beatniks, deserters, Chinese spies. Let's **exorcise** all politicians, generals, publishers, businessmen, Popes, American Legion, **AMA**, FBI, **narcos**, informers.

And then on Inauguration Day Jan. 20 we will bring our revolutionary theater to Washington to inaugurate Pigasus, our pig, the only honest candidate, and turn the White House into a crash pad. They will have to put Nixon's hand on the bible in a glass cage.

Begin now: resist oppression as you feel it. Organize and begin the word of mouth communication that is the basis of all conspiracies....

Every man a revolution! Every small group a revolutionary center! We will be together on election day. Yippie!!!

What happened next...

For the Yippies, 1968 was a golden year. The Democratic convention had turned into a display of police brutality, which seemed to reinforce the Yippies' contention that America was turning into a police state. Yippie founders Abbie Hoffman and Jerry Rubin were among eight protest leaders who were charged with conspiracy for their activities leading up to and at the convention. This group, known as

the Chicago 8 (and later as the Chicago 7 when charges were dismissed against one defendant, Bobby Seale), went to trial, and both Rubin and Hoffman acted out in court—reading poetry, singing songs, and dressing in outrageous costumes—in ways that were intended to mock the justice system. Many who had once thought of the Yippies as outrageous clowns recognized that the "system" had acted with undue brutality in Chicago.

Following the election of Richard Nixon in 1968, and especially after the end of the Chicago 8 trial in 1970, the Yippies began to fade from the public eye. Their brand of political action required events like elections and trials to gain attention; without such events, they had no political program. Both Hoffman and Rubin published books that drew attention to the Yippie cause. Hoffman wrote *Revolution for the Hell of It* in 1968 and the best-seller, *Steal This Book* in 1971. In 1970 Rubin penned *Do It! Scenarios of the Revolution,* which recounted Yippie history and extended the call for revolution.

Taking any opportunity to mock the U.S. justice system, Yippie leader Jerry Rubin appears in Washington, D.C., at a hearing of the House Committee on Un-American Activities in December 1968. Rubin wears a Santa Claus suit and holds a toy gun to protest the hearing as a "total circus." *AP/Wide World Photos. Reproduced by permission.*

By the early 1970s, the counterculture movement as a whole had begun to lose energy, for reasons that continued to puzzle historians into the early 2000s. Some argued that the movement was simply exhausted from trying to change a system that was far more durable than its critics had imagined. Others complained that radical leaders had sold out, taking places of their own in the "establishment"; to be fair, the only establishment place that many of the most vocal leaders ever occupied was a jail cell. Still others believe that the counterculture was simply absorbed into the mainstream, though the mainstream did become more permissive in the process. Hippies lived on in the 1970s but were characterized more by their long hair and their funky clothes than by their politics. By 1975 Richard Nixon had resigned the presidency and the United States had withdrawn from Vietnam. American culture and American politics had left the Yippies behind.

Did you know...

- Jerry Rubin, the colorful Yippie co-founder, left revolution behind in the 1980s when he became a successful businessman, or Yuppie (which stood for young, urban, professional). In the mid-1980s he and Abbie Hoffman held a series of debates called "Yippie or Yuppie," in which they debated the values of revolution versus capitalist excess.

- Abbie Hoffman died in 1989 of an apparent suicide; Jerry Rubin died in 1994 when he was struck by a car while jaywalking across a busy street in Los Angeles, California.

Consider the following...

- What were the strengths and weaknesses of the Yippies' political stance? You might compare their methods to those of other protest groups in the 1960s.

- Historians have long puzzled over why the counterculture movement faded so quickly after reaching its high point in 1968. Why do you think the movement faded from prominence?

- The Yippies' pronouncements were extremely radical in the 1960s. Do they still seem radical today? Explain why or why not.

• Pretend that you are a Yippie from the 1960s and that you travel forward in time to the present day. How have things changed since that time? Are there elements of the early 2000s culture that you would criticize? If so, do you think anyone would listen?

For More Information

Books

Alonso, Karen. *The Chicago Seven Political Protest Trial: A Headline Court Case.* Berkeley Heights, NJ: Enslow, 2002.

Bloom, Alexander, and Wini Breines, eds. *"Takin' It to the Streets": A Sixties Reader.* New York: Oxford University Press, 2003.

Miller, Timothy. *The Hippies and American Values.* Knoxville, TN: University of Tennessee Press, 1991.

Rubin, Jerry. *Do It; Scenarios of the Revolution.* New York: Simon and Schuster, 1970.

Barry Goldwater

Excerpt from Goldwater's 1964 acceptance speech for the Republican presidential nomination

Originally given at the Republican presidential nominating convention, San Francisco, California, July 16, 1964.

Reprinted from *Our Nation's Archive: The History of the United States in Documents*, 1999; also available online at www.nationalcenter.org/Goldwater.html.

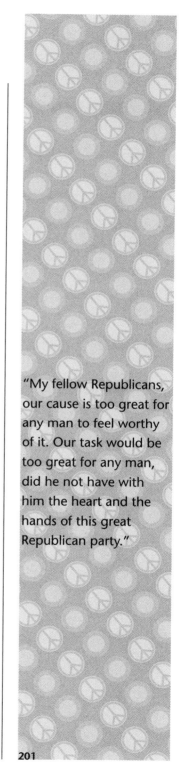

By the early 1960s, American conservatives had been unhappy with the direction of American government for many years. Beginning with the New Deal programs of Democratic president Franklin D. Roosevelt (1882–1945), who served as president from 1933 to 1945, the size of the American government had grown sharply. Roosevelt's New Deal created programs like social security, welfare, and government subsidies that expanded the size of the government and established the precedent for the federal government protecting or preserving the rights of certain social groups. Conservatives believed the expansion of the government and its intrusion into the lives of Americans was wrong-minded and unconstitutional. When both Democrats and liberal Republicans began to support the efforts of the growing civil rights movement in the early 1960s, conservatives started to look for a champion of individual liberties and limited government. They found that champion in Barry Goldwater (1909–1998).

A former Air Force pilot, Goldwater had a fiery personality and striking good looks. He rose through the Republican ranks, moving from city government in Phoenix, Ari-

"My fellow Republicans, our cause is too great for any man to feel worthy of it. Our task would be too great for any man, did he not have with him the heart and the hands of this great Republican party."

Barry Goldwater greets an enthusiastic crowd during a presidential campaign stop in Indianapolis, Indiana, October 1964. *AP/Wide World Photos. Reproduced by permission.*

zona, to a seat in the U.S. Senate in 1952. He soon became known as a spokesman for the most conservative elements in the Republican Party. Backed by wealthy businessmen who resented government regulation, and by fervent young conservatives like members of Young Americans for Freedom, a youth group formed in the late 1950s, Goldwater challenged moderate Republicans and won the primary race for the Republican presidential nomination in 1964.

The Goldwater candidacy was based on certain fundamental principles: Goldwater was for individual freedom, self-reliance, and decentralized government. He was against federal intrusion in civil rights issues in the South, including the creation of national legislation to guarantee voting rights and integrated public facilities for African Americans. Goldwater was not personally a racist; in fact, he was a member of the National Association for the Advancement of Colored People (NAACP). He simply believed that most issues should be settled on a local level. However, Goldwater's opposition to civil rights legislation made him the candidate of southern racists.

Though Goldwater wanted the government out of the lives of Americans, he was not opposed to the use of government power to combat Communism. A fervent anticommunist, Goldwater was an early advocate of increasing American involvement in Vietnam. In fact, Goldwater spoke publicly about the possibility of dropping atomic bombs on communist nations.

Goldwater accepted the Republican presidential nomination in a fiery speech delivered on July 16, 1964, at the Republican nominating convention held at the Cow Palace in San Francisco, California. In the speech, Goldwater expressed his hopes for the country.

Things to remember while reading the excerpt of Barry Goldwater's 1964 acceptance speech…

- Barry Goldwater had fought hard to win the Republican presidential nomination. His leading opponent was Nelson Rockefeller (1908–1979) of New York, a moderate from a distinguished Republican family. Goldwater took 38.2 percent of primary votes to Rockefeller's 22 percent. Other candidates included James A. Rhodes (10.4 percent), Henry Cabot Lodge (6.5 percent), John W. Byrnes (5 percent), and William Scranton (4.1 percent).

- Goldwater selected New York congressman William Miller as his vice presidential running mate. Convention goers chanted: "Here's a riddle, it's a killer. Who the hell is William Miller?"

Barry Goldwater delivering his acceptance speech at the Republican National Convention in San Francisco, California, July 1964.
AP/Wide World Photos. Reproduced by permission.

• Goldwater's opponent in the fall election would be Lyndon B. Johnson (1909–1973; served 1963–69), who had assumed the presidency following the assassination of President John F. Kennedy in 1963. Goldwater carefully crafted some of his positions in opposition to Johnson.

Excerpt of Barry Goldwater's 1964 acceptance speech

From this moment, united and determined, we will go forward together, dedicated to the ultimate and undeniable greatness of the whole man. Together we will win.

I accept your nomination with a deep sense of humility. I accept, too, the responsibility that goes with it, and I seek your con-

tinued help and your continued guidance. My fellow Republicans, our cause is too great for any man to feel worthy of it. Our task would be too great for any man, did he not have with him the heart and the hands of this great Republican party. And I promise you tonight that every fiber of my being is consecrated to our cause, that nothing shall be lacking from the struggle that can be brought to it by enthusiasm, by devotion, and plain hard work.

In this world no person, no party can guarantee anything, but what we can do and what we shall do is to deserve victory, and victory will be ours. The good Lord raised this mighty Republic to be a home for the brave and to flourish as the land of the free—not to stagnate in the swampland of **collectivism**, not to cringe before the bully of communism.

Now, my fellow Americans, the tide has been running against freedom. Our people have followed false prophets. We must, and we shall, return to proven ways—not because they are old, but because they are true.

We must, and we shall, set the tide running again in the cause of freedom. And this party, with its every action, every word, every breath, and every heartbeat, has but a single resolve, and that is freedom.

Freedom made orderly for this nation by our constitutional government. Freedom under a government limited by laws of nature and of nature's God. Freedom balanced so that liberty lacking order will not become the slavery of the prison cell; balanced so that liberty lacking order will not become the license of the mob and of the jungle.

Now, we Americans understand freedom; we have earned it, we have lived for it, and we have died for it. This nation and its people are freedom's models in a searching world. We can be freedom's missionaries in a doubting world.

But, ladies and gentlemen, first we must renew freedom's mission in our own hearts and in our own homes.

During four, futile years **the administration** which we shall replace has distorted and lost that faith. It has talked and talked and talked and talked the words of freedom, but it has failed and failed and failed in the works of freedom.

Now failure cements the wall of shame in **Berlin**; failures blot the sands of shame at the **Bay of Pigs**; failures marked the slow death of freedom in **Laos**; failures infest the jungles of **Vietnam**; and failures

Collectivism: One of a number of words used to refer to Communism, a system in which property is owned by the state and theoretically wealth is distributed evenly throughout society.

The administration: The presidential administration of Lyndon B. Johnson, who assumed the presidency in November 1962 after the death of President John F. Kennedy.

Berlin...Bay of Pigs...Laos...Vietnam: Goldwater is referring to a series of foreign policy issues that he perceives to be failures of the Democratic administration.

*haunt the houses of our once great alliances and undermine the greatest bulwark ever erected by free nations, the **NATO** community.*

Failures proclaim lost leadership, obscure purpose, weakening wills, and the risk of inciting our sworn enemies to new aggressions and to new excesses.

And because of this administration we are tonight a world divided. We are a nation becalmed. We have lost the brisk pace of diversity and the genius of individual creativity. We are plodding at a pace set by centralized planning, red tape, rules without responsibility, and regimentation without recourse.

Rather than useful jobs in our country, people have been offered bureaucratic make-work; rather than moral leadership, they have been given bread and circuses; they have been given spectacles, and, yes, they've even been given scandals.

Tonight there is violence in our streets, corruption in our highest offices, aimlessness among our youth, anxiety among our elderly, and there's a virtual despair among the many who look beyond material success toward the inner meaning of their lives. And where examples of morality should be set, the opposite is seen. Small men seeking great wealth or power have too often and too long turned even the highest levels of public service into mere personal opportunity.

Now, certainly simple honesty is not too much to demand of men in government. We find it in most. Republicans demand it from everyone. They demand it from everyone no matter how exalted or protected his position might be.

The growing menace in our country tonight, to personal safety, to life, to limb and property, in homes, in churches, on the playgrounds and places of business, particularly in our great cities, is the mounting concern—or should be—of every thoughtful citizen in the United States. Security from domestic violence, no less than from foreign aggression, is the most elementary and fundamental purpose of any government, and a government that cannot fulfill this purpose is one that cannot long command the loyalty of its citizens.

*History shows us, demonstrates that nothing, nothing prepares the way for tyranny more than the failure of public officials to keep the streets from **bullies and marauders**.*

Now, we Republicans see all this as more—much more—than the rest: of mere political differences or mere political mistakes. We

NATO: North Atlantic Treaty Organization.

Bullies and marauders: This is a direct reference to civil rights and antiwar protestors, who Goldwater felt should not have the right to disrupt society.

The Sixties in America: Primary Sources

see this as the result of a fundamentally and absolutely wrong view of man, his nature, and his destiny.

Those who seek to live your lives for you, to take your liberty in return for relieving you of yours, those who elevate the state and downgrade the citizen, must see ultimately a world in which earthly power can be substituted for divine will. And this nation was founded upon the rejection of that notion and upon the acceptance of God as the author of freedom.

Now, those who seek absolute power, even though they seek it to do what they regard as good, are simply demanding the right to enforce their own version of heaven on earth, and let me remind you they are the very ones who always create the most hellish tyranny.

Absolute power does corrupt, and those who seek it must be suspect and must be opposed. Their mistaken course stems from false notions, ladies and gentlemen, of equality. Equality, rightly understood as our founding fathers understood it, leads to liberty and to the emancipation of creative differences; wrongly understood, as it has been so tragically in our time, it leads first to conformity and then to despotism.

Fellow Republicans, it is the cause of Republicanism to resist concentrations of power, private or public, which enforce such conformity and inflict such despotism.

It is the cause of Republicanism to ensure that power remains in the hands of the people—and, so help us God, that is exactly what a Republican president will do with the help of a Republican Congress.

It is further the cause of Republicanism to restore a clear understanding of the tyranny of man over man in the world at large. It is our cause to dispel the foggy thinking which avoids hard decisions in the delusion that a world of conflict will somehow resolve itself into a world of harmony, if we just don't rock the boat or irritate the **forces of aggression**—*and this is hogwash.*

It is further the cause of Republicanism to remind ourselves, and the world, that only the strong can remain free: that only the strong can keep the peace.

Now, I needn't remind you, or my fellow Americans regardless of party, that Republicans have shouldered this hard responsibility and marched in this cause before. It was Republican leadership under **Dwight Eisenhower** *that kept the peace, and passed along*

Forces of aggression: Goldwater is alluding to communist nations such as the Soviet Union and China, which he believes should be challenged directly.

Dwight Eisenhower (1890–1969): President of the United States from 1953 to 1961.

to this administration the mightiest arsenal for defense the world has ever known.

And I needn't remind you that it was the strength and the unbelievable will of the Eisenhower years that kept the peace by using our strength, by using it in the **Formosa Strait**, and in **Lebanon**, and by showing it courageously at all times.

It was during those Republican years that the thrust of Communist imperialism was blunted. It was during those years of Republican leadership that this world moved closer not to war but closer to peace than at any other time in the last three decades.

And I needn't remind you—but I will—that it's been during Democratic years that our strength to deter war has been stilled and even gone into a planned decline. It has been during Democratic years that we have weakly stumbled into conflicts, timidly refusing to draw our own lines against aggression, deceitfully refusing to tell even our people of our full participation and tragically letting our finest men die on battlefields unmarked by purpose, unmarked by pride or the prospect of victory.

Yesterday it was **Korea**; tonight it is Vietnam. Make no bones of this. Don't try to sweep this under the rug. We are at war in Vietnam. And yet the president, who is the commander in chief of our forces, refuses to say—refuses to say, mind you—whether or not the objective over there is victory, and his secretary of defense continues to mislead and misinform the American people, and enough of it has gone by.

And I needn't remind you—but I will—it has been during Democratic years that a billion persons were cast into Communist captivity and their fate cynically sealed.

Today, today in our beloved country, we have an administration which seems eager to deal with communism in every coin known—from gold to wheat, from consulates to confidence, and even human freedom itself.

Now, the Republican cause demands that we brand Communism as the principal disturber of peace in the world today. Indeed, we should brand it as the only significant disturber of the peace. And we must make clear that until its goals of conquest are absolutely renounced and its rejections with all nations tempered, communism and the governments it now controls are enemies of every man on earth who is or wants to be free.

Formosa Strait...Lebanon: Goldwater is referring to cases in which the Eisenhower administration stood up to the Soviet Union and its allies.

Korea: Referring to U.S. involvement in the Korean War, 1950–53.

Now, we here in America can keep the peace only if we remain vigilant, and only if we remain strong. Only if we keep our eyes open and keep our guard up can we prevent war.

And I want to make this abundantly clear—I don't intend to let peace or freedom be torn from our grasp because of lack of strength, or lack of will—and that I promise you Americans.

I believe that we must look beyond the defense of freedom today to its extension tomorrow. I believe that the communism which boasts it will bury us will instead give way to the forces of freedom. And I can see in the distant and yet recognizable future the outlines of a world worthy of our dedication, our every risk, our every effort, our every sacrifice along the way. Yes, a world that will redeem the suffering of those will be liberated from tyranny.

I can see, and I suggest that all thoughtful men must contemplate, the flowering of an Atlantic civilization, the whole world of Europe reunified and free, trading openly across its borders, communicating openly across the world.

*This is a goal far, far more meaningful than a **moon shot**.*

[...]

...I pledge that the America I envision in the years ahead will extend its hand in help in teaching and in cultivation so that all new nations will be at least encouraged to go our way, so that they will not wander down the dark alleys of tyranny or to the dead-end streets of collectivism.

*My fellow Republicans, we do no man a service by **hiding freedom's light under a bushel** of mistaken humility.*

I seek an America proud of its past, proud of its ways, proud of its dreams, and determined actively to proclaim them. But our examples to the world must, like charity, begin at home.

In our vision of a good and decent future, free and peaceful, there must be room, room for the liberation of the energy and the talent of the individual, otherwise our vision is blind at the outset.

We must assure a society here which, while never abandoning the needy, or forsaking the helpless, nurtures incentives and opportunity for the creative and the productive.

We must know the whole good is the product of many single contributions.

Moon shot: The attempt by NASA to send a man to the moon, widely criticized by those who resisted the growth of government.

Hiding freedom's light under a bushel: This is an allusion to the "Sermon on the Mount," one of the most famous sermons from the Bible, reputed to be delivered by Jesus.

A campaign button from Barry Goldwater's 1964 presidential race, citing a memorable quote from his speech accepting the Republican nomination.
© David J. and Janice L. Frent Collection/Corbis. Reproduced by permission.

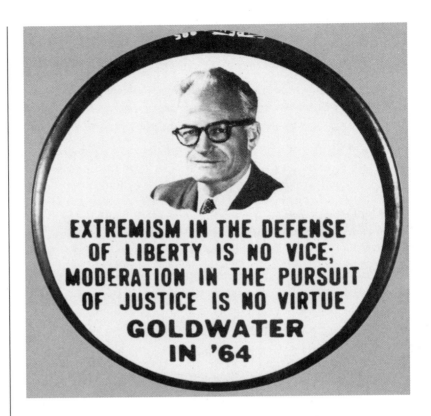

And I cherish the day when our children once again will restore as heroes the sort of men and women who, unafraid and undaunted, pursue the truth, strive to cure disease, subdue and make fruitful our natural environment, and produce the inventive engines of production–science and technology.

This nation, whose creative people have enhanced this entire span of history, should again thrive upon the greatness of all those things which we—we as individual citizens—can and should do.

During Republican years, this again will be a nation of men and women, of families proud of their role, jealous of their responsibilities, unlimited in their aspirations—a nation where all who can will be self-reliant.

We Republicans see in our constitutional form of government the great framework which assures the orderly but dynamic fulfillment of the whole man as the great reason for instituting orderly government in the first place.

We see in private property and in economy based upon and fostering private property the one way to make government a durable ally of the whole man rather than his determined enemy.

We see in the sanctity of private property the only durable foundation for constitutional government in a free society.

[…]

Today…the task of preserving and enlarging freedom at home and safeguarding it from the forces of tyranny abroad is great enough to challenge all our resources and to require all our strength.

Anyone who joins us in all sincerity, we welcome. Those, those who do not care for our cause, we don't expect to enter our ranks in any case. And let our Republicanism so focused and so dedicated not be made fuzzy and futile by unthinking and stupid labels.

I would remind you that extremism in the defense of liberty is no vice!

And let me remind you also that moderation in the pursuit of justice is no virtue!

The beauty of the very system we Republicans are pledged to restore and revitalize, the beauty of this federal system of ours, is in its **reconciliation of diversity with unity**. We must not see malice in honest differences of opinion, and no matter how great, so long as they are not inconsistent with the pledges we have given to each other in and through our Constitution.

Our Republican cause is not to level out the world or make its people conform in computer-regimented sameness. Our Republican cause is to free our people and light the way for liberty throughout the world. Ours is a very human cause for very humane goals. This party, its good people, and its unquestionable devotion to freedom will not fulfill the purposes of this campaign which we launch here now until our cause has won the day, inspired the world, and shown the way to a tomorrow worthy of all our yesteryears.

I repeat, I accept your nomination with humbleness, with pride, and you and I are going to fight for the goodness of our land. Thank you.

Reconciliation of diversity with unity: Goldwater is referring to the idea that individual states can have diverse social and cultural customs within a unified nation.

What happened next...

Goldwater's presidential candidacy marked the beginning of the modern conservative movement in America. Although his ideas frightened some during the 1960s, within twenty years of his campaign his ideas had become mainstream with the election of Republican President Ronald Reagan in 1980 and the election of a Republican majority in Congress in 1994. The Goldwater candidacy also began a shift in electoral politics that continued to be felt into the early 2000s. White southerners, who had voted overwhelmingly for Democratic candidates ever since the end of the American Civil War (1861–65), began to shift their support to the Republican Party.

Goldwater waged a hard-fought campaign against Lyndon Johnson. Campaigning behind the slogan, "In your heart you know he's right," Goldwater criticized Johnson for being soft on communism and for contributing to the moral decline of the nation. Johnson, however, found Goldwater to be an easy target. His campaign drove home the charge that Goldwater was a dangerous extremist, particularly targeting Goldwater's willingness to use atomic weapons. In one particularly dramatic television commercial, the image of a young girl picking a daisy dissolves in the fiery blast of an atomic explosion. Johnson intones: "These are the stakes. To make a world in which all of God's children can live, or to go into the dark. We must either love each other or we must die."

In the end, the American public found Goldwater too extreme, and Johnson won the election in a landslide, taking 61.1 percent of the popular vote to Goldwater's 38.5 percent. It was one of the most crushing defeats in modern politics. Goldwater remembered the race for presidency as like "trying to stand up in a hammock." Because he did not run for his senatorial seat at the same time he ran for president, Goldwater spent four years out of political office. By 1968 Goldwater was re-elected to the Senate and remained a conservative leader until he retired in 1987. His last major act as a senator was to help pass the Defense Department Reorganization Act of 1986, which restructured the military command at the Pentagon. He died in 1998, revered as an elder statesman of American conservatism.

Did you know...

- Although Johnson began the 1964 presidential campaign as the candidate for a peaceful solution in Vietnam, he ended up being known as the president who increased American military involvement in the Vietnam War. By the next presidential election in 1968, Johnson was so unpopular because of his policies toward escalating the war in Vietnam that he did not seek reelection.

- Goldwater may have been his own biggest enemy in the 1964 campaign, for he often made outrageous public statements. For example, he triggered national fear of nuclear war when he discussed the effects of using atomic weapons in Vietnam, saying "defoliation of the forests by low-yield atomic weapons could well be done," on ABC-TV's *Issues and Answers* in 1963. Campaign aides once implored the press the "write what he means, not what he says."

- Press coverage of Goldwater's campaign was very unfriendly. Even the usually conservative magazine the *Saturday Evening Post* called him a "wild man, a stray," adding, "For the good of the Republican Party, which his candidacy disgraces, we hope that Goldwater is crushingly defeated."

- Goldwater's detractors had a heyday with the candidate's campaign slogan, "In your heart you know he's right." Humorous turns on the slogan included "In your heart, you know he might [use nuclear weapons]" and "In your guts, you know he's nuts."

Consider the following...

- Goldwater's candidacy, had it succeeded, would have likely created a very different decade. What do you think would have happened with the major issues of the decade—Vietnam and the antiwar movement, civil rights, the rise of feminism, and the existence of the counterculture—if Goldwater had been president?

- Critics of Goldwater charged that his acceptance speech offered approval for segregation, the practice of maintaining separate public facilities for whites and blacks in the South. Can you point to parts of the speech that may be interpreted as supporting this contention?

- In his campaign, Goldwater raised an ages-old American political issue when he claimed that most political issues should be solved on the local level rather than the national level. Can you name other times in history when Americans have debated the need to limit or expand the power of the federal government?

- Which of the issues raised by Goldwater in his acceptance speech continue to have an impact on American politics? Name three and describe their influence today.

For More Information

Books

Bruun, Erik, and Jay Crosby, eds. *Our Nation's Archive: The History of the United States in Documents.* New York: Black Dog & Leventhal, 1999.

Edwards, Lee. *Goldwater: The Man Who Made a Revolution.* Washington, DC: Regnery, 1995.

Goldberg, Robert Alan. *Barry Goldwater.* New Haven, CT: Yale University Press, 1995.

Goldwater, Barry Morris. *With No Apologies: The Personal and Political Memoirs of United States Senator Barry M. Goldwater.* New York: William Morrow, 1979.

Perlstein, Rick. *Before the Storm: Barry Goldwater and the Unmaking of the American Consensus.* New York: Hill and Wang, 2001.

Web sites

"Barry Goldwater's Acceptance Speech." *The National Center for Public Policy Research.* www.nationalcenter.org/Goldwater.html (accessed on August 30, 2004).

"The Living Room Candidate: 1964, Johnson vs. Goldwater." *American Museum of the Moving Image.* www.ammi.org/cgi-bin/video/years.cgi?1964 (accessed on August 29, 2004).

Debating the Power of Television

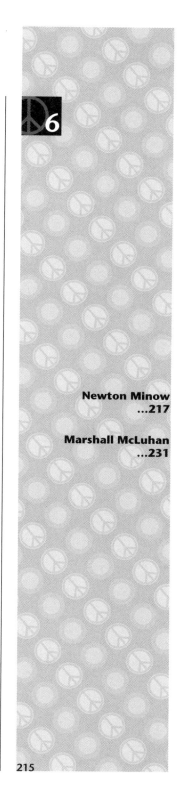

6

Anyone who doubted that television had become an influential force in American culture had only to watch the first televised presidential debates held in 1960. Those who only listened to the debates on the radio thought that Republican vice president Richard M. Nixon (1913–1994) was the clear victor, for he seemed knowledgeable and persuasive. But those who watched the debates on television had a completely different opinion. On TV Nixon looked hot, haggard, and uncertain, wiping his sweaty brow repeatedly. His opponent, the handsome, young Democratic senator John F. Kennedy (1917–1963), appeared calm, cool, and unflappable. Kennedy's appearance persuaded TV viewers more than Nixon's words. TV viewers felt that Kennedy had won the debate. Style had triumphed over content. The differing opinions on the debates of viewers and listeners made Americans keenly aware of the power of this still young medium, television. Into the early 2000s, the role of television in Americans' lives remained an issue of great controversy.

Television first entered American life in the 1940s. By the early 1950s, 20 percent of Americans had a television in their home. By 1960, that number had grown to 90 percent, and this new medium had become a fixture of American culture. Increasingly, Americans turned to the television for their news, their entertainment, and even for some of their education. But what did they find when they turned on the television? Opinions varied widely about the range of subjects and the quality with which they were handled. Some felt that television was an ideal medium to carry news and to tell stories, and they heralded television's educational power. Some critics, however, warned that television was corrupting American youth, undermining literacy, and bringing a constant string of commercials into people's lives.

This chapter presents two influential statements about the importance of television and other media. The first document is a 1961 address given by the chairman of the Federal Communications Commission, **Newton Minow** (1926–), in which he declares that American airwaves are a "vast wasteland." Newton was not the first to complain about the quality of television programming, but he was the first to suggest that the government should do something about it. His address ignited ongoing debates about the role of the government in regulating what goes on television. The second document draws from one of the most influential and misunderstood theoretical statements of the decade: **Marshall McLuhan's** *Understanding Media: Extensions of Man*. Famed for the statement, "the medium is the message," McLuhan offered an intriguing, if difficult, approach to understanding the power that different media have in shaping people's lives. Minow and McLuhan participated in the age-old debate about which is the more important factor in created works: form or content. Is it the television itself or the information it transmits that influences people?

Newton Minow

Excerpt from an address to the National Association of Broadcasters, May 9, 1961

Originally published in *Equal Time: The Private Broadcaster and the Public Interest.* **New York: Atheneum, 1964.**

Reprinted from *Abandoned in the Wasteland: Children, Television, and the First Amendment,* **1995.**

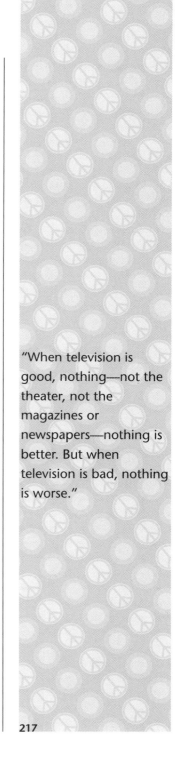

"When television is good, nothing—not the theater, not the magazines or newspapers—nothing is better. But when television is bad, nothing is worse."

When John F. Kennedy was elected president in 1960, he brought to American politics a renewed sense of idealism and commitment to public service. "Ask not what your country can do for you," he proclaimed to the American public at his inauguration in 1961, "ask what you can do for your country." Kennedy, like most American politicians at the time, believed that America was in a race with the Soviet Union to establish dominance in the world. That race was also known as the Cold War (1945–91). Kennedy believed that the United States could win that race if its citizens committed themselves to the highest ideals of education, economic growth, military and public service, even entertainment. He brought to Washington, D.C., a new generation of public servants; among them was Newton Minow (1926–), the new chairman of the Federal Communications Commission (FCC), the government agency charged with overseeing the nation's airwaves.

The FCC was created in 1934 to regulate radio, telephone, telegraph, and other communications systems. Following World War II (1939–45), the FCC had a new technol-

ogy to regulate: television, or TV. Invented in the 1930s, TV went from novelty to common household item in the fifteen years following the war. By 1960, it was estimated that 90 percent of American homes contained at least one TV. The television industry was dominated by a handful of major television networks that produced the majority of programming aired by just over five hundred stations. Every three years, these television stations were required to apply for a license to broadcast using the public airwaves. As part of their license to broadcast, they agreed to act in the "public interest." Newton Minow, a Chicago lawyer, was convinced that American broadcasters were not acting in the public interest. In the 1961 speech before the most important television industry group, the National Association of Broadcasters, he told them so.

Newton Minow pictured in 1961, shortly after being named chairman of the Federal Communications Commission by President John F. Kennedy. *AP/Wide World Photos. Reproduced by permission.*

Things to remember while reading the excerpt of Minow's speech to the National Association of Broadcasters:

- In 1961 the only television broadcast stations available were on channels two through thirteen.

- In 1961 there were 47.2 million television sets in American homes, and fewer than 5 percent of those were capable of receiving signals in color.

- In 1961 the vast majority of Americans received their television signals by antenna from a local television station. Cable television and satellite transmission of TV signals were both in their infancy.

- The FCC only had the power to grant licenses to broadcast stations, not to regulate the content of their programming.

Excerpt of Newton Minow's speech to the National Association of Broadcasters, May 9, 1961

*Thank you for this opportunity to meet with you today. This is my first public address since I took over my new job. When the **New Frontiersmen** rode into town, I locked myself in my office to do my homework and get my feet wet. But apparently I haven't managed to stay out of hot water. I seem to have detected a certain nervous apprehension about what I might say or do when I emerged from that locked office for this, my maiden station break.*

[...]

*It may also come as a surprise to some of you, but I want you to know that you have my admiration and respect. Yours is a most honorable profession. Anyone who is in the broadcasting business has a **tough row to hoe**. You earn your **bread** by using public property. When you work in broadcasting, you volunteer for public service, public pressure, and public regulation. You must compete with other attractions and other investments, and the only way you can do it is to **prove to us every three years** that you should have been in business in the first place.*

I can think of easier ways to make a living.

But I cannot think of more satisfying ways.

*I admire your courage—but that doesn't mean I would make life any easier for you. Your license lets you use the public's airwaves as trustees for 180 million Americans. The public is your **beneficiary**. If you want to stay on as trustees, you must deliver a decent return to the public—not only to your stockholders. So, as a representative of the public, your health and your product are among my chief concerns.*

*As to your health: let's talk only of television today. In 1960 **gross broadcast revenues** of the television industry were over $1,268,000,000; profit before taxes was $243,900,000—an average return on revenue of 19.2 per cent. Compare this with 1959, when gross broadcast revenues were $1,163,900,000, and profit before taxes was $222,300,000, an average return on revenue of*

New Frontiersmen: This is a joking reference to the political appointees of new president John F. Kennedy (1917–1963), who promised to usher in a New Frontier in American history.

Tough row to hoe: A metaphor meaning a difficult job or tough task.

Bread: Money.

Prove to us...: Minow is referring to the process by which broadcasters must apply every three years for a license to broadcast.

Beneficiary: The one who benefits from your work.

Gross broadcast revenues: Total money earned from broadcasting.

*19.1 per cent. So the percentage increase of total revenues from 1959 to 1960 was 9 per cent, and the percentage increase of profit was 9.7 per cent. This, despite a **recession**. For your investors, the price has indeed been right.*

I have confidence in your health.

But not in your product.

It is with this and much more in mind that I come before you today.

One editorialist in the trade press wrote that "the FCC of the New Frontier is going to be one of the toughest FCC's in the history of broadcast regulation." If he meant that we intend to enforce the law in the public interest, let me make it perfectly clear that he is right—we do.

*If he meant that we intend to **muzzle or censor** broadcasting, he is dead wrong.*

It would not surprise me if some of you had expected me to come here today and say in effect, "Clean up your own house or the government will do it for you."

Well, in a limited sense, you would be right—I've just said it.

But I want to say to you earnestly that it is not in that spirit that I come before you today, nor is it in that spirit that I intend to serve the FCC.

I am in Washington to help broadcasting, not to harm it; to strengthen it, not weaken it; to reward it, not punish it; to encourage it, not threaten it; to stimulate it, not censor it.

Above all, I am here to uphold and protect the public interest.

What do we mean by "the public interest"? Some say the public interest is merely what interests the public.

I disagree.

*So does your distinguished president, **Governor Collins**. In a recent speech he said, "Broadcasting, to serve the public interest, must have a soul and a conscience, a burning desire to excel, as well as to sell; the urge to build the character, citizenship, and intellectual stature of people, as well as to expand the gross national product...By no means do I imply that broadcasters disregard the public interest...But a much better job can be done, and should be done." [...]*

Recession: A period of reduced economic activity.

Muzzle or censor: To delete or limit access to material considered objectionable; in this case, Minow is referring to government control over television programming.

Governor Collins: LeRoy Collins (1909–1991), former governor of Florida and president of the National Association of Broadcasters (NAB) from 1961 to 1964.

The Sixties in America: Primary Sources

I could not agree more.

*And I would add that in **today's world**, with chaos in Laos and the Congo aflame, with Communist tyranny on our Caribbean doorstep and relentless pressure on our Atlantic alliance, with social and economic problems at home of the gravest nature, yes, and with technological knowledge that makes it possible, as our president has said, not only to destroy our world but to destroy poverty around the world—in a time of peril and opportunity, the old complacent, unbalanced fare of action-adventure and situation comedies is simply not good enough.*

Your industry possesses the most powerful voice in America. It has an inescapable duty to make that voice ring with intelligence and with leadership. In a few years this exciting industry has grown from a novelty to an instrument of overwhelming impact on the American people. It should be making ready for the kind of leadership that newspapers and magazines assumed years ago, to make our people aware of their world.

*Ours has been called the **jet age, the atomic age, the space age**. It is also, I submit, the television age. And just as history will decide whether the leaders of today's world employed the atom to destroy the world or rebuild it for mankind's benefit, so will history decide whether today's broadcasters employed their powerful voice to enrich the people or **debase** them.*

*If I seem today to address myself chiefly to the problems of television, I don't want any of you radio broadcasters to think we've **gone to sleep at your switch** —we haven't. We still listen. But in recent years most of the controversies and crosscurrents in broadcast programming have swirled around television. And so my subject today is the television industry and the public interest.*

*Like everybody, I wear more than one hat. I am the Chairman of the FCC. I am also a television viewer and the husband and father of other television viewers. I have seen a great many television programs that seemed to me eminently worthwhile, and I am not talking about the much-bemoaned **good old days of** Playhouse 90 and Studio One.*

I am talking about this past season. Some were wonderfully entertaining, such as The Fabulous Fifties, *the* Fred Astaire Show, *and the* Bing Crosby Special; *some were dramatic and moving, such as Conrad's* Victory *and* Twilight Zone; *some were marvelously informative, such as* The Nation's Future, CBS Reports, *and* The

Today's world …: In the list that follows, Minow refers to areas and issues where the United States is contesting with the Soviet Union for supremacy and power in the Cold War (1945–91).

Jet age, the atomic age, the space age: These terms were commonly used to refer to an era that many felt was defined by advances in technology and weaponry.

Debase: To lower in quality or character.

Gone to sleep at your switch: An expression, taken from the railroad industry, meaning to ignore important activities.

Good old days of *Playhouse 90* **and** *Studio One.*: Minow is referring to some high-quality programs from the 1950s.

A scene from the popular TV show *Twilight Zone,* which debuted in 1959 and ran through the early 1960s. Newton Minow counted this program among the best of its time.

Station signs off: In the 1960s, television stations usually ended their programming sometime after midnight and had a brief message in which they "signed off."

Wasteland: A space that is desolate and spiritually barren or empty.

Valiant Years. *I could list many more—programs that I am sure everyone here felt enriched his own life and that of his family. When television is good, nothing—not the theater, not the magazines or newspapers—nothing is better.*

But when television is bad, nothing is worse. I invite you to sit down in front of your television set when your station goes on the air and stay there without a book, magazine, newspaper, profit-and-loss sheet or rating book to distract you—and keep your eyes glued to that set until the **station signs off**. *I can assure you that you will observe a vast* **wasteland**.

You will see a procession of game shows, violence, audience participation shows, formula comedies about totally unbelievable families, blood and thunder, mayhem, violence, sadism, murder, Western bad men, Western good men, private eyes, gangsters, more violence and cartoons. And, endlessly, commercials—many screaming, cajoling, and offending. And most of all, boredom. True, you will see a few things you will enjoy. But they will be very, very few. And if you think I exaggerate, try it.

Is there one person in this room who claims that broadcasting can't do better?

Well, a glance at next season's proposed programming can give us little heart. Of seventy-three and a half hours of prime evening time, the networks have tentatively scheduled fifty-nine hours to categories of "action-adventure," situation comedy, variety, quiz, and movies.

Is there one network president in this room who claims he can't do better?

Well, is there at least one network president who believes that the other networks can't do better?

Gentlemen, your **trust accounting with your beneficiaries** *is overdue.*

Never have so few owed so much to so many.

Why is so much of television so bad? I have heard many answers: demands of your advertisers; competition for ever higher ratings; the need always to attract a mass audience; the high cost of television programs; the insatiable appetite for programming material—these are some of them. Unquestionably these are tough problems not susceptible to easy answers.

But I am not convinced that you have tried hard enough to solve them.

I do not accept the idea that the present over-all programming is aimed accurately at the public taste. The ratings tell us only that some people have their television sets turned on, and of that number, so many are tuned to one channel and so many to another. They don't tell us what the public might watch if they were offered half a dozen additional choices. A rating, at best, is an indication of how many people saw what you gave them. Unfortunately it does not reveal the depth of the penetration, or the intensity of reaction, and it never reveals what the acceptance would have been if what you gave them had been better—if all the forces of art and creativity and daring and imagination had been unleashed. I believe in the people's good sense and good taste, and I am not convinced that the people's taste is as low as some of you assume.

My concern with the rating services is not with their accuracy. Perhaps they are accurate. I really don't know. What, then, is wrong with the ratings? It's not been their accuracy—it's been their use.

Certainly I hope you will agree that ratings should have little influence where children are concerned. The best estimates indicate that during the hours of 5 to 6 P.M., 60 per cent of your audience is composed of children under twelve. And most young children today, believe it or not, spend as much time watching television as they do in the schoolroom. I repeat—let that sink in—most young children today spend as much time watching television as they do in the schoolroom. It used to be said that there were three great influences on a child: home, school, and church. Today there is a fourth great influence, and you ladies and gentlemen control it.

If parents, teachers, and ministers conducted their responsibilities by following the ratings, children would have a steady diet of ice cream, school holidays, and no Sunday School. What about your responsibilities? Is there no room on television to teach, to inform, to

Trust accounting with your beneficiaries: Minow is telling broadcasters that he feels that they need to justify their decisions about programming to television viewers.

A family gathered around the television, circa the 1960s. Newton Minow felt strongly about the responsibility of television broadcasters to provide quality programming for children, not just cartoons and violence. © H. Armstrong Roberts/Corbis. Reproduced by permission.

Trademarks: In this case, the type of program that typifies or represents the network's programming.

uplift, to stretch, to enlarge the capacities of our children? Is there no room for programs deepening their understanding of children in other lands? Is there no room for a children's news show explaining something about the world to them at their level of understanding? Is there no room for reading the great literature of the past, teaching them the great traditions of freedom? There are some fine children's shows, but they are drowned out in the massive doses of cartoons, violence, and more violence. Must these be your **trademarks**? Search your consciences and see if you cannot offer more to your young beneficiaries, whose future you guide so many hours each and every day.

What about adult programming and ratings? You know, newspaper publishers take popularity ratings, too. The answers are pretty clear; it is almost always the comics, followed by the advice-to-the-lovelorn columns. But, ladies and gentlemen, the news is still on the front page of all newspapers, the editorials are not replaced by more comics, the newspapers have not become one long collection of advice to the lovelorn. Yet newspapers do not need a license from the government to be in business—they do not use **public property**. But in television—where your responsibilities as public trustees are so plain—the moment that the ratings indicate that Westerns are popular, there are new imitations of Westerns on the air faster than the old **coaxial cable** could take us from Hollywood to New York. Broadcasting cannot continue to live by the numbers. Ratings ought to be the slave of the broadcaster, not his master. And you and I both know that the rating services themselves would agree.

Let me make clear that what I am talking about is balance. I believe that the public interest is made up of many interests. There are many people in this great country, and you must serve all of us. You will get no argument from me if you say that, given a choice between a Western and a symphony, more people will watch the Western. I like Westerns and private eyes too—but a steady diet for the whole country is obviously not in the public interest. We all know that people would more often prefer to be entertained than stimulated or informed. But your obligations are not satisfied if you look only to popularity as a test of what to broadcast. You are not only in show business; you are free to communicate ideas as well as relaxation. You must provide a wider range of choices, more diversity, more alternatives. It is not enough to cater to the nation's whims—you must also serve the nation's needs.

And I would add this—that if some of you persist in a relentless search for the highest rating and the **lowest common denominator**, you may very well lose your audience. Because, to paraphrase a great American who was recently my law partner, the people are wise, wiser than some of the broadcasters—and politicians—think.

[...]

Another, and perhaps the most important, frontier: television will rapidly join the **parade into space**. International television will be with us soon. No one knows how long it will be until a broadcast from a studio in New York will be viewed in India as well as in Indiana, will be seen in the Congo as it is seen in Chicago. But as surely as we are meeting here today, that day will come—and once again our world will shrink.

What will the people of other countries think of us when they see our Western badmen and good men punching each other in the jaw in between the shooting? What will the Latin American or African child learn of America from our great communications indus-

Public property: Newton is referring to the airwaves, which are owned by the public.

Coaxial cable: This was a kind of high-speed wire used to carry television signals from the dawn of the industry in the 1930s.

Lowest common denominator: Derived from mathematics, the term refers to the desire to produce television shows that can be understood by the simplest or least educated audience.

Parade into space: Newton is referring to the coming of satellite broadcasting, which will allow television signals to be sent around the world.

try? We cannot permit television in its present form to be our voice overseas.

There is your challenge to leadership. You must reexamine some fundamentals of your industry. You must open your minds and open your hearts to the limitless horizons of tomorrow.

I can suggest some words that should serve to guide you:

> Television and all who participate in it are jointly accountable to the American public for respect for the special needs of children, for community responsibility, for the advancement of education and culture, for the acceptability of the program materials chosen, for decency and decorum in production, and for propriety in advertising. This responsibility cannot be discharged by any given group of programs, but can be discharged only through the highest standards of respect for the American home, applied to every moment of every program presented by television.
>
> Program materials should enlarge the horizons of the viewer, provide him with wholesome entertainment, afford helpful stimulation, and remind him of the responsibilities which the citizen has toward his society.

*These words are not mine. They are yours. They are taken literally from your own **Television Code**. They reflect the leadership and aspirations of your own great industry. I urge you to respect them as I do. And I urge you to respect the intelligent and farsighted leadership of Governor LeRoy Collins and to make this meeting a creative act. I urge you at this meeting and, after you leave, back home, at your stations and your networks, to strive ceaselessly to improve your product and to better serve your viewers, the American people.*

I hope that we at the FCC will not allow ourselves to become so bogged down in the mountain of papers, hearings, memoranda, orders and the daily routine that we close our eyes to the wider view of the public interest. And I hope that you broadcasters will not permit yourselves to become so absorbed in the chase for ratings, sales and profits that you lose this wider view. Now more than ever before in broadcasting's history the times demand the best of all of us.

We need imagination in programming, not sterility; creativity, not imitation; experimentation, not conformity; excellence, not mediocrity. Television is filled with creative, imaginative people. You must strive to set them free.

Television in its young life has had many hours of greatness...and it has had its endless hours of mediocrity and its moments of public disgrace. There are estimates that today the av-

Television Code: A code of conduct adopted by television broadcasters.

erage viewer spends about 200 minutes daily with television, while the average reader spends thirty-eight minutes with magazines and forty minutes with newspapers. Television has grown faster than a teenager, and now it is time to grow up.

What you gentlemen broadcast through the people's air affects the people's taste, their knowledge, their opinions, their understanding of themselves and of their world. And their future.

The power of instantaneous sight and sound is without precedent in mankind's history. This is an awesome power. It has limitless capabilities for good—and for evil. And it carries with it awesome responsibilities—responsibilities which you and I cannot escape.

*In his stirring inaugural address, **our president** said, "And so, my fellow Americans: ask not what your country can do for you— ask what you can do for your country."*

Ladies and Gentlemen, ask not what broadcasting can do for you—ask what you can do for broadcasting.

I urge you to put the people's airwaves to the service of the people and the cause of freedom. You must help prepare a generation for great decisions. You must help a great nation fulfill its future.

Do this, and I pledge you our help.

What happened next...

Minow's speech caused a real sensation in the television industry. Critics of television were pleased, for they had long charged that the highest interest of the industry was making money and that programmers cared little for creating quality programming. They hoped that the government would use its power to increase the educational value of TV programming. On the other hand, network executives and station owners reacted angrily. They were upset that Minow had called television a "vast wasteland" and feared that Minow and the Kennedy administration would increase federal regulation of the airwaves.

Our president: Refers to President John F. Kennedy.

The FCC conducted a series of hearings in 1962 to examine the programming policies of the major networks, CBS, NBC, and ABC. One television executive accused Minow and the FCC of trying to use the authority of the government to determine the content of the programming seen by the American people. This charge of government censorship was adamantly denied by Minow, who insisted that he merely wanted TV stations to live up to their civic commitment to broadcast programming that was in the public interest. In the end, however, little changed as a result of Minow's address. Broadcasters chose programming based on ratings, the data that showed which programs the public preferred. The shows with the highest ratings fetched the highest dollar from advertisers and were thus aired most consistently. Television remained very commercial and dedicated to entertainment not education.

Over time, however, there were changes that increased the amount of educational programming on television. Perhaps the most important change was the creation, in 1967, of the Corporation for Public Broadcasting (CPB). This government-funded agency funneled government dollars into the creation of quality education programming, especially for television. One product of the CPB was the introduction of the children's show *Sesame Street* in 1969. In 1969 the CPB also created the Public Broadcasting System, a network used to distribute programs to public television stations. Other forces encouraging diversity in TV programming were the introduction of the ultrahigh-frequency (UHF) broadcasting spectrum and the spread of cable television. Both of these innovations allowed for more television stations, which served the more specialized interests Minow felt were being ignored by major stations.

Did you know ...
- In a 1991 speech called "How Vast the Wasteland Now?" Minow claimed that the two most important words in his 1961 speech were not "vast wasteland" but "public interest."

- The ability of the FCC to regulate TV programming was limited to its right to deny a license to those stations that did not broadcast in the "public interest." But the very idea of the "public interest" was poorly defined, and most stations met their obligation by airing a few educational programs at off-peak hours. Minow knew that he could do little to change broadcasters' activities, but he hoped that he could inspire them to higher ideals.

- By the end of the 1960s the majority of TV programming was broadcasting in color, and most TV sets could receive color signals.

- By the end of the 1960s eighty-two channels were available to viewers.

Consider the following...

- If television broadcasters had followed Minow's advice, how might television have been changed?

- What role do you think the government should play in regulating television? Do you think there should be more government intervention in controlling the content of programming, or less? Explain your answers.

- Do you believe, as Minow seems to, that the content of television has a direct influence on the behavior of television viewers? Can you explain your answer using specific evidence?

- Suppose that Newton Minow was the chairman of the FCC in the early 2000s. What would he think about the state of television today?

- If you were the chairman of the FCC and were asked by the U.S. president to give a speech to broadcasters, what would you advise in your speech? What changes would you like to see?

For More Information

Books

Calabro, Marian. *Zap!: A Brief History of Television*. New York: Four Winds Press, 1992.

Minow, Newton N. *Equal Time: The Private Broadcaster and the Public Interest*. New York: Atheneum, 1964.

Minow, Newton N., and Craig L. Lamay. *Abandoned in the Wasteland: Children, Television, and the First Amendment.* New York: Harper Collins, 1995.

Taylor, Ella. *Prime Time Families: Television Culture in Postwar America.* Berkeley, CA: University of California Press, 1989.

Web sites

"The FCC History Project." *FCC: Federal Communications Commission.* www.fcc.gov/omd/history (accessed on August 5, 2004).

Marshall McLuhan

Excerpts from Understanding Media: The Extensions of Man
Originally published in 1964; excerpts taken from 1994 reprint.

In 1961 Federal Communications Commission chairman Newton Minow (1926–) argued that the content of television programming played a crucial role in the cultural life of the nation. In 1964 media theorist Marshall McLuhan (1911–1980) argued that the content of programming mattered far less than the underlying form of televised communication. He claimed, in one of the most famous expressions of the 1960s, "the medium is the message." But what did McLuhan mean by his famous pronouncement, and why did it seem to open up a whole world for those who claimed to understand it?

Marshall McLuhan was one of the most celebrated intellectuals of the 1960s. His most notable books are *The Mechanical Bride: Folklore of Industrial Man* (1951), *The Gutenberg Galaxy: The Making of Typographic Man* (1962), *Understanding Media: The Extensions of Man* (1964), and *The Medium Is the Massage* (1967). ("Massage," rather than *"Message,"* is correct. The title of McLuhan's 1967 collection of works has caused much confusion. Long viewed as another of McLuhan's plays on words, it was later revealed to be a publisher's mistake that the author liked so much he kept it.) The books themselves were difficult: using specialized terminology and

"In a culture like ours…it is sometimes a bit of a shock to be reminded that, in operational and practical fact, the medium is the message."

Marshall McLuhan was one of the most celebrated intellectuals of the 1960s.
© Bettmann/Corbis. Reproduced by permission.

long quotations from a dizzying array of authors, McLuhan advanced his ideas in complex, halting arguments that took much work to decipher. David Skinner, assessing McLuhan's career in *Public Interest,* claimed that "Quoting [McLuhan] at any length can have the unfortunate effect of mystifying the reader.... At the high point of his fame, McLuhan's often impenetrable writing style seemed to offer proof of his importance as a thinker." In any case, most people did not read his books. Instead they encountered his intriguing ideas in unusual and attention-grabbing phrases quoted on television, on radio, and in print.

McLuhan was fascinated with the ways that media, which he called "extensions of man," reshaped human experience. He argued that the introduction of print technology had reshaped culture in the past and that the introduction of radio and television were changing contemporary culture, creating a "global village" in which everyone was connected. He was less interested in the content of newspapers or television programs than in the way the form of the medium determined how people behaved; it was this insight that led him to declare that "the medium is the message." Many people responded to McLuhan's ideas, believing that they unlocked the door to understanding some of the sweeping social changes that were gripping the United States in the 1960s. For his followers, McLuhan's theories explained everything from the Hippie movement to the sexual revolution to the anti-Vietnam War movement. Critics claimed that his ideas were nonsense and did not stand up to scrutiny. Reading McLuhan's works allows people to make up their own minds regarding this controversy.

Things to remember while reading the excerpts from *Understanding Media*:

- David Skinner wrote in *Public Interest*: "Many a McLuhan sentence will work like a koan, which once explained loses its purpose along with its edge." (In Zen Buddhism, a koan is a seemingly contradictory statement that one meditates on in order to come to enlightenment.) Can you identify some sentences that might work like koans?

• McLuhan was a favorite of those who felt that the world was transforming during the 1960s. His works helped them understand the sweeping changes that were coming about as a result of the various social movements of the period. Novelist Tom Wolfe once said that McLuhan was "the most important thinker since Newton, Darwin, Freud, Einstein, and Pavlov."

• McLuhan was born in Edmonton, Alberta, Canada, on July 21, 1911. He was a professor of English at a variety of universities, and he was one of the pioneers of the study in American universities of popular culture.

Excerpts from Understanding Media: The Extensions of Man

Introduction by Lewis H. Lapham

James Reston wrote in the New York Times *(July 7, 1957):*

> *A health director...reported this week that a small mouse, which presumably had been watching television, attacked a little girl and her full-grown cat....Both mouse and cat survived, and the incident is recorded here as a reminder that things seem to be changing.*

After three thousand years of **explosion***, by means of fragmentary and mechanical technologies, the Western world is* **imploding***. During the* **mechanical ages** *we had extended our bodies in space. Today, after more than a century of electronic technology, we have extended our central nervous systems itself in a global embrace, abolishing both space and time as far as our planet is concerned. Rapidly, we approach the final phase of the extensions of man—the technological simulation of consciousness, when the creative process of knowing will be collectively and corporately extended to the whole of human society, much as we have already extended our senses and our nerves by the various media. Whether the extension*

Explosion: Expansion outward.

Imploding: Collapsing inward.

Mechanical age: McLuhan is referring to the industrial age, before the introduction of electric and electronic technologies that allowed communication to be instantaneous.

of consciousness, so long sought by advertisers for specific products, will be "a good thing" is a question that admits of a wide solution. There is little possibility of answering such questions about the extensions of man without considering them all together. Any extension, whether of skin, hand, or foot, affects the whole psychic and social complex.

Some of the principal extensions, together with some of their psychic and social consequences, are studied in this book. Just how little consideration has been given to such matters in the past can be gathered from the **consternation** of one of the editors of this book. He noted in dismay that "seventy-five per cent of your material is new. A successful book cannot venture to be more than ten per cent new." Such a risk seems quite worth taking at the present time when the stakes are very high, and the need to understand the effects of the extension of man becomes more urgent by the hour.

In the mechanical age now receding, many actions could be taken without too much concern. Slow movement insured that the reactions were delayed for considerable periods of time. Today the action and the reaction occur almost at the same time. We actually live mythically and integrally, as it were, but we continue to think in the old, fragmented space and time patterns of the pre-electric age.

[…]

The **aspiration** of our time for wholeness, empathy and depth awareness is a natural **adjunct** of electric technology. The age of mechanical industry that preceded us found vehement assertion of private outlook that natural mode of expression. Every culture and every age has its favorite model of perception and knowledge that it is inclined to **prescribe** for everybody and everything. The mark of our time is its **revulsion** against imposed patterns. We are suddenly eager to have things and people declare their beings totally. There is a deep faith to be found in this new attitude—a faith that concerns the ultimate harmony of all being. Such is the faith in which this book has been written. It explores the contours of our new extended beings in our technologies, seeking the principle of **intelligibility** in each of them. In the full confidence that it is possible to win an understanding of these forms that will bring them into orderly service, I have looked at them anew, accepting very little of the **conventional wisdom** concerning them. One can say of media as Robert Theobald has said of economic depressions: "There is one additional factor that has helped to control depressions, and that is a better understanding of their development." Examination of the

Consternation: Confused amazement or dismay.

Aspiration: Strong desire.

Adjunct: Something added.

Prescribe: To lay down as a guide or pattern.

Revulsion: Reaction against.

Intelligibility: Capable of being understood.

Conventional wisdom: That which is commonly known.

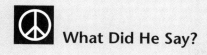 **What Did He Say?**

Marshall McLuhan (1911–1980) was one of the most celebrated and intriguing figures of the 1960s. His dramatic and controversial statements about the impact of various media on humans changed the way people understood their relation to television, magazines, and each other. Some people believed that McLuhan's ideas were profound; others thought he was full of nonsense. Let's take a look at some of McLuhan's more obscure statements:

"In the electric age we wear all mankind as our skin" (1964).

"The new clothing of the planet is garbage" (1967).

"The future of the future is the present" (1967).

"The electronic age...angelizes man, disembodies him. Turns him into software" (1971).

Such statements make his more famous announcements—such as "the medium is the message"—seem straightforward. It helps to remember that McLuhan did not intend his statements to make perfect sense. He wanted his readers to be puzzled.

According to McLuhan's son, Eric McLuhan, quoted in *Forward Through the Rearview Mirror: Reflections on and by Marshall McLuhan,* McLuhan's favorite form for communication was the aphorism. An aphorism is a highly compressed statement of an idea or a principle. "The aphorism," wrote Eric McLuhan, "is a poetic form that calls for a lot of participation on the part of the reader. You have to chew on an aphorism and work with it for a while before you understand it fully. A good aphorism could keep you busy for a week." McLuhan wanted people to work at understanding his ideas and to discover their own ideas in the process. The last thing he wanted was for people to mindlessly agree with his ideas. For McLuhan, thinking very hard was the highest form of human activity.

---

origin and development of the individual extensions of man should be preceded by a look at some general aspects of the media, or extensions of man, beginning with the never-explained numbness that each extension brings about in the individual and society.

Chapter 1: The Medium Is the Message

In a culture like ours, long accustomed to splitting and dividing all things as a means of control, it is sometimes a bit of a shock to be reminded that, in operational and practical fact, the medium is the message. This is merely to say that the personal and social consequences of any medium—that is, of any extension of ourselves—result from the new scale that is introduced into our affairs by each extension of our-selves, or by any new technology. Thus, with automation, for example, the new patterns of human association tend to eliminate jobs, it is true. That is the negative result. Positively, automation creates roles for peo-ple, which is to say depth of involvement in their work and human asso-ciation that our preceding mechanical technology had destroyed. Many people would be disposed to say that it was not the machine, but what one did with the machine, that was its meaning or message. In terms of the ways in which the machine altered our relations to one another and to ourselves, it mattered not in the least whether it turned out cornflakes or Cadillacs. The restructuring of human work and association was shaped by the technique of fragmentation that is the essence of ma-chine technology. The essence of automation technology is the opposite. It is integral and decentralist in depth, just as the machine was fragmen-tary, centralist, and superficial in its patterning of human relationships.

*The instance of the electric light may prove illuminating in this connection. The electric light is pure information. It is a medium without a message, as it were, unless it is used to spell out some verbal ad or name. This fact, characteristic of all media, means that the "content" of any medium is always another medium. The con-tent of writing is speech, just as the written word is the content of print, and print is the content of the telegraph. If it is asked, "What is the content of speech?," it is necessary to say, "It is an actual process of thought, which is in itself nonverbal." An **abstract paint-ing** represents direction manifestation of creative thought processes as they might appear in computer designs. What we are consider-ing here, however, are the psychic and social consequences of the designs of patterns as they amplify or accelerate existing processes. For the "message" of any medium or technology is the change of scale or pace or pattern that it introduces into human affairs. The railway did not introduce movement or transportation or wheel or road into human society, but it accelerated and enlarged the scale of previous human functions, creating totally new kinds of cities and new kinds of work and leisure. This happened whether the railway functioned in a tropical or northern environment, and is quite inde-pendent of the freight of content of the railway medium. The air-plane, on the other hand, by accelerating the rate of transportation, tends to dissolve the railway form of city, politics, and association, quite independently of what the airplane is used for.*

Let us return to the electric light. Whether the light is being used for brain surgery or night baseball is a matter of indifference. It could be argued that these activities are in some way the "content" of the

Abstract painting: A painting which does not contain realis-tic representations of life.

electric light, since they could not exist without the electric light. This fact merely underlines the point that "the medium is the message" because it is the medium that shapes and controls the scale and form of human association and design. The content of uses of such media are as diverse as they are ineffectual in shaping the form of human association. Indeed, it is only too typical that the "content" of any medium binds us to the character of the medium. It is only today that industries have become aware of the various kinds of business in which they are engaged. When IBM discovered that it was not in the business of making office equipment or business machines, but that it was in the business of processing information, then it began to navigate with clear vision. The General Electric Company makes a considerable portion of its profits from electric light bulbs and lighting systems. It has not yet discovered that, quite as much as A.T.&T., it is in the business of moving information.

The electric light escapes attention as a communication medium just because it has no "content." And this makes it an invaluable instance of how people fail to study media at all. For it is not till the electric light is used to spell out some brand name that it is noticed as a medium. Then it is not the light but the "content" (or what is really another medium) that is noticed. The message of the electric light is like the message of electric power in industry, totally radical, pervasive, and decentralized. For electric light and power are separate from their uses, yet they eliminate time and space factors in human association exactly as do radio, telegraph, telephone, and TV, creating involvement in depth.

[...]

*If the formative power in the media are the media themselves, that raises a host of large matters that can only be mentioned here, although they deserve volumes. Namely, that technological media are staples or natural resources, exactly as are coal and cotton and oil. Anybody will concede that society whose economy is dependent upon one or two major staples like cotton, or grain, or lumber, or fish, or cattle is going to have some obvious social patterns of organization as a result. Stress on a few major **staples** creates extreme instability in the economy but great endurance in the population. The **pathos** and humor of the American South are embedded in such an economy of limited staples. For a society configured by reliance on a few **commodities** accepts them as a social bond quite as much as the metropolis does the press. Cotton and oil, like radio and TV, become "fixed charges" on the entire psychic life of the*

Staples: Commonly used goods, such as wheat or sugar.

Pathos: Emotional content that produces sympathy or pity.

Commodities: A synonym for staples, or commonly used goods.

Configure: Shape or define.

Psychologist C. G. Jung: A Swiss psychologist (1875–1961) who believed that society had a "collective unconscious," an underlying sense of how the world was defined and ordered.

community. And this pervasive fact creates the unique cultural flavor of any society. It pays through the nose and all its other senses for each staple that shapes its life.

That our human senses, of which all media are extensions, are also fixed charges on our personal energies, and that they also **configure** the awareness and experience of each one of us, may be perceived in another connection mentioned by the **psychologist C. G. Jung:**

> Every Roman was surrounded by slaves. The slave and his psychology flooded ancient Italy, and every Roman became inwardly, and of course unwittingly, a slave. Because living constantly in the atmosphere of slaves, he became infected through the unconscious with their psychology. No one can shield himself from such an influence (Contributions to Analytical Psychology, London, 1928).

What happened next...

There are rarely direct or tangible results that arise from the work of intellectuals such as McLuhan. No legislation was passed declaring that the United States was the capital of the global village, and no one was barred from controlling the messages carried by the media. Yet the indirect results of McLuhan's work were significant ... and they remain into the twenty-first century. McLuhan helped people understand the ways that different media control and condition the ways that things like news, entertainment, and communication are received and understood. Thanks in part to McLuhan and others like him, people in technologically advanced nations are intensely aware of the impact of the media and commercialism on their lives.

McLuhan himself was at the height of his celebrity following the publication of *Understanding Media* in 1964. For the next several years, he was one of the West's leading intellectuals. His works were dissected in literary journals, he was interviewed in *Playboy* magazine in 1969, and he and his sayings—especially the phrase "Marshall McLuhan, what are you doin'?"—were played for laughs on the popular TV program *Rowan and Martin's Laugh-In*. According to *Playboy*, he was called "the guru of the boob tube" and "the Dr. Spock of pop culture" (referring to the doctor who had popularized new theories of child-rearing). By the mid-1970s, however, intellectuals and academics began to criticize and take apart his theories, and his work fell out of fashion. McLuhan died in 1980, and before long most of McLuhan's books went out of print. Yet his influence remained alive in the early 2000s. The rise of a new form of media, the Internet, prompted many to revisit McLuhan's theories, and his rambling, sometimes disjointed writings fit right in with the academic writing styles of the 1990s. In 1994, the University of Toronto established the McLuhan Program in Culture and Technology to continue academic study in the tradition of the man once called "the oracle of modern times" (an oracle is a person who reveals hidden knowledge).

Marshall McLuhan was one of the first to argue that a successful political candidate must convey a pleasing personality on television. Here, Richard Nixon wipes his sweaty face during a televised presidential debate in 1960, giving viewers the impression that he was nervous and less competent than his opponent, the calm and collected John F. Kennedy.
AP/Wide World Photos. Reproduced by permission.

Did you know...

- McLuhan was one of the first people to analyze the importance of television as a tool of political campaigns in advanced societies. He argued that a successful political candidate must convey a pleasing personality on television, for personality now has become as important as policy.

- One of McLuhan's theories was that print culture—books, magazines, and newspapers—was in decline while video culture was growing in importance. The facts proved his case: the circulation of both magazines and newspapers declined dramatically during the 1950s and 1960s. Television became a powerful tool for communicating news, for it brought high-impact events like the 1963 assassination of John F. Kennedy and the Vietnam War (1959–75) directly into the homes of Americans.

Consider the following ...

- Can you explain, in your own words, what Marshall McLuhan meant by the statement "the medium is the message"? Do you agree with McLuhan that the medium is the message?

- McLuhan concludes his chapter with a quote about the impact of slavery in Roman times. What is the purpose of this quote? How does the institution of slavery in the past compare to the institution of television in advanced societies?

- McLuhan very consciously decided to present his ideas in challenging and difficult terms. Do you think this was a wise decision? Evaluate the merits of trying to communicate complicated ideas in complicated prose versus simplifying them by using a style that is easier to understand.

- Many observers feel that McLuhan was ahead of his time and that his ideas make more sense in the early 2000s than they did in the 1960s. Explain how you think McLuhan's theories can be applied in the twenty-first century.

For More Information

Books

Benedetti, Paul, and Nancy DeHart, eds. *Forward Through the Rearview Mirror: Reflections on and by Marshall McLuhan.* Cambridge, MA: MIT Press, 1996.

Gordon, W. Terrence. *Marshall McLuhan: Escape into Understanding: A Biography.* New York: Basic Books, 1997.

Levinson, Paul. *Digital McLuhan: A Guide to the Information Millennium.* New York: Routledge, 2001.

McLuhan, Marshall. *Understanding Media: The Extensions of Man.* New York: McGraw-Hill, 1964; reprinted, with introduction by Lewis H. Lapham, Cambridge, MA: MIT Press, 1994.

Periodicals

"The Playboy Interview: Marshall McLuhan." *Playboy* (March 1969).

Skinner, David. "McLuhan's World—And Ours." *Public Interest* (Winter 2000): p. 52.

Web sites

The McLuhan Program in Culture and Technology. www.mcluhan.utoronto.ca (accessed on August 7, 2004).

Where to Learn More

Books

Altman, Linda Jacobs. *The American Civil Rights Movement: The African-American Struggle for Equality.* Berkeley Heights, NJ: Enslow, 2004.

Anderson, David L. *The Columbia Guide to the Vietnam War.* New York: Columbia University Press, 2002.

Archer, Jules. *The Incredible Sixties: The Stormy Years that Changed America.* San Diego, CA: Harcourt Brace Jovanovich, 1986.

Austin, Joe, and Michael Nevin Willard. *Generations of Youth: Youth Cultures and History in Twentieth-Century America.* New York: New York University Press, 1998.

Bloom, Alexander, and Wini Breines, eds. *"Takin' It to the Streets": A Sixties Reader.* New York: Oxford University Press, 2003.

Breuer, William B. *Race to the Moon: America's Duel with the Soviets.* Westport, CT: Greenwood Publishing, 1993.

Burner, David. *Making Peace with the 1960s.* Princeton, NJ: Princeton University Press, 1996.

Cantwell, Robert. *When We Were Good: The Folk Revival.* Cambridge, MA: Harvard University Press, 1996.

Collier, Christopher, and James Lincoln Collier. *The Changing Face of American Society: 1945-2000.* New York: Benchmark, 2002.

Dougan, Clark. *A Nation Divided.* Boston: Boston Publishing Co., 1984.

Dudley, William, ed. *The 1960s*. San Diego: Greenhaven, 2000.

Dunn, John M. *A History of U.S. Involvement.* San Diego, CA: Lucent Books, 2001.

Edelstein, Andrew. *The Pop Sixties*. New York: Ballantine Books, 1985.

Farber, David. *The Age of Great Dreams: America in the 1960s.* New York: Hill and Wang, 1994.

Farber, David, and Beth Bailey, with others. *The Columbia Guide to America in the 1960s.* New York: Columbia University Press, 2001.

Feinstein, Stephen. *The 1960s from the Vietnam War to Flower Power.* Berkeley Heights, NJ: Enslow, 2000.

Finkelstein, Norman H. *The Way Things Never Were: The Truth about the "Good Old Days."* New York: Atheneum Books for Young Readers, 1999.

Galt, Margot Fortunato. *Stop This War!: American Protest of the Conflict in Vietnam.* Minneapolis, MN: Lerner, 2000.

Gitlin, Todd. *The Sixties: Years of Hope, Days of Rage.* New York: Bantam, 1987; revised, 1993.

Goldberg, RoseLee. *Performance: Live Art since 1960.* New York: Harry N. Abrams, 1998.

Holland, Gini. *The 1960s*. San Diego, CA: Lucent, 1999.

Isserman, Maurice, and Michael Kazin. *America Divided: The Civil War of the 1960s.* New York: Oxford University Press, 2000.

Jay, Kathryn. *More Than Just a Game: Sports in American Life Since 1945.* New York: Columbia University Press, 2004.

Kallen, Stuart A. *The Kennedy Assassination.* San Diego, CA: Lucent, 2003.

Kallen, Stuart A. *Political Activists of the 1960s.* San Diego, CA: Lucent Books, 2004.

Kallen, Stuart A., ed. *Sixties Counterculture.* San Diego, CA: Greenhaven Press, 2001.

Katz, William Loren. *The Great Society to the Reagan Era, 1964-1990.* Austin, TX: Raintree Steck-Vaughn, 1993.

Lebrecht, Norman. *The Companion to 20th-Century Music.* New York: Simon & Schuster, 1992.

Levy, Debbie. *The Vietnam War.* Minneapolis, MN: Lerner, 2004.

Lobenthal, Joel. *Radical Rags: Fashion of the Sixties.* New York: Abbeville Press, 1990.

Lowe, Jacques. *The Kennedy Legacy: A Generation Later.* New York: Viking Studio, 1988.

Lucie-Smith, Edward. *Visual Arts in the Twentieth Century.* Upper Saddle River, NJ: Prentice Hall, 1996.

MacNeil, Robert, ed. *The Way We Were: 1963, the Year Kennedy Was Shot.* New York: Carroll & Graf, 1988.

Marsden, George M. *Religion and American Culture*. San Diego, CA: Harcourt Brace Jovanovich, 1990.

McCormick, Anita Louisa. *The Vietnam Antiwar Movement in American History*. Berkeley Heights, NJ: Enslow Publishers, 2000.

McWilliams, John C. *The 1960s Cultural Revolution*. Westport, CT: Greenwood Press, 2000.

Miller, Jim. *Democracy Is in the Streets: From Port Huron to the Siege of Chicago*. Cambridge, MA: Harvard University Press, 1994.

Miller, Jim, ed. *The Rolling Stone Illustrated History of Rock and Roll*. New York: Rolling Stone Press, 1980.

Miller, Timothy. *The Hippies and American Values*. Knoxville: University of Tennessee Press, 1991.

Mordden, Ethan. *Medium Cool: The Movies of the 1960s*. New York: Knopf, 1990.

Moss, George. *America in the Twentieth Century*. Upper Saddle River, NJ: Prentice-Hall, 1988.

Northrup, Cynthia Clark, ed. *The American Economy: A Historical Encyclopedia*. Santa Barbara, CA: ABC-CLIO, 2003.

O'Neill, William L. *Coming Apart: An Informal History of America in the 1960s*. Chicago, IL: Quadrangle, 1971.

Parker, Thomas, and Douglas Nelson. *Day by Day: The Sixties*. New York: Facts on File, 1983.

Roberts, Randy, and James S. Olson. *Winning Is the Only Thing: Sports in America Since 1945*. Baltimore, MD: Johns Hopkins University Press, 1989.

Schwartz, Richard A. *Cold War Culture: Media and the Arts, 1945–1990*. New York: Facts on File, 1997.

Sloman, Larry. *Steal This Dream: Abbie Hoffman and the Countercultural Revolution in America*. New York: Doubleday, 1998.

Stevens, Jay. *Storming Heaven: LSD and the American Dream*. New York: Atlantic Monthly Press, 1987.

Stern, Jane, and Michael Stern. *Sixties People*. New York: Knopf, 1990.

Summers, Harry G., Jr. *Historical Atlas of the Vietnam War*. New York: Houghton Mifflin, 1995.

Treanor, Nick, ed. *The Civil Rights Movement*. San Diego, CA: Greenhaven Press, 2003.

Tucker, Spencer C. *Encyclopedia of the Vietnam War: A Political, Social, and Military History*. 3 vols. Santa Barbara, CA: ABC-CLIO, 1998.

Turbulent Years: The 60s. Alexandria, VA: Time-Life Books, 1998.

Unger, Irwin, and Debi Unger, eds. *The Times Were a Changin'*. New York: Random House, 1998.

Uschan, Michael V. *Life on the Front Lines: The Fight for Civil Rights*. San Diego, CA: Lucent Books, 2004.

Witcover, Jules. *The Year the Dream Died: Revisiting 1968 in America*. New York: Warner Books, 1997.

Wormser, Richard. *Three Faces of Vietnam*. New York: F. Watts, 1993.

Young, Marilyn B., John J. Fitzgerald, and A. Tom Grunfeld. *The Vietnam War: A History in Documents*. New York: Oxford University Press, 2002.

Web Sites

American Presidents Life Portraits. http://www.americanpresidents.org.

"The Cuban Missile Crisis, 1962: The 40th Anniversary." *The National Security Archive.* http://www.gwu.edu/~nsarchiv/nsa/cuba_mis_cri/.

Divining America: Religion and the National Culture. http://www.nhc.rtp.nc.us/tserve/divam.htm.

Hippies on the Web: Haight-Ashbury Music and Culture. http://www.rockument.com/links.html.

John F. Kennedy Library and Museum. http://www.jfklibrary.org.

"The Living Room Candidate: Presidential Campaign Commercials, 1952-2004." *American Museum of the Moving Image.* http://livingroomcandidate.movingimage.us/index.php.

Lyndon Baines Johnson Library and Museum. http://www.lbjlib.utexas.edu.

National Civil Rights Museum. http://www.civilrightsmuseum.org.

"The Presidents of the United States." *The White House.* http://www.whitehouse.gov/history/presidents.

The Richard Nixon Library and Birthplace. http://www.nixonfoundation.org.

The Sixties Project. http://lists.village.virginia.edu/sixties/.

The 1960s—Social Unrest & Counterculture. http://www.historyteacher.net/APUSH-Course/Weblinks/Weblinks27.htm.

Vietnam Online. http://www.pbs.org/wgbh/amex/vietnam/.

Voices of Civil Rights: Ordinary People, Extraordinary Stories. http://www.voicesofcivilrights.org.

Index

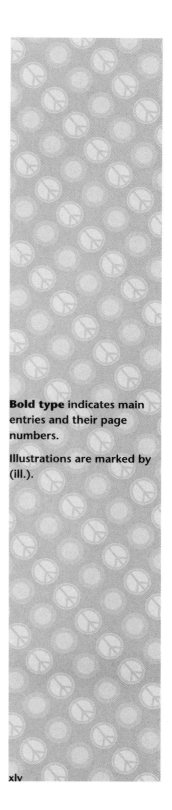

Bold type indicates main entries and their page numbers.

Illustrations are marked by (ill.).

Elijah Muhammad, 26, 26 (ill.)
Equal Employment Opportunity
    Commission (EEOC), 87
Equal Pay Act, 60
Equal Rights Amendment (ERA),
    72, 91–93
Extremism. *See* Goldwater, Barry;
    Left (political viewpoint);
    Radicals; Right (political
    viewpoint); *specific names of
    political groups*

F

Farber, David, 133–134, 138
FCC. *See* Federal Communica-
    tions Commission.
Federal Communications Com-
    mission (FCC), 215, 217–218
Feminine Mystique, The (Friedan),
    58, 71, 72, 73–86
Feminism, 102. *See also* National
    Organization for Women;
    Women; Women's Liberation
    Movement
Feminist perspectives, 55–58
Folk music, 154
Foreign policy. *See* Cold War;
    Vietnam War
Forman, James, 146
Freedom riders, 2, 141. *See also*
    Civil rights movement; Stu-
    dent Nonviolent Coordinating
    Committee (SNCC) 83 (ill.)
Friedan, Betty, 58, **71–86**, 72
    (ill.), 83 (ill.), 88 (ill.)
    childhood, education and
        young womanhood of, 71–72
    on frustration of American
        homemakers, 78–79, 80
    on marriage in America,
        73–78, 81
    on need to offer women new
        education and work options,
        81–83
    on old solutions to womens'
        problems, 79–81
    research performed by, 72

G

Gay liberation, 92, 93

Geneva Convention, 113, 114,
    115
Ginsberg, Allen, 192
"Global village," 232
Goldstein, Betty Naomi. *See*
    Friedan, Betty
Goldwater, Barry, 201–214, 202
    (ill.), 204 (ill.), 210 (ill.)
    anticommunism of, 203,
        206–207, 208–209
    background and career of,
        201–202
    conservatism of, 202–203
    election of 1964 and, 186
    on extremism, 211
    foreign policy intentions of,
        205–208
    media treatment of, 213
    racism and, 203
    states' rights and, 203
    Vietnam War viewpoint of,
        111, 122, 208
    Young Americans for Freedom
        and, 202
Great Depression, 161–162
Guerilla warfare. *See* Vietcong;
    Vietnam War
Gulf of Tonkin, 112

H

"Hawks," 122
Hayden, Tom, 167, 171 (ill.),
    186–187
Hippies, 191–193
Ho Chi Minh, 106, 117, 119
Hoffman, Abbie, 192, 195,
    196–197, 198
House Committee on Un-Ameri-
    can Activities, 197
"House Joint Resolution 1145,
    August 7, 1964" (Johnson),
    116–117
"How Vast the Wasteland Now?"
    (Minow), 228

I

"I-Feel-Like-I'm- Fixin'-to-Die
    Rag" (McDonald), 154
"I Have a Dream" (King), 14, 44